The Right Way to Hire Financial Help

The Right Way to Hire Financial Help

*A complete guide to choosing and managing brokers,
financial planners, insurance agents, lawyers,
tax preparers, bankers, and real estate agents*

Charles A. Jaffe

The MIT Press
Cambridge, Massachusetts
London, England

This book was set in Stone Serif and Stone Sans on the Monotype 'Prism Plus' PostScript Imagesetter by Asco Trade Typesetting Ltd., Hong Kong.

Printed and bound in the United States of America.

Library of Congress Cataloging-in-Publication Data

Jaffe, Charles A.
  The right way to hire financial help: a complete guide to choosing and managing brokers, financial planners, insurance agents, lawyers, tax preparers, bankers, and real estate agents / Charles A. Jaffe.
     p.   cm.
  Includes index.
  ISBN 0-262-10070-3 (alk. paper)
  1. Financial planners. 2. Investment advisors. 3. Finance, Personal. 4. Financial services industry. I. Title.
HG179.5.J34   1998
332.6—dc21   97-30595
                                                                                                      CIP

For every consumer who has signed up with a financial adviser expecting answers, but come away with self-doubt and more questions

And for my girls—Susan, Thomson, and Whitney

Contents

Acknowledgments

Just as it takes a team of advisers to secure a person's finances, so did it take a team of people to make this book a reality. Several teams, actually.

In almost everything I have done in my career, first credit has gone to Ripley Hotch, my one-time editor, long-time mentor, role model, and friend, who convinced me that I could actually do a project like this and, in our all-too-rare phone conversations, always made me laugh at my own travails. Ripley, who helped me start my career in newspapers, then helped me start writing for magazines, and who finally moved to books himself, kept telling me the finished product would be worth it, and I believe he is right.

Next there is the team from *The Boston Globe*, most notably business editor Larry Edelman who encouraged me to pursue this project and who believed me when I said I could write both the book and my columns and never miss a beat. Then there are the editors who have handled my copy—Anne Eisenmenger, Alison Bethel, and Maria Shao during the time it took me to write and edit—all of them playing a vital role in making sure that my work was of such high quality that Larry never noticed the few beats I missed.

Then comes the team from The MIT Press. Ann Sochi started me on this journey, waited for its completion and then made a career change before I had the chance to work with her. Terry Vaughn and Victoria Richardson, who inherited this work from Ann, had enough patience to make Job seem like a guy with a short attention span. Best of all, they gave me the freedom to switch gears midstream, and the book is much better for that. Dana Andrus didn't give me so much freedom; she made sure the book was written in plain English—and the book is better for that too.

Of course no journalist comes without a team of sources. I am privileged to talk every day with some of the brightest minds in the investment and money management world. I have quoted many of these experts throughout the book, but many more helped form the opinions and ideas you will read here. This legion of people is too big to mention individually; suffice it to say that if you talked with me about financial services between 1995 and 1997, you are likely to see yourself in here somewhere and I thank you for the input.

Then there is the home team, my friends and family. My father, father-in-law, and brother acted as my test audience, the folks who saw the first big chunk of this book. Their input and feedback not only improved the work but made it much easier for me to complete. Jenny Lamont Johnson, a long-time friend, also merits special mention; she let me use her apartment at Harvard (once the home of T. S. Eliot, I might add) so that I could go on long, uninterrupted writing-and-cigar binges. Perhaps the most important contributor to the whole thing was my wife Susan, who never once asked me "How's the book coming?" because she knew it would add pressure to the process. She was the person most affected by this undertaking; without her efforts, I never could have finished and stayed sane.

Last, I owe a special debt to the people who read my columns, who write or call me with feedback, and who share their stories with me every week in the hope that I can impart some wisdom that might help them navigate choppy financial waters. They are the ones who made me realize that a book like this one is necessary and are the reason why the book was worth the effort.

The Right Way to Hire Financial Help

Introduction

A friend listened to me describe this book and the philosophy behind it, the whole time bobbing his head like one of those ceramic paper-weight dolls.

"So," he said at last, "it's a self-help book for people who have decided they can't help themselves."

I winced.

The reaction was not unexpected because it highlights a popular misconception—and because it came from a friend who would rather botch the bedroom wallpaper job than pay someone to do it right.

There is a perception among some people—most notably the do-it-yourself crowd—that paying for help to manage your money and affairs is a move borne from desperation or ignorance.

Bzzzt. Wrong answer.

One of the most responsible actions anyone can take toward managing their money is to own up to their shortcomings and to pursue assistance for those weaknesses in a strong, self-assured manner.

There is virtually nothing in money management that you cannot do yourself, but there is a big difference between simply taking on the task and actually doing it well. Whether it is buying stocks without a broker, building a portfolio of mutual funds, or purchasing life insurance, dabbling almost always leads to disaster.

I'm a big believer in doing as much as possible on your own, provided you understand this simple strategy for managing things yourself: Go strong or don't go at all.

The problem is that many people do neither. They don't have the know-how to do it themselves and don't want to take the time to learn, but they also don't want to hire outside counsel. They get their information in snippets, from friends, in the papers or magazines, from radio and television programs, at the barber shop or beauty salon, or in online chat rooms, and they wind up with a patchwork of products instead of a blanket of financial security.

Worse yet, the decision to hire an adviser becomes an abdication of responsibility, rather than an aggressive move to make things better.

Instead of choosing their helpers carefully—matching skills to needs and doing the interviews necessary to create the appropriate level of comfort—they look upon the hiring decision as a means to an end, as in "If I hire this person to do my taxes, I'll never have to worry about my taxes again."

And that's where folks like my friend come to the conclusion that people who want or need assistance simply can't help themselves. They perceive financial relationships as an all-or-nothing proposition, either done on your own or handed off to someone in exchange for a hefty fee.

Like most, they fail to recognize that the person who hires advisers must then manage those helpers and remain intimately involved in making decisions.

This book is not about seeking help, it's about taking control. During the course of a lifetime, people need advice in many different financial arenas, and this book seeks to make sure that you get that assistance on your own terms. Whether you choose to do as much as possible on your own or hire help for every task, you play the single most important role in managing your finances.

As you go through the chapters, there may be times when it seems like I am stating the obvious, telling you things you already know. There will be plenty of times when I am repetitive, re-stating key points over the course of several chapters. Don't give up on the book when that happens.

Likewise you may be looking for advice on one type of adviser, say, a real estate agent, and see examples—particularly in the early chapters—that pertain to the other specialties. Believe me, there is plenty of overlap between the specialties, and in most situations I could have culled my examples from any of the six fields. There are specific chapters dedicated to each type of adviser so that no one type of adviser gets short shrift in the end.

This book is designed to encompass both a wide audience and broad subject matter. It is for people who are new to managing their own affairs, as well as people who must decide if they need help or who simply want to manage their managers better and need to figure out just how to do that.

How you use this book will depend on your personal situation. If you have never managed your money before or hired a financial adviser of any type, you may actually sit down and read it cover to cover. If you have some market savvy, you may skip chapters that rehash material you are familiar with to get to the parts of the book that focus on the next adviser you need to hire.

And if you already have one or more financial helpers, you may decide to use this book not as a guide to hiring financial assistance, but for seeing whether you are getting the most for your money. To do that, you might jump directly to the chapters on hiring each type of expert, where you can review the selection process to see whether you had enough information to make a good decision in the first place and determine whether your adviser passes muster in hindsight. If not—or if your current dealings with any adviser leave something to be desired—you might use the book as an excuse to sit down with your counselors to redraw the boundaries and guidelines of your relationship.

Over the course of your lifetime, as you need to hire new and different advisers or to evaluate current helpers, I hope you will revisit the book to ensure that you have asked the right questions and not overlooked potential trouble spots.

Remember, there is no serendipity in managing your affairs. If you are thinking of hiring a financial planner or an accountant, and you meet one at a party whom you like and think could satisfy your needs, that is not fate, it's coincidence.

If you sign on with that person and receive lousy advice—or good counsel for that matter—that is happenstance.

By controlling the process, by choosing and managing advisers wisely, you eliminate fate, coincidence, and all of the other "signs" that lead people to make ugly mistakes.

Luck, as legendary football coach Vince Lombardi noted, is what happens when preparation meets opportunity; this book is designed to prepare you to meet and interview financial intermediaries, so that someday you will be able to say you are lucky enough to work with good people.

Picking financial advisers, as I explained to my friend, is tricky, filled with subjective judgments that can affect a lifetime's worth of work and savings. It is not an exercise to be taken on with a cavalier attitude.

Having decided to read this book, you are not giving up your role in managing your money, but you also have decided not to leave key financial relationships to chance. Nothing will help you have a bright financial future more than that.

1   *How to start looking for help*

From the time we are old enough to spend money, we start picking financial advisers.

It starts with emulating our parents' habits, or deciding not to. It goes on to school days, where we caucus with the other kids about what is cool and what we "must" spend our money on.

By the time we get to adulthood, there are plenty of direct and tangential influences on how we manage money, ranging from the media to friends and family to the people we meet every day.

Each of those connections is a *de facto* adviser.

The lone person with the responsibility for managing your affairs, however, remains the same. It's *you*.

So take a good look at your needs, interests, and lifestyle. Over the course of a lifetime, at the very least you will need to manage investments; secure and work out loans; buy or sell a house; insure that home, your property, and family against catastrophic losses; develop a plan to pass that home and your investments along to heirs; and pay taxes on the whole thing.

A lot of that you can do on your own, if you have the interest and choose to develop the expertise to represent yourself well. That knowledge is available to you in adult-education classes, seminars, and hundreds of personal finance books. More often than not, however, you will want help, even if it is only in the form of a consultant who looks over your shoulder to make sure, everything is well thought out.

Say hello to a broker or financial adviser, banker, real estate agent, insurance agent, lawyer and/or estate planner, and a tax preparer or accountant.

If you agree that it's a given that you are likely to need the services of each of these people at some point during your lifetime, then it's important that you learn the right way to hire them.

It starts with the idea that you will "shop" for financial help, the same way you shop around for a car, refrigerator, home, or any big-ticket item.

I'm always amazed that people spend more time researching a new microwave oven than checking into the background of the person who will determine a big chunk of their financial future, but it must be that no one fears offending the microwave with tough personal questions.

Shopping for financial services, from tax preparation to investment advice, is no different than purchasing any other commodity. There are certain key factors to consider:

Price

It's not the most important factor on everyone's list, but it is always a key consideration. No one, no matter how wealthy, has the ability to say "cost is no object" when it comes to their financial affairs; that is how large fortunes unravel in lurid tales of greed, fraud, or ineptitude.

No one thinks twice about eyeballing a can of peas for a price check, or even about getting an estimate before hiring a contractor to do some home repairs, yet people get scared about whether they can ask a lawyer how he bills for his services, as if somehow that professional would explode into an "If you have to ask, you can't afford me!" rage.

Well, maybe you can't afford him. Or maybe you simply don't want to. But if you ask the question and a financial adviser gets angry about it, then you know right away that this is not the person for you. Smart financial advisers of all stripes are happy to explain their charges and to justify the reasons behind their rates; it is up to you to decide if you want to pay the freight.

What's important is that you seek out a price that you feel good about paying—because that encourages you to use the services regularly and develop a relationship with the provider—and that you understand exactly how the adviser will be compensated and are comfortable with that means of payment.

Quality

The toughest area of financial advice to assess,this is where you will have to do the bulk of your work in order to be happy with the outcome.

There is a natural tendency to equate high price with high quality, as in "this broker doesn't deal with low net worth clients, so he must be good." Conversely, any adviser who comes on the cheap must be suspect.

Not so fast.

Those are assumptions, not truisms.

There are many big-dollar advisers with a slew of unhappy customers in their wake. The size of their fees is more the result of their time in the business and, in some cases, overblown reputations that allow them to charge as if they are providing exclusive service.

At the other end of the spectrum, there are plenty of lower-paid advisers whose biggest crime is inexperience, lack of time developing a client base, or simply poor marketing. It's important to remember that almost everyone in financial advisory roles today started out doing grunt work like cold calls and scraping to get customers.

The quality of financial advice is not a quantitative issue, although many people try to make it one. Quality advice simply cannot be measured exclusively in terms of getting the highest rate of return on your money or taking more deductions on your tax return, because those goals can be accomplished in bad ways such as taking on too much risk or deducting items the IRS is likely to disallow.

You will determine the quality of a financial adviser in several ways: professional accomplishments and credentials, satisfied customers, a record of integrity, the perceived value of the work, and gut feeling. Paying for advice boils down to purchasing trust, and your gut about someone will go a long way toward determining how comfortable you are with them in the future.

In financial services, as in refrigerators, there is some name-brand consciousness, which gives a Big Six accountant recognition that a sole practitioner won't get, for example, or makes H&R Block more trusted than "Joe's Tax Service." But the difference between large and small firms often has to do with size and advertising budget more than quality; you will be better off focusing on ability than preconceived notions.

To find advisers who really are worth keeping, you will have to sort through all kinds of fancy packaging. Some of the dumbest financial advice I have ever heard has been dispensed in the most posh offices in the country, the personal finance equivalent to having a fancy Italian restaurant serve you a toaster pizza.

Need

A critical factor in most of your other purchases, need plays a direct role in your choice of advisers. The more advanced your needs, the more you will tilt your decision-making process to paying the full ticket price.

That's why you must do a real needs assessment, a self-examination of what you want in an advisory relationship, what you expect from your banker, insurance agent, or other counselor.

This is particularly important in financial services, where so many products are "sold" rather than purchased based on the consumer's knowledge. I have yet to meet anyone who can say they set out to buy variable life insurance. Most were looking for a savings vehicle, and perhaps a safety blanket, when they bumped into an adviser pushing the policies. Only years later have they started second-guessing their decisions.

I equate purchasing financial help to the first time I bought a computer, when a young salesman simply could not stop pushing the "fast printer," which would knock out my papers more quickly, all for just a few hundred dollars that I could not afford to pay. Faster printing sounded great, but I simply didn't need it; paying for it might not have been a waste of money, but it would have made me less comfortable with the overall deal I negotiated, and that loss in satisfaction might have made the entire affair a downer.

Knowing your needs and being able to explain them to an adviser will go a long way toward making the people you work with advisers for a lifetime.

Affordability

This is different from price because it is the factor where you decide how an adviser's costs fit into your budget. It is also where you look for low-cost alternatives.

Most people don't realize that there is financial assistance at virtually every price point, from ultra-discount to through-the-nose chic.

On the low end, it might be free advice offered by a public agency such as the Internal Revenue Service or a consultation using toll-free hotlines that hook you up with a certified financial planner or certified public accountant who bills you on a per-minute basis for the advice provided. The upper end of the scale includes some of the top financial planners in the country, who charge hundreds of dollars just for an initial interview—regardless of whether you hire them to work for you—and money managers who take a big slice of the assets they run for you each year.

It is not enough to simply look at what you are being charged, you must see how it fits into your budget. If you want ongoing financial planning services but cannot afford a $300-an-hour planner, then you will have two shopping choices; either you change your expectations about how often you actually work with this adviser, or you set your sights on a lower-priced adviser who can meet your quality expectations and still deliver the service you need.

If neither of those options is pretty, then consider doing-it-yourself, although if you only decide to be your own adviser after you have an established a need for the services of others, it is probably too late to help yourself without outside assistance.

You may lust after your neighbor's financial planner—the one that helped the neighbor buy the BMW and put in the swimming pool—but you may not be able to afford that adviser and you will be a lot better off picking someone whose price is better aligned with your budget.

The product itself

In the case of financial services, it's not quite, as static as purchasing a computer, where you can see the hardware. Still, whenever possible, examine the hardware that is available.

For example, if you are working with an insurance agent, you will want one who deals only with high-grade companies. In the stock arena, if you are paying for a full-service broker, you want to know how many top-flight analysts—called industry all-stars—are with the firm. Similarly you will want to know if brokers are discouraged from using anything but house opinions, which means they might stifle their own intuition and knowledge so that they can sell the stocks in which the brokerage firm makes a market. (They may get paid extra for selling those stocks, too.)

If your selections are limited, you must review the available products to see whether the firm is realistically capable of meeting your changing long-term needs. There is nothing worse than feeling that your adviser can't deliver—or isn't delivering—because they don't have the kind of high-quality product you need to succeed.

Services/features

This is where you determine what to expect for your money, not from a qualitative standpoint but in simple "here's what you get from me" terms.

Unless you have a lot of money savvy, the adviser will be educating you on what they offer. Even if you think you know what to expect from an adviser, find out about everything available. Most people consider a banker simply as the person who holds deposits, for example, without knowing that some bankers offer valuable trust services.

Just as you would want a refrigerator salesman to explain the different ways that the removable shelves can improve your life and allow you to decide whether it is worth paying for a second "crisper," so can you talk to a prospective financial adviser about what the relationship is going to be like and what you can expect. Will it be regular phone calls and the ability to chat without receiving a bill every time you need a consultation because you anticipate a major event in your life? Will the broker accept your calls whenever the market makes you nervous? Does the accountant or financial adviser offer a regular newsletter to customers, and is that publication merely a pass-along from a national office, or does it reflect the adviser's feelings about the market, economy, law changes, investment strategies, and more?

Before signing up with any adviser, determine what they are offering and match that against your needs and desires.

All of that research—determining what a financial adviser's services cost and what you can afford to pay, what their services are and what you need, and whether they have the ability to deliver on their promises—simply requires that you think of financial services like every other good or service that you buy, no different from hiring a plumber or a television repairman except that you feel a bit out of your league.

To ease that problem, do your legwork in advance of your need so that you will have plenty of time, and don't have to rush a decision.

Robert Clark, editor-in-chief at *Dow Jones Investment Advisor* magazine, once told me that most people deal with a lot of financial counselors over the course of a lifetime, typically taking advice from one, then moving to another and another without ever establishing a cohesive plan. Bouncing between advisers leads to short-term thinking and mistakes, creating a hodgepodge of holdings and sabotaging the investment portfolio.

If people did the work up front, Clark noted, they could pick one adviser who they could work with comfortably for a lifetime.

If you want advice and advisors who last you a lifetime, it's time to get to work.

2 *A pocketful of money beats a mouthful of excuses*

Life is what is speeding by us while we put things off.

Nowhere is that more true than in our finances, where time truly is money.

You can see that in virtually every advisory relationship. If you save or invest a little bit today and let it grow, you will need to put away a lot less tomorrow. If you take care of your insurance needs today, you don't run the risk of having no coverage in your time of need. If you talk to a tax preparer in June, you can turn tax preparation into actual tax planning. Talking to a lawyer or estate planner can ensure that your heirs don't lose a fortune to inheritance taxes or suffer through emotional times burdened by demanding financial decisions. If you meet with a real estate agent, you can find out how to get the most from your home while you own it, instead of making savvy property moves only as you prepare to sell.

There are plenty of excuses for not doing any of those things right now, but there is also no excuse for not hiring the help we need to manage our money wisely. When it comes to managing your money, putting off today for tomorrow is not a fair trade; your investments have a day less to compound, you spend another day playing at life without a financial safety net.

So now you have purchased this book and are either about to hire advisers or are evaluating the ones you have.

The right way to pick advisers is complicated and requires a lot of discipline and attention to detail. It is a subjective decision where your gut will determine a lot, but where your brain has to know enough to figure out what makes your stomach queasy.

And it can be a daunting task.

Knowing how to choose an adviser doesn't mean you will actually sign the contract.

Most people even considering the need for financial help have a pocketful of excuses as to why they haven't done it already. Even as they acknowledge their need for help, they want to come up with a reason to ignore it.

So here are the most common excuses I have heard for not hiring financial helpers—perhaps one of them has been your thinking—and why you need to overcome this kind of reasoning.

"I plan to do that stuff myself—when I need to"

This is a hard-to-overcome alibi because we all like being self-reliant and believe we can do things ourselves. Plus this raises the why-should-I-pay-for-help issue.

No one really *wants* to pay for financial help, especially when there is so much readily available information out there designed to help us manage our affairs. Invariably we have neighbors or friends who seem to be living proof that everyone can manage money on their own (and do well at it) provided they commit the time and effort.

Likewise plumbing is something that everyone can do.

You can buy do-it-yourself books on fixing leaky pipes or how to replace copper tubing, can get all of the necessary tools—if you don't already have them—at the local hardware store and probably save a lot of money taking care of the problem on your own.

But for some reason, there is neither stigma nor second-thought to calling in a plumber when the sink is stopped or the shower won't drain. In time of need, most people may pull out a plunger, but they will pick up the phone if the problem can't be solved in just a few minutes.

Just as a plumber can save money by fixing things before leaks and clogs force major repairs, so can an adviser help clean up money problems before they become major.

If you haven't hired financial help because you intend to do it yourself, look immediately at your situation. Financial planning—a real program of setting and pursuing goals—should be started early; if you haven't got that kind of comprehensive plan in mind already (and a portfolio of investments is not enough), then you should consider whether you really are a "do-it-yourselfer."

Remember too that the reason many people do things themselves is because they want the "ideal" financial plan.

To the average consumer the ideal plan has three qualities: it is cheap, easy, and successful.

You can get all of those things in your financial relationships, but almost never more than two of them at any one time.

You can get hassle-free, no-time-involved planning that carries you toward your financial goals, for example, but it won't be cheap. Conversely, if you do all your own planning, it will be free and might be successful, but it won't be easy.

It is very easy to let things slide, to stick with what you know and are comfortable with and to avoid mounting problems that you have never before addressed.

A perfect example would be life insurance. Most people starting out don't need it; you should only insure what you can't afford to lose or replace, and singles or young marrieds without a lot of assets frequently don't require coverage.

But that has a way of changing as marriage, a home, and family and other issues creep into the picture.

The result is a person who needs insurance and knows it but hasn't done anything about it—until a call comes from a salesman or someone at a business lunch mentions of. People take this chance meeting as a sign that Providence has smiled upon them, giving them someone who can answer their insurance concerns just at their time of need.

Hundreds of people have told me their personal version of this story, usually including how it wound up as a disaster.

Hiring help does not mean giving up on doing it yourself, it means shoring up the areas where you lack the confidence to make decisions. If you know you need to work on one area of your finances, ask why you aren't doing it right now—or at least educating yourself so that you will be ready to do it on your own when the time comes.

And as for waiting until you have a need to hire an adviser, the issue is whether you will be smart enough to recognize when that moment is—and whether you can get appropriate service in your moment of need. It's pretty easy to figure out when you absolutely must have a relationship with a real estate agent because you have taken a new job or decided to uproot the family or are being transferred.

It's a lot harder to recognize just how your insurance needs have changed, or how your investment strategy is inadequate.

Studies show, for example, that the vast majority of people with retirement savings in a 401(k) plan are too conservative for their own time horizon. That means they may be saving "enough money," but they have not invested it aggressively enough to build a sufficient nest egg.

Presumably many of these people feel they do not need help allocating their retirement savings. They expect their time of financial planing need to come five or ten years before they retire, when they figure out how to protect what they have and how to save enough to retire on their own time schedule.

What they will find out when they hire that adviser is that they have fallen short of their goals, and that they will have to save more aggressively or perhaps put off their retirement date in order to secure the future.

Later in this book you will find out why it is important to hire advisers when you do not have a pressing need for their services. Evaluate your own situation honestly; if you expect to hire help "when I need it," then chances are that you need help now but the situation has not turned desperate.

"I don't know enough and am afraid of being ripped off"

Being scammed is a legitimate fear. And it's always scary hiring an adviser to whom your level of knowledge will always make you feel like a subordinate.

If anything goes wrong—even if it is the kind of simple investment misjudgment that periodically impairs the greatest stock-picking minds —you are likely to feel taken.

But the chances that you will hire a scoundrel are slim, especially if you know enough to remain in control of the situation and have all of your choices spelled out to you. The rule of thumb in financial relationships is very simple: Never do anything you don't understand.

That being the case, you are hiring someone to explore your options. You are then making the choices from the menu prepared by the adviser. Continuing that analogy, if your waiter can't adequately explain the way a meal is prepared or describe how it tastes, you should stick with something that you feel certain will be satisfying.

If the waiter suggests that you are making a bad choice—that he or she knows a lot more about this menu than you do and that they know exactly what you should eat—then they are trying to control your behavior. That's when it's time to find a restaurant where the staff has better table manners.

If you maintain an active role, regardless of your expertise, you greatly reduce the risk of being swindled. But not having a world of financial knowledge doesn't mean you can't manage a team of experts, it simply means that you have to be more pro-active and possibly more demanding of the players your select.

Not hiring financial advisers is indeed a great way to ensure that you don't get scammed, but unless you are prepared to take on the tasks yourself, it is equally likely to guarantee that you will never reach your financial goals.

"Those people wouldn't be interested in working with me right now"

The other version of this excuse is "I'm not wealthy enough to afford (or need) help."

This excuse is debunked as follows: You never know until you try.

No one has ever said that financial help must be expensive. It certainly can be, but it depends on the level of service you are looking for and the mindset of the adviser.

These days, there are many discount providers, pre-paid plans, employer-sponsored assistance programs and more than can help you out. But whether you are paying a flat rate of $69 for a "fiscal physical" offered by a financial planner or $400 an hour for detailed, individualized service, there is probably an adviser who can help you regardless of your current financial situation.

"There is help out there for everyone at every income level," says David H. Diesslin, former president of the National Association of Personal Financial Advisors and head of Diesslin & Associates, a Houston-based financial planning firm. "But it is not always easy to find the right match—the person who does what you want and need, who thinks you make an attractive client and who will do it at a cost you consider reasonable. If you are flexible, you will be able to find people who can do a good job for you."

You can bet that the hotshot broker with the $100,000 minimum account is not interested in placing your first-ever $500 purchase of stocks. But there will be people in the very same firm for whom that order would represent an inroads to a relationship and a start toward what they hope will someday be a $100,000-plus client (namely you).

There are plenty of established advisers out there who take on small clients at reasonable prices. And while experience is a wonderful thing, it is also important to remember that every star adviser started out as a raw rookie and worked up.

As a result, if you have a concern about an area of your finances and worry that you can't take care of it yourself, you can both afford and find someone who will help you.

There are financial professionals—in all areas of expertise—whose interest is in building a clientele. Just as you are looking at developing financial relationships, so are they—and that means they value some things a bit more highly than the money you can put in their pocket today.

The smart real estate agent, for example, doesn't just want to sell you a house now but wants to be in on the deal in the future when you decide it's time to move. The local banker doesn't just want your checking account and credit card business, he wants your mortgage, college savings, trust funds, and your children's birthday-gift money.

One of the first rules that applies to any financial adviser: if they lose interest when you "run out of money," dump them for someone who cares. Anyone who you feel you can't "afford" to work with, or who loses interest in you because you don't generate enough money, obviously is not a good fit.

Even small clients represent big opportunities for advisers. If your money and earnings potential grows, it translates to future business and enhanced opportunities for the adviser; if you are satisfied with their service, your referrals could become future clients.

Don't undervalue yourself.

"I don't want people meddling in my business"

Good advisers don't mess things up for you, they work with you.

Ironically most people get advice from other people who actually are meddling, as opposed to a financial adviser who is paid to come in and analyze the situation.

You can get stock tips form the people you meet at cocktail parties, the post office, or the hairdresser, in supermarket checkout lines, and from strangers you meet on the Internet. You can call a radio station, write a newspaper columnist, and detail your situation to friends and family, all of who will offer their advice, most of it less than expert.

You still make the decisions, so no one really butts into your business unless you let them.

In hiring advisers, however, you are arming yourself to make those choices. You understand the options, the potential consequences, and hopefully, you have explored the alternatives.

The chances of making a mistake are therefore significantly reduced.

That's not having people meddle in your affairs, it's having them counsel you—and it's worth encouraging.

"My father (or friend or other relative) will tell me who to go to"

Every financial situation is different. What works for your neighbor or Uncle Bob or the person at the next desk is not necessarily right for you.

Chances are pretty good that your financial situation is a whole lot different than that of your parents (or children). Say, for example, your father is in retirement. His stockbroker has a lot of clients who are retired; you, on the other hand, are just entering your prime earning years and need to be more aggressive than the rest of the broker's clients. Just because he is a good broker for a conservative set does not make him right for you.

Most people find their financial advisers through word of mouth, and referrals are a big part of the process, but you have to do the legwork yourself.

Again, think of this in terms of services you are more familiar with. If your life depended on it—and your financial life may depend on the advice you get from your financial helpers—would you go to your father's barber or mother's hairstylist, would you trust your brother's mechanic (even if he doesn't normally work on the type of car you own), and would you let your neighbors decorate your home?

Probably not.

Turn to others for referrals and ideas, but be prepared to go your own route. When it comes to financial advice, one size does not fit all.

"I don't have time to interview people right now"

This discussion has come full circle, back to time being money. In this case, if you don't have the time to hire financial helpers the right way, you run the risk of losing money either to people who are frauds or just aren't good at this stuff.

With the exception of lawyers, every other realm of financial advice requires virtually no specialized training and knowledge. If you want to be a tax preparer or a financial planner, for example, you need only hang out your shingle (and maybe complete a registration form with a state agency). Some states require that certain types of advisers pass an exam to gain their license, but even this is no guarantee of formal education.

The investment in picking the right adviser will be rewarded not only with a good relationship and sound money management, but with time. In the future you won't be wasting time trying to resolve disputes, pick a different adviser, or clean up for the mistakes of the adviser you picked in a hurry.

"I don't know how to select an adviser"

Well, that's what this book is for. Keep reading—or keep the book handy when hiring new counselors—and this excuse should evaporate.

The problem with all of these excuses is that they become the rationale for future failure. They are why someone who doesn't get the right price when they sell a house blames the agent—"I signed up with her because Joe and Marge had such good experience with her"—or why someone who discovers they made bad financial planning decisions blames their insurance agent ("He said he could advise me on investing, and I didn't want to have to go out and hire someone else").

What we most want to avoid is the failure to reach our goals and control our life's savings. If you fall short in those arenas, no alibis will be satisfactory. Do the financial chores that you can on your own; there is no excuse for not hiring helpers for the rest of it.

3 Recruit advisers before you need them

Mark Twain once wrote that a banker is a fellow who "lends you his umbrella when the sun is shining and wants it back the minute it begins to rain."

Truth be told, that description would be apt for a lot of advisory relationships. There are plenty of people who are happy to deal with you when it will make them a quick buck but who aren't going to be there for you when the time comes to make tough decisions.

With that in mind, it is very difficult to shop for help when you have a pressing need.

If you have just inherited a large sum of money, for example, every financial adviser in your neighborhood is likely to be clamoring after you. When you don't have that money—or maybe don't yet know how much you will someday inherit—finding a planner to help you devise an investment strategy is not nearly so easy.

One of the biggest problems people have in hiring financial help is that they pick their advisers at the wrong time, either doing it when the pressure is on and there is some sort of financial deadline to meet or looking for help when they don't have the time to do adequate research into their prospective advisers.

But think of the consequences of forging a relationship with an adviser in the crucible of an immediate need for service:

- You could learn that you disagree with your real estate agent on the pricing of your house once the first offer has been received.

- You could discover that your bank relies exclusively on formulas to make its decisions, right at the time that you need money and your finances don't fit into the bank's equation.

▪ You could find out that the broker whose eyes lit up at the prospect of investing your inheritance has taken more risks than you are comfortable with.

▪ Your tax preparer could play a little fast and loose with the rules, a strategy you might not discover until you are on your way to the audit.

A big part of this book discusses the selection process involved in picking various financial specialists. In each case I suggest interviewing at least three prospective advisers before making a choice. In the most crucial positions—notably financial planners, tax preparers, and insurance agents—it could easily take five interviews before you have found someone with whom you are comfortable.

It's impossible to do that kind of work in a hurry, which is why most people never do it at all.

Instead, they go out and talk to a financial planner, for example, hear a bunch of stuff that sounds goods, and then figure they have heard enough. Almost every planner I know is willing to let potential clients come for an interview, but I know of almost no financial planners who have gone through these interviews and then didn't get the client.

That tells me one of two things: either the planners I know are much more impressive than their peers during interviews, or more likely, the clients never bothered to talk to more than one adviser.

When I get a chance to talk to readers, invariably they want to know the name of the one planner I would recommend. I don't give that name for several reasons:

1. By contract, I am not allowed to work with a financial planner in New England—it could be perceived as a tacit endorsement and, therefore, a conflict of interest—so while I have reviewed the work and checked the background of the planners I use as sources, none of them has ever handled my money.

There is a big difference between talking to the media and performing for a client.

2. No matter my selection, the adviser may not be appropriate given the circumstances of the person asking for my help. Since I am never intimately familiar with the finances of readers, there is no way to make a match that I could feel comfortable with.

Personally I would pick one adviser for my mother, a different one for my father, and a third adviser if the job were to manage their money together.

But the important thing isn't why I don't recommend planners, it's why the people ask for the names in the first place. Invariably they want to abdicate the decision or take the fast route out of the selection process. I have heard more than a few groans when I say that the right way to choose a planner is to start by interviewing three of them.

By failing to forge relationships in advance—when there is no sense of urgency—and then hiring an adviser in a pinch, they are likely to find that they have applied a Band-Aid to their financial woes rather than discovered a cure.

When it comes to personal financial relationships, the time to develop a rapport with an adviser is when you have little or no need for service, when you can ask questions with impunity, without fear that the counselor will take offense and leave you in the lurch.

Your multiple interviews don't have to be within one week. You can network with friends, family, and current advisers to get an idea of the specialists to call, and then spread the selection process over a month or two; keep notes on the first interviews so that you have a reminder of how you felt after the sessions.

Similarly you should always be able to make an excuse to visit or interview or chat with potential or current team members. When my wife Susan and I moved from Pennsylvania to Massachusetts, we knew that we would need to hire a local attorney to handle our eventual home purchase, update our wills, and more. We have a terrific attorney in Pennsylvania, but even he acknowledges that we need a local to handle the basics.

Throughout the course of our transition to the Bay State, we had a few papers that needed to be notarized. Susan used that paperwork as the opportunity to interview various local attorneys who would notarize the documents for free; while she had a moment with them, she asked a few questions about the type of work they do, how they handle certain issues, and so on.

As we got closer to actually needing to hire a lawyer to review our home purchase contract and refresh the wills, we had a short list of candidates. We did the requisite background checks, arranged for me to ask some questions either by phone or in person, and—despite needing a lawyer quickly to review a sudden home-purchase offer— we didn't rush into a decision.

Not surprisingly, the lawyer we chose was the one who spent the most time visiting with Susan and talking to me. What is surprising—especially because we live in a very small town—is that he was not the attorney recommended to us by friends. They had suggested the other people who made the short list. Had we been rushed into a decision, we probably would have chosen one of those attorneys; in the long run we would not have been as satisfied to have that lawyer on our team. (From now on, by the way, the new attorney will notarize our signatures whenever necessary, if only because it gives us a reason to chat and a few minutes to discuss life changes that might require legal maneuverings. In most states plenty of people can notarize paperwork; we turn a chore into part of our advisory relationship.)

Managing a financial team—and that is essentially what happens once you hire a financial planner, an insurance agent, a tax preparer, lawyer, et al.—and having relationships with various advisers is not difficult. It's about stepping inside a branch to meet with the banker to talk about financing options on a car or to ask how the Federal Reserve Board's movement on interest rates might affect your ability or desire to refinance in the future.

With a broker, it's a call or two where you ask about stock tips that you heard, but where you were not anticipating making any changes to your portfolio; with a financial planner, it might be a moment to talk about a mutual fund that both sounds good and seems to be a fit into your portfolio. With a real estate agent, it is any time you consider making major changes to your house, or when a house sells on your street or in the immediate neighborhood. You should contact your attorney and insurance agent any time there might be a major event in your life, ranging from additional children to the purchase of new valuables to a change of address.

And in each instance, asking for a breakfast or lunch meeting—especially if the person knows you value them as an adviser—is a great way to develop a rapport. It may be a once-a-year get-together —"Take your broker to lunch" is an old bit of stock market advice— but it gives you an opportunity to talk and brainstorm without the pressure and immediacy of having work in progress.

Throughout the financial services business, specialists break down into two basic categories—"relationship oriented" or "transaction oriented."

Later in this book, in the chapter describing what makes for an ideal relationship, there is a brief discussion of the difference in these two genres of adviser. For now, suffice it to say that recruiting advisers early virtually eliminates the entire group of "transaction-oriented" helpers. Transaction-driven advisers want to make a deal, not to chat about what they can do for you at some unnamed point in the future.

These are the folks who lose interest when they find out you can't deliver something for them right now. I call it the "Brendan Byrne" syndrome, an inside joke that dates back to my high school days.

When I was in high school in New Jersey, the then-Governor Brendan Byrne came to visit during a campaign run. He flew in by helicopter, and it was a big deal for the school and the community. The buildup preceded him for weeks.

Byrne was rushed into the auditorium, where the upper classes were assembled; the lower classes were listening over the intercom. After getting settled in at the podium, the first thing Byrne did was ask how many students would be eligible to vote in the next election.

Seven kids raised their hand.

Nine minutes later Byrne's speech was over and he was out the door.

Byrne, obviously, was transaction oriented. When we couldn't deliver the votes, we got the five-cent talk, instead of getting the dollar's worth the students and administration had been hoping for.

Transaction-oriented advisers often betray themselves during the early recruiting process. They are the ones who want to do everything "now," for whom there is never a reason to slow down and reflect when they "have the answer" to your needs. If there is a big enough pot of gold at the end of your rainbow, they will stick around and try to close the deal, but it will always feel like a sales pitch rather than concerned counsel.

By comparison, relationship-oriented advisers are a little less worried with what your business means to them now. They make the assumption that a relationship will lead to years of work and, as a result, are willing to do the little things now that help you become a lifetime business partner.

It is that attitude that you need to foster in order to make your financial relationships blossom.

Let's use your banker as an example.

Banking is a business fraught with formulas. Some banks, for example, won't make auto loans on used cars that are more than four model years old. But say for a moment that you car of choice is an eight-year-old Mercedes-Benz with low mileage and a lot of life left.

If you are calling various banks trying to get used car loan rates by phone, you routinely will be told that the institutions don't make loans on cars that old. In fact, however, they do—provided they understand the situation better.

If your banker knows that you are a good credit risk with a solid payment history and that the car is worth the money being loaned to buy it, the deal will happen. Getting that preferential treatment without hassles and holdups generally involves asking for it in advance, going in and talking to your banker about financing options, the same way you should have once discussed the various features on a checking account or the trust services the bank offers.

Without a banker on the team, you will find the car first, then look for a loan, and wind up taking less favorable terms because the institution is bailing you out of a jam rather than being your partner in the purchase.

You should be able to envision similar circumstances with almost every type of financial arrangement you are involved in.

One of the biggest reasons to have a team assembled is purely for counseling reasons, to get advice when a situation arises. But the reason you can get sound advice in a pinch from your personal stable of advisers is that all of the players know you, your risk tolerances, your goals, and so on.

The lack of that comfort zone—and the time it takes to try to learn a client—is one reason why even the best financial advisers don't always look so good when they are hired on the spur of the moment.

By recruiting advisers early, you also establish your management style before the big financial issues hit home. That makes it much easier to ensure that you will be on your own terms when your life enters financial crunch-time.

Don't be one of the millions of people who spends more time shopping for or repairing television sets than they do for financial services. Recognize that the advisers you choose have a huge impact on the financial well-being of you and your entire family.

The majority of consumers who hire advisers in a pinch wind up dismissing them later on, moving from one stop-gap helper to the next. They make do with Band-Aid solutions instead of trying to cure their financial ills, losing faith in their helpers whenever the market turns, or they see something that looks just a little bit better than what they have now; they chase inferior alternatives and throw away financial plans that can achieve their goals, or they work at least once in their lives with a fraud or charlatan.

The idea in seeking financial assistance is to make your counselors partners in your success, capable of giving you good advice for years to come.

Don't settle for Mark Twain's banker. Instead, get to know your advisers and take the time to let them know you; it's the only way you can feel comfortable that you will be protected even in the worst of storms.

4   *Overcoming sins of commission*

There's an old country song where the singer tells his loved one: "Don't pay the ransom, honey, I've escaped."

When it comes to managing your money, paying for help has a tendency to feel like paying ransom. You want to get the object of your payoff—in this case financial security—but can't be sure it will arrive safe and sound and that you won't just lose your money to some thief.

At the same time, escape is a real possibility. You can always do this stuff on your own.

But therein lies a quandary.

On the one hand, that escape is difficult—truly impossible for many.

On the other, no one likes being taken hostage or paying ransom for their safety, and yet they can feel like a prisoner when looking at commissions, management fees, and retainers.

The result is that people focus on the payment structure, rather than the process and results. They go to great lengths to avoid commissions.

I'm all in favor of getting things cheaply and not paying more than you have to for financial counsel, but many people who brag about avoiding hefty fees can't be quite so boastful about performance. They rely on hearsay, cocktail party gossip, or luck to make and manage their money; all are sources of information sure to be disappointing at one point or another.

The idea is not necessarily to get everything at low or no cost. Instead, you want to get what you pay for.

For example, if you know the next stock you want to purchase, have figured out how it will impact your overall investment portfolio, and do not want to hear about other options, then you clearly do not need a full-service broker to execute the trade. A discount broker—who will take you order, buy the shares, and offer no ancillary advice or counsel—will do just fine.

If, on the other hand, you want an adviser who helps you pick appropriate stock investments, who reviews the fundamentals of companies that fit your investment profile, and who develops a stock selection and asset allocation strategy, then a discount broker would be a bad call. You would save on the execution, but you wouldn't get the service you need.

Somewhere between managing money on the cheap and paying through the nose lies the ideal payment structure for the average consumer.

There are several ways to pay for financial help. Bankers typically are not paid directly for their efforts, but have their pay built into loans and other basic services. Bank advisers, however, may work on a commission basis if they are dispensing more sophisticated advice. Tax preparers, by comparison, work almost entirely on a fee-for-service basis, getting paid either for the time spent preparing the return or by-the-form, where each completed piece of paperwork is worth a set price.

The majority of real estate agents work strictly on commission, while brokers, financial planners, and insurance agents can be paid in several ways, from commissions to a fee based on a percentage of the money involved in the transaction to a flat hourly fee. Some payment structures, such as "fee offset" combine two forms of payment, with set fees being reduced by the amount of any commissions paid.

The big reason people hate paying commissions is that it seems so cheesy. Here is someone who is pushing a product that is supposedly for your benefit, yet the only way they can make money on the deal is if you buy. That removes a lot of incentive for someone to watch out for your best interests in the deal. (The one exception to that basic conflict is the real estate agent working for the seller; real estate agents get the biggest commission if the seller gets the best price, so their interests tend to lie in concert with their client on matters of pricing changes and how to negotiate the bidding process. But that does not ensure that an agent won't cut a quick deal that brings in a commission, even though the client might have been better off waiting for a second bidder.)

Because so many people find commission sales disarming, the financial services industry has been moving toward flat fees. These are pitched as safe, no-conflict ways to do business.

Wrong.

Truth be told, there are potential conflicts of interest in virtually every type of advisory relationship, no matter how neatly it is structured.

In an hourly rate basis, the answer is obvious: it is in the best interest of the service provider to rack up the hours on your behalf. Even if the number of hours is limited, it may seem like a lot to you. ("Could it really take two hours of a lawyer's time to prepare a no-frills, simple will?")

In the piece-of-the-deal arrangement, the adviser has two potential biases. One is to get the highest possible price, which is no conflict at all unless they put off anything that doesn't maximize their commission. There are plenty of circumstances, most notably with lawyers and real estate agents, where getting the transaction done immediately is better for the client than waiting to squeeze every possible penny from the deal. The other conflict is the exact opposite, which is adviser pushing to get the deal done so that it generates their fee now. In that situation the client might be better off waiting for a more lucrative offer, but the adviser wants to close the deal now in order to get paid.

And in the assets-under-management scenario, a conflict is equally easy to envision, in that the adviser wants to maximize the assets they manage. (Say you come into a major inheritance and are torn between investing the money and paying off your mortgage. It is in the adviser's best interest to get as much of that inheritance under management—where it generates a bigger fee—which might create a bias against conservative options like paying off the mortgage.)

In other words, in all payment forms an adviser may have a reason to want to do something untrustworthy.

The National Association of Personal Financial Advisers has created a special designation for financial-service providers who operate on a fee-only basis. The new F-O mark—which stands for fee-only—is an instant signal of the adviser's compensation method, but it says nothing of expertise and competence.

But the words "fee-only" do not mean "no conflict." Moreover, because so many advisers now use "fee-for-service" or some other inconclusive terms to describe their practice, you need to keep these potential trouble spots in mind at all times.

Knowing that actually makes it easier to shop for financial advisers. Instead of being embarrassed to ask about the price for someone's services—fearing the snooty "If you have to ask, you can't afford me" routine—simply make it a regular part of your interviews. Any financial adviser who is not forthcoming about disclosing the ways they get paid and what they actually get paid for is not worth trusting.

Armed with cost information and having interviewed a few practitioners, you can make sensible decisions. You may have found a tax preparer who is cheap, for example, but you might prefer the experience and education level of an accountant who costs a bit more. Conversely, you might look at an accountant and an enrolled agent —another form of tax preparer—and decide that you do not need to pay a premium to have a super-expert handle your ordinary, plain vanilla tax return.

Once you break financial help down to its costs—no matter how they are calculated—you will see that these are services not unlike many everyday tasks that you currently choose to pay for help with.

Let's look at the financial world in terms of another business that affects almost everyone, automotive repair.

For just a moment, we'll pretend that *Money* and *Kiplinger's Personal Finance* magazines are actually *Auto Mechanic* and *Fix Your Own*. Instead of being about mutual funds and certificates of deposit, the magazines run stories about assembling the right tool kit, or five ways to a faster and neater oil change; the ads are for sparkplugs, replacement pistons, and fuel injectors.

If we create a culture where average folk frown upon the people who pay a mechanic to do the job—and I compare the work of most financial advisers to that of most auto mechanics, despite the angry letters I get from the financial services community—then we will have approximated the atmosphere surrounding financial services today.

The result would be the same that you can currently see by talking with friends and neighbors about their finances.

There will be a group of people who really know what they are talking about, a group of people trying to get along with inadequate knowledge—discernable by cars that run but make a lot of noise and break down a little too frequently—and a group of people who pay for help to fix their car and have few or no car troubles as a result. (This last group might still wash its own cars, but it will leave the big stuff to the pros.)

The trick in that kind of society would be to wind up in the first or last group, either knowledgeable enough to use the auto magazines and the other available data to help yourself or smart enough to know how uninformed you are and to pay for help before messing things up on your own.

One more key point: For most people, the car is only the third or fourth biggest investment in their life. It falls somewhere behind a home and a retirement/college savings portfolio, at the very least.

So consider the logic in someone who has no trouble paying a mechanic, yet can't stomach the thought of paying a financial counselor who is watching over their very biggest investment vehicles.

That makes no sense.

Neither does picking or avoiding any type of financial adviser solely on the basis of cost.

Once you have identified your need, the object is to find counselors who will take care of it. Cost is an object but not the only object.

Instead, look at what you are getting for the money and determine where the reasonable balance lies. If someone wants a big fat fee for selling you a mutual fund without developing an asset allocation plan or providing other advisory services, then you are paying a lot of money for something you could accomplish just as easily with a $29 piece of software or a $40 magazine subscription.

But if an adviser completes a needs analysis, determines a plan of action that will get you from where you are now to where your financial goals are, they deserve some level of compensation.

Getting back to that auto-mechanic analogy, you may decide that you like one mechanic better than another because he speaks in plain English and you believe his repairs are of a superior quality. You will pay a premium for that level of service, even though you might know in your heart that you could be satisfied with lower-grade service at a discounted price.

When it comes to hiring financial help, the issue is not price, but rather a combination of service, quality, and cost. By comparison-shopping for advisers, you can get past the cost issue and look at the bigger picture. You're not going to like paying for advice any better—it may still feel like ransom—but you will have a better idea that the "goods" will be delivered when you pay your bill.

5   *Do you want your mother's decorator? A guide to referrals*

Shortly after I began writing this book, my wife and I started asking friends for the names of contractors who had done work on their hardwood floors.

Quickly, we had a short list of four names.

We took notes as our friends bragged about their contractor's best attributes.

One was cheap. (Okay, "reasonable" might be a better word.)

One was happy to work on the weekends to get the job done more quickly.

One was "the guy who everyone in town uses."

One "took extra time to do the job right," and didn't charge more when the work took longer than expected.

Presumably, if you were looking at the same kind of refinishing job we were considering, one of those attributes would stand out. Someone would jump to the top of your list, whether it is the guy who costs less—in our home, some of those refinished floors are almost entirely covered by rugs, so cheap is good—or the floor man with the status to get jobs from all of the right people in the community, a kind of blanket endorsement from the town we love.

What was interesting about the list was that it came from close friends, all of whom have a lot in common with each other. They all care enough about the appearance of their home enough to want quality craftsmanship, they all have lives similar to ours where refinishing the floors would be a disruptive inconvenience they want to minimize, and they all have limited funds available for this kind of work.

Given that background on the people actually making the referrals—and having seen in their homes the handiwork of these craftsmen—there is a good chance that any of the contractors could meet our basic needs, albeit some a little bit better than others.

Yet each of our friends made their referral by citing the one thing that stuck out in their mind about the contractor.

And that referral, in many ways, was an attempt to justify their own decision, to say that they had picked the right floor man because he was hard-working, successful, diligent, or reasonable. Our choosing the same floor man—especially since they know we shop around—validates their opinion.

Therein lies one of the inherent problems with referrals, the potential for conflict of interest. With referrals, you always have to wonder whether the advice being proffered—even when you have gone out of your way to ask for it—really is in your best interest.

With professional referrals—when, say, a banker recommends an accountant—there is reason to question the motives of the advisers involved. In some cases there can be kickbacks or financial incentives involved, either monetary or in the form of returned favors. In some full-service financial firms, the adviser working with you on investments has a concrete reason to want to see you stay within the firm when you buy insurance, which may be a motivation for the glowing endorsement of the firm's policy seller.

Many trade groups are happy to provide you with the names and numbers of counselors who work in your area, but those groups tend to have a bias toward their own membership, which means that anyone who is not a member or who has not achieved a certain credential that the organization happens to espouse won't be on there. Your state society of certified public accountants, for instance, will not give you referrals to enrolled agents, a different status of tax preparer that may be better suited—and less expensive—to the tax-preparation needs of many individuals.

Many referral services are paid referrals, where a provider only gets on the list if they agree to advertise. The need to advertise for more clients is not necessarily an endorsement for the adviser's business.

With referrals from friends, there can be the same potential judgment-coloring factors, from rewards—advisers who offer gifts or financial incentives for bringing in new customers—to the need to validate personal decisions. (Sadly you never find out about that last condition until it is too late, when a regular conversation becomes "Isn't Joe great? We just can't believe how pleased we could be with an accountant.")

And even if the referral is honest and true, it still may not deliver the right person for you. Think of it in terms of interior decorators. Your mother may have a lovely home, but it might not be your style and taste; when she refers you to her decorator, it's entirely possible that you wind up with someone who does lovely work—so long as it's for your mother.

When it comes to financial advisers, a referral should be a starting point, not a selling point.

My favorite referral story involves a very prominent stockbroker in Allentown, PA, a city where I was once business editor of the local newspaper, *The Morning Call.*

It is often assumed that you only get great monetary advice in big money-center areas, a fallacy that I wanted to dispel by holding a public stock-picking contest between some prominent local brokers. One of the people who agreed to participate—much to the surprise of almost everyone in the local investment community, I found out later—was a guy I'm going to call Jim. (I'd use his real name, but given how much he wants this episode to go away, I fear the wrath of his lawyers.)

Jim was *the* broker in town, the one who handled the local money elite, the name routinely kicked around as the biggest shot in the neighborhood. He was efficacious and personable, handsome and very well connected. He had the highest minimum in the area for establishing an account, and the highest-profile clientele. When I went searching for players in the game, I sought out the recommendations of regional executives, and three of every four referrals were to Jim; I began to question whether any other area brokers were doing significant business.

But we found a few other good stock-pickers and started the year-long process of investing and managing imaginary portfolios for the benefit of our readers. The contest had rules that were a bit stilted—most money managers do not shoot for big short-term results, and we were running a contest to see who could achieve the most growth in twelve months—but all of the brokers understood the situation, the same way you would hope they would understand the special needs of an individual client.

When the year was gone, so were a lot of Jim's clients.

Three of the brokers' portfolios had gained more than 40 percent, a fourth more than 20.

Jim had lost nearly 40 percent.

Worse yet, he had done it with the exact same strategy he used for his real-life clients, a particularly dumb move since the vagaries of a one-year competition are a lot different than the long-term investment concerns of a wide-ranging clientele. Those customers started to realize over the course of the year, that Jim pigeon-holed all of his customers into the same investments, regardless of their specific needs.

Just as those investments were inappropriate for the imaginary client in our contest, so were they poor choices for some of his real clients. His one-strategy-fits-all style had never been apparent to customers until it was in the paper and, by then, Jim couldn't sweet-talk his clients into walking around wearing his poorly fitted portfolio.

Jim's performance was so bad that his brokerage firm—one of the nationwide biggies—no longer allows its representatives to take part in such contests without written consent from headquarters.

When the whole episode was finished, Jim told me that his greatest mistake was not his strategy so much as participating in the first place. He said—and this is one of my favorite quotes ever—"A whale only gets harpooned when it comes to the surface."

But what stuck with me was not just that line, or Jim's lack of performance, but rather a comment made to me over breakfast by a prominent local executive, one of the clients who left Jim about nine months into the game. "What the game made me realize," the executive said, "is that he's been losing my money with a smile on his face for a long, long time."

The last time I checked, Jim was selling a lot of insurance and annuity products, mostly to the long-time customers who at least left some of their money with him.

Jim had the best word-of-mouth in town, but as it turned out, everyone who kicked around Jim's name was, essentially, justifying their own decision. By making the recommendation, they got to raise his good points and re-convince themselves that their decision was a good one, and that he was "the best choice in town." His business had survived for years more on his ability to generate referrals than his ability to generate profits.

"Some people re-sell themselves when they give a referral," says Dr. Harry Clarke Noyes, who runs Psychological Motivations, a Dobbs Ferry, NY, firm that examines consumer behavior. "They list the attributes of someone to you, and they are also re-examining the decision on their own. They may want you to choose the same person because it confirms their decision—and because if you choose someone else it could raise more doubt in their mind.

"It's not that everyone who makes a referral does this, but it certainly happens."

All of this does not mean that referrals should be taken with a grain of salt. Getting counsel from someone else remains the single best way of starting with a short list of specialists, be it insurance agents or contractors who restore hardwood floors.

But referrals need to be fleshed out.

Most people make virtually no distinction between a "referral"—you ask for the name of someone to turn to—and a "reference," someone who you grill on their experience working with the adviser.

In practice, however, there tends to be one major difference. Referrals are taken at face value, where a reference undergoes questioning to ascertain their level of satisfaction. (In both cases there is the presumed conflict of interest that one reason to vouch for the adviser is to justify their own benefit. There may be other benefits such as discounted services, gifts, and other incentives for helping to bring clients into the fold; all potential conflicts should be asked after.)

Getting a name from someone who answers the question "Who do you buy insurance from" is not enough. You want to know why they recommended someone, if that person is especially suited for your needs (something that a paid adviser making a professional referral should be able to answer) and more.

There is more later in the book about questioning a reference.

With the potential for conflict of interest—especially when one adviser is passing your business to another—you might wonder whether it is smart to discount referrals altogether.

Clearly the answer is no.

My last car purchase came from an establishment where every time you refer someone who buys a car, you get $100 off your next purchase or repair job. The incentive is there for me to make the referral, but I wouldn't do it if I expected someone to be dissatisfied with the dealer. Such disappointment could potentially erode the friendship.

And so while my friends who recommended hardwood floor specialists may have had their own conflicts of interest, chances are that they would have told me to avoid anyone with whom they had a bad experience.

Referrals put you squarely in the middle, somewhere between a friend or adviser wanting you to be satisfied and wanting to justify their own selections.

When it comes to referrals and your financial team, what you need to guard against is the "instant trust" factor, where you impart so much faith in someone else that you let your guard down. It is too easy to use a referral as the sole basis to hiring a financial adviser.

You trust your friend, who got a big fat tax refund check, so you believe they must have a good tax preparer.

Or, you have a problem that your hired gun for taxes can't solve; they suggest a specialist who can get the job done. You trust your tax preparer—or already should have dumped them—which creates instant trust in the referral.

That trust may be well-founded and the referral may be perfect, but the basic rule holds true: no one gets a position on your financial team until you have checked them out and feel comfortable that they belong.

Referrals are a great way to make a short list of candidates for any position on your team. Asking your financial planner and banker for the names of an estate-planning attorney can yield you very good choices (particularly if they name the same person), and the word of a trustworthy friend should generate your confidence in an adviser. But the crucial thing is to compile a short list and not to stray from the process of selecting a financial helper just because one candidate was built up by friends and colleagues as the "right" choice.

Remember too that you may not take the same approach to financial relationships as your friends or need the same kind of assistance. Your neighbor may drive a fancy car and be a "wealthy doctor," but that may also make him self-employed and dealing with a completely different kind of retirement-savings situation than what you face working for a big public company.

Your other neighbor might be satisfied getting an update on their portfolio every six months, while you want a report every time the market hiccups. If the two of you are, in reality, completely disparate personality types—one is nervous, the other calm—you will need to examine whether an adviser can meet your needs, no matter how they differ from your neighbor's. It's kind of like your mother's decorator; competent and skilled, perhaps, but just not your style.

The key with referrals is to find out what kind of relationship your friend has with their hired help. What is the tenor of the relationship? How often do they get updates? Does the adviser return calls promptly? How does he or she react when proffered advice is not taken? Just what makes this adviser so great?

In essence, once you have the referral, you need to treat your friend like a reference so that you can make your own decision rather than simply confirming theirs.

Gather a series of referrals, decide which candidates sound the most promising to interview, and then make your selection. And if someone who makes a referral is offended that you went your own way and found someone without their help, that's not your problem. You'll be prepared to justify your decisions, if need be, and they will get over it.

Remember, it's a referral, not a sales pitch. There may be a lot of advisers who can satisfy your needs—just as my wife and I had the pick of experts for our floor—but no one knows your criteria for a financial relationship better than you do. More important, no one else has to live with the consequences of your selection decision.

6   *Friends don't let friends become clients, most of the time*

Years ago my wife was convinced by a friend that we needed to do some financial planning.

The friend just happened to be a new financial adviser.

She of course wanted to be the one to advise us.

I explained to my wife that I felt pretty comfortable doing my own financial planning, but Susan sold me on the idea that her friend Sandra could help us find better financing options for our first new car. Sandra also could provide a counterbalance to my judgment—something I have always sought out—by which I might learn if my early forays into mutual funds were properly thought out.

Best of all, and Sandra gave us this in writing, it was a money-back deal. If we weren't satisfied or Sandra did not provide us with ideas and information we didn't have on our own, we could get our money back.

And so I signed the contract.

As you can easily figure out this far into the book—even before we get to specifics on how to pick advisers—the selection process was all wrong. I did not contact references, interview other planners, do a complete background check on the firm and perform all of the other tasks necessary to a good hiring decision.

Worse yet, Sandra did not deliver.

Her fund selections were mediocre at best; I had done significantly better on my own, so I would not pay a commission to buy her suggestions. Beyond that, her advice consisted largely of trying to help us improve our cash flow so that we could purchase insurance products that, at the time, we had no need for and no real way to afford. Sandra's advice on the car boiled down to suggesting that we pursue a great loan deal that I had found all by myself.

Which brings us to the money-back part.

I'm still waiting.

Susan couldn't bring herself to push for it; she didn't want to lose a friend or have me come off like a jerk. Sandra ran in the small circle of friends we had at the time; although saying something to friends about our professional relationship would have been a breach of ethics, we feared that kind of gossip. In short, we were young and didn't put up much of a fight.

Despite telling Sandra that I was disappointed, I never got it, nor did I pursue, my money back.

The two lessons to take from this experience are:

1. Hire advisers the right way. If you have a friend or relative who can pass muster and with whom you still feel most comfortable after interviewing several candidates, so be it.

2. When possible, don't do business with friends or relatives. It's a good way to lose both.

A recent survey by the American Society of Chartered Life Underwriters & Chartered Financial Consultants said that 40 percent of all people take financial advice from friends, family, and business associates. While the remaining populace relies on some type of financial adviser, the study did not say how many of those planning relationships had some sort of friendship or family tie.

Clearly, however, people feel comfortable relying on loved ones for financial advice, which makes it a tough call when a relative is selling financial services.

In fact, if a friend or family member goes into the financial services arena, you can expect a phone call about becoming a client. Every new financial adviser, no matter whether they are in banking, real estate, accounting, or selling stocks and bonds, must start by building a client base. To get their business off the ground, most people contact friends and relatives.

Clearly some of these situations turn into wonderful financial relationships. The initial clientele for most new mutual funds is the family and acquaintances of the manager, and surely somebody knew every mutual fund management genius before the media discovered that person as a genius.

But remember that for every guru, there are countless advisers who don't make the grade; if you aren't one of the truly lucky—related by some freak of nature to a person who is a real freak of nature and, therefore, a world-class money manager at a young age—you are almost guaranteed to be disappointed in more ways than one.

In our case, with the financial relationship going nowhere, Susan and Sandra grew distant; both women surely must have known that family get-togethers would eventually lead to shop talk.

So we lost a friend and about $200. In the long run it's the latter that still bothers me, because I learned that Sandra valued our friendship differently than I did or she never would have jeopardized it with a business proposition.

Indeed, one of the key considerations to doing business with a friend is whether the offer of financial help is being made out of altruism—"I see your plight and think I can help"—or from the need to get clients.

"F&R selling"—sales-speak for selling to friends and relatives—is a crutch for the person making the sale. Think of it like someone selling Girl Scout cookies. A girl may start sales at home, then with neighbors, then hitting up people in her parents' office, but generating lucrative returns requires selling to strangers.

If someone is established in business and is just now getting around to making a sales pitch to you, be skeptical; good advisers—and good salesmen—don't have to rely on the friends-and-family crutch for too long.

Not long ago a friend in our new hometown pitched financial services to Susan. Susan explained that I have a strict no-business-with-friends policy, yet she still feared offending this man and his wife. As far as I'm concerned, "friendship" shouldn't be that fragile; had he taken offense at our refusing to do business, this man would have been showing little respect for our judgment and character. That would mean we don't have much of a friendship.

For most people, doing business with a friend or family member spells trouble for one big reason: you let your guard down.

There is an assumption that friends and family get special treatment, a little extra hand-holding, an insider's edge on hot information or some extra level of dependability. In addition the crucial element of trust—the cornerstone to your search for any financial adviser—tends to be in place with both your kin and your playmates. Clearly, unless they are a complete fraud, you can assume that your friend or family member wants both the personal and professional relationships to prosper.

Still, their good intentions do not mean they can deliver the goods. The nephew with the ink still fresh on a real estate license, for example, may not have enough experience to get you the best deal on the sale of your home. Compounding the problem is a reluctance to question advice—or terminate an advisory relationship if it's going poorly—because it could lead to family/friendship problems.

Unless you are willing to sacrifice that best deal for the sake of the relationship, then you don't want to do business with relatives.

But even if you plan to separate business from friendships, that will not make the offers go away, nor will it make them any less tempting. Now mater how much you try to avoid mixing business and pleasure, the comfort level you have with relations and friends always is alluring.

The important thing to remember about doing business with friends is that it can be emotional on all sides. If you ask your best childhood friend to provide a written history of their business experience and credentials, they may take offense.

That reaction is one more reason why it is hard to mix business and personal relationships. If they blanch when you want an interview and ask about dispute resolution or want something in writing, how will they treat you if you ever decide not to follow a piece of their advice?

If anything but a where-do-I-sign-up answer will be treated as an affront, the friendship is guaranteed to be strained or you are surrendering control of your decision-making powers.

If you are considering a business relationship with a relative, stick to the selection process you would use on a complete stranger. It will increase your odds for success.

If, for example, you interview several prospective insurance agents and come away feeling that your brother-in-law is not a good adviser, you avoid the unpleasantness of having to sever the business relationship later when it falls short of your expectations. On the other hand, if he truly is the best option, you will never second-guess whether the relationship colored your selection.

As you put a friend or relative through the adviser-selection process, put particular stress on the following five elements.

▪ *Doing a complete background check.* Even if your friend or relative is on the up-and-up, their firm may not be. Plenty of people starting out in financial services wind up working for boiler-room operations, firms with poor reputations and worse.

Again, intentions often differ form reality. I have heard any number of newly minted brokers extoll the virtues of penny stocks—

believing this stuff in their hearts—right up to the day when their firm was shut down by lawmakers for illegal doings by higher-ups.

Then there are those advisers who have burned clients and, now, need new ones. If a friend or relation has been in business for ten years but only recently thought to call you up and offer their services, find out if there is a regulatory reason for their sudden interest.

Checking financial advisers of all sorts requires little more than one or two phone calls—how to do it is in the chapters on picking individual advisers—and your friend or relative will be none the wiser for your efforts, so it won't hurt any feelings.

▪ *Asking "Why do you want me as a client?"* One key to a successful financial relationship is finding someone who wants to "hire" you. When it comes to friends and family, try to find out their motive in seeking you out.

Just as you might worry about some relative constantly calling to hit you up for money, so should you be concerned about someone who sees the value of your friendship as a meal ticket. The answer you want to hear is one based on demographics, on what they have learned about people in your financial situation, of how they can fulfill your financial needs.

Be sure that your situation is one they are familiar with, that you are a good match with their typical client. You do not want to be anybody's test case, their maiden effort into complex financial waters.

If you do not resemble that average client and they do not have a good reason for wanting to hire you—beyond the mere paycheck you can provide—then consider whether this is a relationship where the benefits will be a bit one-sided.

▪ *Getting it in writing.* If they are truly think well of you, they won't mind setting down the terms of the relationship in writing, even if such a contract is not required by law. You want specifics on how the relationship will work, what you are getting for your money, the name of a supervisor (when applicable), and how you will get your money back if you are not satisfied.

If you ever are so unhappy as to ask for your money back, there's a good chance the friendship will be shot. In that circumstance, in order not to feel taken advantage of, you want better recourse than having to tell a judge or arbitrator that you thought this friend would take care of you.

▪ *Seeking out references.* You may have held your nephew since he was in the cradle, but that doesn't mean you have any idea whether he is any good at this job. Ask for the name of a customer whose situation is similar to yours so that you can hear an impartial observer—one who presumably likes the adviser's services—extoll their virtues.

Again, a friend or relative may be offended that you would ask; that's a sign that they do not have enough respect for you as a client to meet your requirements for making a business relationship work.

- *Drawing the lines between business and pleasure.* Try to make it clear that you do not want the business side of your relationship to spill over into the personal side, and determine what the two of you can do to keep that from happening.

My stockbroker, for example, is a former lacrosse teammate with whom I started working before I made my personal prohibition on mixing friends and finances. The reason the relationship works is that it is clearly defined; Tommy knows that the day he calls with a hot stock tip—something I do not want from my broker because I do my own investment research—is the day our business relationship ends. He offers suggestions and guidance when I ask, executes the trades I want to make, and stays clearly within the bounds of what I want from a broker. When we're done with business, we swap stories about our families.

Express what you want from the financial relationship, and discuss how the two of you can set up limits that keep any shortfalls from spilling over and hurting the personal relationship. Tell the adviser under what circumstances you would cut and run; your expectations —perhaps you want a counselor who can deliver 15 percent returns per year, even though that is tough to do with a balanced investment portfolio—go a long way to determining whether the two of you are destined for a successful financial relationship. By talking about this in advance, the two of you may decide that any financial relationship would jeopardize the personal side of things and not be worth it.

Remember, there is more than money at stake when you do business with friends and family. While you are going through the adviser selection process, include the extra value of your friendship in your decision-making. You stand to lose a lot more than your cash if a financial relationship with a friend or relative turns sour.

Defining an ideal financial relationship is a bit like describing love.

Words may escape us, but we know when we are in it.

When it comes to financial relationships, ideal is an individual concept.

I have one friend who insists his stockbroker call every time the market drops 100 points, in order to talk strategy (and to calm my friend's nervous stomach). By comparison, I wouldn't expect to hear from my broker if the Dow Jones Industrial Average lost 1,000 points—unless I called him to buy, sell, or talk strategy.

Both relationships are ideal, however, because the broker acts in accordance with his client's wishes, and both clients are pleased with the level of service they receive.

That means that in order to have an ideal relationship with an adviser, you must first decide what you want, and then express it to the adviser up front in order to set appropriate expectations.

That's a bit tricky; you are paying for someone to advise you, and in that capacity, they are the ones who are supposed to help you determine what's going to work.

So you can't create your ideal in a vacuum. You must enter the interview process with a framework that you consider the "right" way to go and then see how the adviser's ideal fits in with that.

Regardless of whether you are choosing a lawyer, a broker, a banker, or any member of the team, there are a few things involved in ideal financial relationships.

Personal service

Service in financial relationships is kind of like the involvement a college student has with professors, particularly at a big college where it is easy to remain anonymous.

In those situations you can sit in the back of the class, do your assignments, and go largely unnoticed, or you can work with the professor, visit during office hours, and develop a relationship.

You can be well served by either type of relationship, but the important thing is to get the education you are paying for and to have the relationship you want to receive for your money.

Throughout the financial services business, specialists break down into two basic categories—"relationship oriented" or "transaction oriented."

The transaction-oriented providers want to rack up the deals. It is the bank that charges you a fee for using a teller—don't laugh, it's probably coming to your neighborhood soon—or where there is no one in your branch who has basic decision-making powers. Or it is the stockbroker who wants to sell you the stock and has to rush off to the next customer, rather than discuss with you how the purchase fits in with your overall portfolio and strategy. It is the insurance agent who is pushing new products that he wants you to sign up for before you have a full understanding of how the coverage works. Or it is the lawyer who signs you up, brings you "into the firm," and then passes all responsibility to a subordinate who really represents you. It is the grind-it-out tax preparation services, or the real estate agent who has too many current listings to recall without a printout.

Some firms are transaction oriented for cost reasons. You can save money buying life insurance direct from a provider rather than through an agent, for example, but the trade-off for the savings is the level of service, advice, and hand-holding you can expect. Similarly you can save money buy using a discount broker, but that's only a wise idea if you don't want or need the "full-service" part of working with a full-service broker.

Even when cost is not the big issue in choosing an adviser, there is nothing necessarily wrong with using transaction-driven providers, especially if you have some do-it-yourself initiative with your finances. For example, plenty of people—I would wager that it's a majority—don't know the names of the people who serve them at the bank but are not unhappy with that. So long as they don't want to buy an older-model used car, get an interest-only mortgage, or do anything out of the ordinary, the do-it-by-machine or drive-thru bank customer can be completely satisfied.

But for most people—especially those who bought this book to improve their fortunes by managing a team of helpers—financial counsel requires more than an interface with a machine.

That being the case, the first thing you need to do is determine the level of personal service you want, and what the adviser is willing to provide.

It sounds obvious, but you want to know who will actually deal with you—will it be the broker or will you also be talking to an assistant, for example—and under what conditions will you hear from them. (There are times when it is perfectly acceptable to deal with an adviser's assistant or with a firm's specialist in the area of a particular need, but you should know who you will be working on your account and whether you will be getting the service you expect from the counselor you want.) You want to know what will prompt the adviser to call you—new opportunities or products, changes in the status of your situation, changes in the law that could affect you, the periodic need for review—and how they will respond when you call.

In a time of crisis, for example, you may want your insurance agent to walk you through a claim, rather than dealing on an impersonal basis with an insurance company adjuster to whom you are just another case number. Your agent may tell you that he or she just processes policies, and that they leave the claims to the adjusters; you may prefer to have someone who has a track record, borne out by references, of pushing the insurer for quicker settlements and fast resolutions.

"The easiest way to be let down by your adviser is to not spell out your expectations in advance," says Ross Levin of Accredited Investors in Minneapolis, a former president of the International Association of Financial Planners. "That is especially true in service, because what works well for an adviser—the way they deal with all of their clients—may not be what you are looking for. Maybe they like to deal by telephone, you want to meet face to face.

"Find out how someone likes to do business—how do they typically interact with the customer—and decide if that is something you can live with."

Consultation

There is a slight difference between the personal service you receive and the ability to consult with your advisers. The difference might be clear this way: sometimes you need to use your adviser's services, other times you just want to talk.

If your lawyer or financial planner recommends a particular tax strategy, for example, you might want to run it past your tax preparer for a second opinion. If you are having your advisers act like a team, an approach that I advocate and cover later in this book, you may want the two advisers to discuss the situation before you make your decision.

Consultations—whether they are a quick tax question for your accountant or a major sit-down to have a financial planner retitle assets to follow an estate plan—are sometimes necessary, but they aren't always free.

Advisers sometimes squirm at the thought of free time, but if the commodity involved in advisory relationships is trust, then having the meter running on every conversation discourages interaction. At the same time you should not be abusive of your adviser's time, or expect them to donate a few hours to answer a complex question for you.

Define the terms of the quick-opinion/knowledgeable-resource portion of your relationship. Unless you are working with someone who charges based on a percentage of the assets involved (or who is being paid on a contingency), you should expect a bill if you need repeated, lengthy consultations. But you also want an adviser to whom you will be meaningful enough that the periodic "What does this mean for me?" phone call does not generate a bill.

Willingness to work with other financial specialists

To get different specialists to function as one unit, you need team players. Yes, your broker or financial adviser should be the lead expert on investments but that does not mean they should be unwilling to discuss your investment situation with an accountant, banker, or lawyer.

Not every one of these discussions is adversarial, pitting one player against the other. If, for example, you are considering establishing trusts or are involved in estate planning, having your lawyer and financial adviser talk makes good financial sense. Aside from bouncing ideas around to determine, say, what type of trust is best for you, they need to coordinate your plan. The best estate plan can be rendered useless if you do not retitle assets to follow it.

Some advisers like to wear more than one hat, acting as say an accountant and financial planner, or money manager and lawyer, but you may only use them for one particular skill. If they must consult with your hired gun in their second area of expertise, you need to make sure they will not be upset because they don't have that slice of your business. (Another chapter of this book deals with what I call the "utility infielders" of the financial world.)

Every adviser you consider should know who your other counselors are, particularly if there could be circumstances where you would want them to interact.

"No one wants to think they are going to fight with your other advisers," says Dick Wagner, a partner in the Denver advisory firm of Sharkey, Howes, Wagner & Javer, "but they aren't really providing you the kind of service you need if they won't even talk to your other advisers. If they fight the idea that they may have to deal with your accountant—or argue that they can do everything themselves or within their firm—then you have to wonder if they will be able to handle direction and hard questions, whether it comes from another adviser or from you."

Understanding

No good adviser wants you to buy something you don't understand.

It is hard to tell from an initial interview spent feeling each other out, rather than talking heavy-duty finances, whether an adviser can explain things to you clearly. (If the first meeting is either over your head or includes a heavy-handed sales pitch, that would be the signs of a rush job, which is an instant turnoff).

But in an ideal advisory relationship, decisions are made only after you have complete understanding and agreement. Every key decision —whether it is why you should purchase a tax-free investment to why you should price your home at a certain level—should be explained to you until you are comfortable with it.

If you never grasp the whys and hows, the adviser should be willing to change tactics—without getting frustrated or angry with you— as opposed to trying to convince you that they are the expert and know so much about the situation that you should trust them.

Tolerance for "stupid" questions and "excessive" requests

If you intend to actively manage your finances, you will have a lot of questions. They may be as simple as "Can you tell me what a municipal bond is and why I keep reading that I should invest in them?" or they may involve more complex issues based on your desire to understand something like how the government taxes mutual funds (a subject that should be easy but which the Internal Revenue Service has made difficult).

Assume that you will be a high-maintenance client because you intend to manage the managers. Some advisers hate that, even when they say they want to build long-term relationships; that dislike shows itself when you start asking questions and making the adviser really work on your behalf.

Clear, and clearly followed, instructions

A financial adviser I met in Pennsylvania used to argue with me that the "planner-as-a-doctor" analogy was a good one.

"You go to a doctor, explain what is bothering you and then wait for a diagnosis," he said. "The doctor then takes the steps needed to make you feel better or to give you the cure."

I granted him that situation was possible, especially the part where the doctor does the work without explaining his or her assessment/ recommendation.

"But what worries me," I said, "is that a lot of people go to financial 'doctors' and say 'Hey Doc, I have a headache,' and the doctor starts examining the patient's feet. That's when you've got a problem."

One of the biggest troubles individuals have with advisers involves instructions.

You may recall the story about "Jim," the stockbroker who lost the investment contest and a lot of his business in the process. The scenario for the competition was an investor who had a sum of money that, for personal reasons, needed to be withdrawn in a year. There was a time deadline, and a reason to invest and trade the account aggressively.

Clearly that is not most individuals; most people looking at a short time horizon are very conservative with their money, for fear of downturns in which there is no time to recover and paper losses become real ones.

Long-term investors might buy more of a stock when it declines provided that they believe the long-term prospects of the company will prompt a rebound. Short-term investors unload losers and looks for faster horses.

Jim kept buying more of his losers—and his losers were plentiful. When his initial results were not good, he stopped listening to the imaginary client and didn't even attempt a short-term strategy, investing instead with a longer-term outlook. If the game had been a five-year contest, where the investments had time to rebound, Jim might have done just fine; in the case of the imaginary client for the contest, his decisions meant losses in a year when the market was up.

An adviser should be comfortable with the relationship you set up. If that means you don't want to hear about "hot" investments, then you should never get a sales pitch on the latest tip or fad. If it means you are investing with a short-term time frame, then the decisions should fit into that context.

Experts assume they know more than you do. They might know more about investments but not about when you have a tuition bill due, how your spending habits have changed, or how your financial situation disrupts your sleeping habits.

Mutual understanding over the roads not taken

One key mantra for managing your financial help is "I'm the boss." If they do their job and lay out everything in a way that you understand, then you should have easy-to-explain reasons why you do or do not follow their suggestions. But no matter how good their logic, or poor your reason for balking, it is still your move to make.

If an adviser waves his or her expertise in your face—"I do this every day, and you don't and yet you trust your judgment over mine"—run away as fast as you can.

With ideal financial counseling, there are no hard sells—a trusted adviser should not have to pitch you hard, and should know when you are reluctant to make a move—no "be grateful to work with me" guilt trips, no threats of "maybe you will have to work with my associate in the future."

If the adviser understands what you want from the relationship, they should ask questions about why you rejected their advice, about what made you uncomfortable, and they should try to determine why the two of you did not connect.

With that kind of discourse, the relationship evolves, and the adviser's future ideas probably will be more in line with your own.

No underlings, unless previously approved

You are going through a rigorous selection process to pick an adviser, someone you trust, to help with your finances. If you subsequently find out that your affairs will be handled by someone else in the firm, you had better either meet that person or take your money elsewhere.

If you go to a broker who then passes you along to a junior associate, you are suddenly dealing with an entirely new entity. The background checks, the references or referrals, the initial interview, and all of the rest of your work is out the window.

In all various realms of personal finance, there are advisers who farm out some of the work or summon subordinates or peers to handle specific problems. You need to know of that possibility before it takes place.

Unless you approve of the people you will be working with, there are no substitutions or exchanges. A good adviser knows this and will not take on so much work that they cannot devote the proper amount of time to you.

Approval of your spouse, partner, heirs, or executor

In the event something happens to you, your adviser needs to be prepared to work with the folks who will manage your estate. They should not be condescending or demeaning—even if they are used to dealing with you.

You want someone who can work comfortably with you and your heirs, even if there is a radical difference in your levels of financial sophistication. If an adviser wants to work exclusively with the knowledgeable partner in a relationship, then the less-savvy person could be headed for trouble if they ever need to manage household affairs or the estate.

Smart advisers recognize this, and they will not do all of their work with one person while leaving the rest of the household in the dark.

If your relationship with an adviser does not meet those basic criteria, chances are that it will come up short down the road, leaving you disappointed with the service (or lack thereof) or the person.

Remember too that almost every adviser will jump through hoops and promise the moon to get you in the door as a client. Determining whether they can craft the kind of relationship you want and need will be a big part of your hiring decision; knowing what you want from the relationship will go a long way toward helping you find that ideal.

8 *Your first meeting with an adviser*

A colleague of mine once complained about a financial planner he was working with, someone he had been "meticulous" in choosing. My friend was disappointed with the planner's level of service, responsiveness, and fee structure.

"If you were so meticulous in picking this planner, why didn't you know what to expect?" I asked. "Hadn't you discussed fees, what you would be getting, and how fast she would respond to you?"

"Well," my friend said sheepishly, "we never really got to that."

It seems that my friend let the planner take charge of the initial interview. Instead of a wide-ranging feel-each-other-out chat, the planner asked a raft of questions, all designed to determine how much money was involved and the goals and objectives my friend planned to shoot for. Then the adviser asked if she should go ahead and prepare a basic financial plan.

She seemed excited to do the work—more so than the other two planners my colleague interviewed—and he liked her energy, so he gave the go-ahead.

He was told the plan would be ready in three weeks.

The planner then dismissed my friend to get to work. Interview over.

Not quite a month later, my friend received—by mail, no less—exactly what had been promised, an action plan for how to reach his goals. The plan was devoid of investment selections, advice on allocating 401(k) retirement plan savings and specific suggestions on how and where to cut spending to improve cash flow and reduce debt.

Lacking as it was, the plan was more costly than expected.

The planner in this situation—considered one of the nation's elite advisers, by the way—clearly thought she was being hired to do a one-time periodic review; my friend, just as plainly, thought he was going to receive much more specific advice.

The miscommunication—cleared up to everyone's satisfaction after I prodded him to request a second meeting to express both his displeasure and what he expected from the relationship—occurred because the interview went from being a how-do-you-do? to a "You're on the job."

It should never happen that way.

Your initial meeting with any adviser is a physical and mental handshake, an exercise in sizing someone up and deciding which one of several people will be the best to work with. It is a working session only in the sense that the adviser presumably is working to earn your business, you are struggling to pick the best adviser, and everyone involved wants the first interview to be the cornerstone of a long and rewarding financial relationship.

But it should never be a foregone conclusion that your first meeting will lead to working together, particularly since you will be interviewing more than one candidate—hopefully three—before making a decision.

Unless you simply need someone to facilitate a transaction, plan to interview between two and five advisers.

The reason, in financial terms, is the difference between qualitative and quantitative analysis, known in the real world as art and science.

The science part of any financial relationship is how well someone does with "procedures." Just about any lawyer can draft a will, and you will seldom meet a tax preparer or accountant who would back down from a challenging tax return. Presumably they are qualified to do the work and to make the necessary arrangements for your affairs to be in order.

What distinguishes one adviser from the pack is how he or she finesses the science and blends it with art. It's how they go from simply producing a will to knowing all the right steps to take to craft a protective legal document, or how they minimize your tax liability without increasing the likelihood of an audit. And it's how they make you feel in the process, which should be comfortable and in control.

The first adviser you talk with is always going to sound good; they will be able to answer your questions—the very questions that drove you to hire financial help rather than trying to do it yourself—and you are very likely to spend the most time with them because most of the discussion will be new territory for you.

Most advisers I talk with say that to the best of their knowledge, the bulk of their clients never did multiple interviews. They were hired by the end of the get-acquainted meeting and figure they have gotten the brush-off when a prospective client has to "think it over." All have had the occasional client washout, where either the adviser or the consumer did not do enough work to make a good match and the relationship dissolved down the road.

No matter what kind of financial adviser you are looking for, the search and initial meeting should follow a similar pattern. In the chapters discussing how to select each type of counselor there are the specific questions to ask during an initial interview, covering the unique circumstances of each specialty.

Here, however, are the elements that are crucial to every adviser meeting—regardless of what kind of specialist you are hiring—and to the interview process itself.

Do some advance work by telephone

You don't want to waste an adviser's time—or your own—so try to ensure that you and the adviser make a good match before scheduling a get-acquainted meeting.

For example, you will want to ask about costs upfront; it makes no sense to talk to a lawyer who charges $200 an hour when you were hoping the work could be done for $100. Similarly many advisers have account minimums; it's silly to interview a financial planner with a $500,000 account minimum when you have $50,000 in assets.

This is also where you get the basics on whether you fit with the profile of the adviser's average client. If you are scheduling meetings with financial planners to work on estate-planning issues, for example, make sure prospective advisers actually work on those matters regularly. Many financial planners specialize in money management and may not be focused on the need that has driven you to seek assistance.

Whenever possible, talk directly with the adviser, rather than an assistant. While most advisers will not turn away potential business unless they are too busy to handle new accounts, what you hear in their voice will go a long way toward helping in your decision. Obviously, as you lay out the basics of what you are looking for— and the size and scope of the job—you should be listening for interest and energy.

Schedule your meeting at least ten days in advance

Once you are certain that you want to meet with an adviser, set up an appointment, but leave yourself time to do some necessary background checks. With the exception of bankers and real estate agents —where background checks are cursory—it could take a few days to check on an adviser's background; unless you have checked on their regulatory history before ever calling to chat, you will want to have that work done before you get acquainted. (You will find the information needed to make background checks on most advisers later in this book.)

In addition many advisers will want to send you material to streamline the interview process. Leave enough time to read everything, complete any paperwork they send, and gather necessary documents and records.

If you are married, your spouse should look everything over, even if he or she is not the primary decision-maker on these matters. Remember that you are purchasing trust, so you want to make sure your partner knows what is going on and has faith and confidence in the adviser.

When you schedule the initial interview, find out whether you will be charged for it. Some advisers are on the clock, even for a first-time sit-down, while others waive the initial consultation fee if you become a client. The majority of advisers I come in contact with do not charge any fee whatsoever for a get-acquainted meeting.

Charging for a how-do-you-do is a privilege advisers earn when they are successful; time is their currency, precious enough that they don't want to waste it on unproductive interviews.

I know a prominent Boston planner who charges $500 for an initial sit-down, regardless of whether you become his client. If you had to interview three planners of his ilk, that would cost $1,500; if all you are looking for is someone to give you a simple financial checkup, that's more than you would expect to pay for the entire job.

The problem when someone charges for an interview is that it puts pressure on you to choose that adviser because you don't want to waste your money (and the entire point of picking a financial adviser is to make the most of your money). That said, try to avoid initial consultation fees where possible, and never pay a consultation fee to someone who stands to make big money from you on contingency (if they sell your home, win your court case, etc.).

And while it is important to value and respect an adviser's time, don't throw money into a first interview until sufficiently checking out those candidates who do not charge for a first sit-down. There are many qualified advisers out there, and there will always be someone—perhaps with less of a track record, but not necessarily with less expertise—for you to choose from.

Do your background checks

Everyone has their own tolerance levels, and you need to make sure an adviser falls within yours before the first meeting.

Over time, many financial counselors will have disagreements with clients, often nothing more than simple misunderstandings. In today's litigious society that means that there are a lot of good advisers out there with one or two black marks in their past.

Before your first sit-down, you want to arm yourself with information about those incidents. You can either do this when you are first sorting out advisers—doing the work on your short list of candidates before the initial interview—or immediately after your phone conversation when you have decided to set up an interview.

You want the background data in hand before your initial interview so that you can ask about any black marks or red flags and get an explanation as to what happened and how problems were resolved. Clients may have had unrealistic expectations; the adviser may have created that kind of problem. Whatever it is, you want the adviser's side of the story—and you don't want to see too many of these problems in someone's past.

Again, this comes under the heading of trust, which is the first thing you must establish in a financial relationship. If an adviser won't talk about what you have found on their record, or if the story sounds implausible or just plain sloppy, look elsewhere.

In addition any adviser whose file comes back with several black marks on it may have exceeded your tolerance level. In that case, cancel the interview.

Do your homework

Before an initial sit-down, prepare a written statement of what you want from this relationship. In addition complete whatever materials the adviser sends you.

Again couples must read the materials and prepare the statement together. A good adviser will want to hear from both of you; if one partner sits in the room silently, a high-quality counselor will try to draw them out. Equally important, you will want your partner to concur on your written statement and to have given thought as to the household's financial goals.

Bring everyone involved to the meeting

A *Boston Globe* retiree once came to me with questions about his adviser. The big thing he wanted to know was how to get his wife to like the guy. Apparently, she didn't "like the looks of him," not to mention the fact that he talked over her head, using financial jargon that, to her, was the equivalent of speaking in Latin. (To be honest, the husband didn't understand everything the adviser was saying either, but that's another story.)

I told the retiree that it was time to get a new adviser.

He objected, saying he liked the guy.

You are doing financial planning for the entire family, not just yourself. For that very reason, you want both partners—or parents or children if the planning is on their behalf—at the initial meeting.

If you or your partner dislikes the adviser's clothing, dress, manner, or whatever, find a different adviser. It may seem silly to get rid of a potential financial helper because you don't like, say, his haircut, but it is also valid if it makes you uncomfortable. (Truth be told, the convenience of an adviser's office, their gender, age, and personality always have a lot to do with the selection process, no matter how much detail and science we apply to choosing helpers. All are acceptable factors in differentiating one potential adviser from the next.)

In the case of the retiree, his wife no longer wanted to go to planning meetings with him because of her feelings toward the adviser. If he didn't honor his wife's wishes and, later, died before her, she would be stuck during her time of grief dealing with someone she hates.

Yes, she can get another adviser at that time, but the one thing this book is proving to you is that selecting financial help is neither fast nor easy.

If an adviser is working on behalf of the entire household, they must have the trust of everyone. Both partners must be comfortable with any adviser chosen and have veto power if, for any reason, the chemistry just doesn't seem right.

Come out from under the covers

If you can't trust someone enough to open up to them, they have no business advising you on financial matters.

You must disclose all relevant information so that your advisers can make informed decisions; it is hard to live up to a consumer's expectations and to reach their goals without a complete picture of their finances.

For example, some people meeting with a financial planner for the first time fudge their debt amount because the mistakes of their past make them embarrassed.

The problem is that a good adviser may not work with you unless you provide them with a clear financial snapshot at the very first meeting. Moreover, since you want an adviser whose clientele is similar to you and who wants to hire you, giving too little information can lead to a bad fit.

Be honest about yourself, what kind of person you are—if you intend to call every day, they should know that up front, for example —and about your needs. Be honest about your assets too. Understand that every house has faults, for example, and that the real estate agent will want to hear them from you; similarly an insurance agent or financial planner is in the best position to help you if they have a true picture of your earnings, assets, and liabilities.

Reveal any unusual life circumstances that might affect the adviser's work. A gay individual or couple in a nontraditional relationship may be reluctant to share this information right away. Yet there are special rules and strategies that come into play in these situations, and you will want to be sure the adviser has the technical expertise to help you.

Last, be sure to tell the adviser why you are in the office. It might be that you have a specific need, are nervous about what you have done on your own, or that you are unhappy with the services of your current adviser. That disclosure will lead the discussion over ground that you absolutely must cover in order to make a good selection.

If you are going to pay someone to advise you, make sure they have the same information you would have if you were making all decisions on your own.

Don't try to show how smart you are

A good adviser figures this out pretty quickly. Besides, you are hiring someone who, on these matters, is supposed to know more than you do. So just as you would not talk to your doctors using words like "subdural hematoma" instead of a bruise, don't try to be flashy with what you know when meeting an adviser for the first time.

This does not just apply to what you say but also what you hear. If the adviser is talking over your head and you make believe you understand, the adviser might believe you. That's how people wind up with arbitration or court cases.

If an adviser talks over your head or is "moving too fast for you," make them slow down and explain things at your level. If they can't do that in the initial meeting—when things should be pretty simple—then you undoubtedly will want to hire someone else.

Decide on the services you need, and what they cost

Remember my colleague whose initial interview led to overpriced planning-by-mail? Find out specifically what this adviser intends to do for you and how (and how much) they will be compensated for their services.

Yes, you asked questions like these during your initial phone contact, but the face-to-face meeting may have brought out new circumstances and changed things. Leave the meeting with a clear understanding of what you will get if you sign up as a client and what it will cost you.

Never expect something for nothing

If you think that the adviser will solve all your problems in the initial meeting (and at no charge), you will be disappointed. Most advisers can't help themselves and will offer some free counsel, but they won't solve your problems that fast, nor should you expect them too. If the solutions were that easy, you wouldn't need help.

Just because the initial meeting does not leave you with any solutions is no reason to take an adviser off your prospect list. You may unnecessarily eliminate the best candidate for the job.

If you have reservations, spill your guts

Be fair to the adviser and yourself; if something has been said—or not said—that needs to be addressed (or covered again), ask.

It might be that you want clarification on how you could get your money back if you are not satisfied, it might be the discussion of the red flags raised during a background check or anything that makes you nervous at all, but try to get a better explanation before leaving the office. It could be that you are dissatisfied with your current adviser and haven't heard enough to convince you that the new relationship will be different.

If the adviser cannot adequately address your concerns, hire someone else.

Many times the adviser dominates the interview. They need to get information from you and, since they have these meetings all the time, know the directions this session needs to go in.

Still, you can't afford to be bashful.

If you don't ask about your concerns, you have a big problem. In general, there will be no way for you to answer these nagging questions on your own; since you can't resolve them, your search for financial help will drag on, and you will have a tough time making a good decision because of your reservations. Or, worse yet, you wind up hiring someone who you are nervous about.

Make sure the adviser wants to hire you as a client

This has already been said several times in this book, always applying to your behavior, the type of person and financial situation you represent. In this case, however, it talks about your conduct in the get-acquainted meeting.

If you ignore the previous steps outlined in this chapter, you run the risk of having an adviser label you as a potential problem or a high-maintenance client. Good advisers run away from that kind of trouble—they don't want their next client to become that rare black mark on their record and are not desperate to add new customers—so make sure that you do your part.

Ask for references

Some advisers consider "I have to go home and think about it" to be the brush-off. (You can show them this book, and tell them you are using it to help in the selection process if you feel compelled to reassure them of your sincerity.)

But you also want the time to consider them as an adviser because you would like to check references.

There is a potential problem here, in that some firms do not give references or give only the names of people to whom they give referrals, such as a financial planner using the lawyer to whom he refers estate work as a reference.

Explain, as politely as possible, that references will allow you to ask about the character of a relationship. You expect a reference to be sweet on the adviser; what you want to know is the tone and tenor of the relationship. How does this adviser work with you, how do they respond when you have questions? How did the reference come to choose this adviser?

Those questions and how to treat references is laid out later in the book.

If your adviser is unwilling to give you the names of references (especially clients, rather than professionals, where there might be a business or monetary tie coloring the reference), they may not be worth keeping on your short list.

That's a tough call. References are an additional check and balance, but an adviser who uses confidentiality and convenience as an excuse to withhold names has not necessarily killed the deal, particularly if the adviser has addressed your reservations and if you found the adviser on a referral from a friend or other financial counselor.

Having completed a detailed interview, armed with references (or with the knowledge that you aren't going to get them), you can leave the office, go home, and mull over the adviser. Having repeated the interview process with at least one other adviser, you should be comfortable in making a decision and with the advice you get down the line.

H.D. Vest must like initials.

The founder of a nationwide financial services firm that bears his name, Vest not only goes by his initials, but he drops a lot of other letters too. On the cover of one of his books, for example, he lists eighteen different professional credentials, sometimes two different designations from the same group.

I am not making this up.

According to his latest book, Vest is—try to say this in one breath —an MS, MSFS, MSM, DIBA, CEBS, CFA, CFP, CFS, ChFC, CLU, CMA, CPA/PFS, FLMI/I, AMC, EPTC, PECC.

Wow.

I assume his parents simply gave him the H.D. and that he didn't have to take a class somewhere to get it.

Credentials make an adviser look impressive—and perhaps a bit more intimidating on those occasions when you question their advice —but they don't necessarily make the advice any better.

Truth be told, I ran Vest's credentials past some of the nation's leading financial advisers, and they couldn't identify all of the designations. Neither could I.

Nor should you care if someone has that many professional designations.

Credentials are misleading. Even if you know what a CFP, or Certified Financial Planner, is, chances are you do not know what goes into achieving that designation. And CFP is a common credential, unlike a lot of the business card alphabet soup out there.

What credentials generally prove is that an adviser is furthering their education, knowledge that is crucial as the rules regarding all areas of finance seem to change almost every day.

But all of those credentials don't make someone worthy of being your adviser.

I come to that conclusion from personal experience.

In June 1995 I was one of five journalists who took the two-day, ten-hour exam to become a Certified Financial Planner. It was a media play by the folks who administer the CFP standard; even if we had passed the test, we would not have qualified as CFPs.

I did not study for the test and did not expect to pass it—nor did I want to because I would have lost all respect for both the test and the group if I could ace it without formal training.

None of the journalists passed.

But what I learned was not how tough the test was, but rather that the mark of CFP—a standard I have tremendous respect for—does not make someone a great financial planner. It proves their technical proficiency, their ability to analyze your portfolio and to make appropriate suggestions, but has no bearing on their "relationship" skills.

An adviser could pass the CFP exam largely by boning up on some basic formulas and rules but could be lacking the basic human skills necessary to build a comfortable relationship. Since the entire concept of hiring a financial helper hinges on developing this working partnership, credentials alone are not enough to make someone worthy.

Don't get me wrong, technical expertise is critical, especially when it comes to the legal, insurance, and tax arenas where a mistake could have severe costs.

But I do not know of a single financial planner—and I asked dozens of them after taking the test—who has ever had a client come in and ask for the calculation of the Sharpe Index of Performance on a mutual fund. In fact none of the planners I queried could actually calculate the Sharpe Index without the formula in front of them. (The Sharpe is so esoteric that most mainstream financial dictionaries ignore it, most planners can't adequately explain it, and I'm not even going to attempt it here.)

Yet the Sharpe Index is on the CFP exam.

Meanwhile, subjective decision-making about where someone can cut spending to improve savings or reduce debt is not anywhere on the CFP exam. And all of the same planners who have earned the CFP and have never been asked by a client to calculate a Sharpe Index have dozens of clients who needed help changing their spending habits.

Taking the test answered for me one of the most troubling questions in the financial services business. Until I saw what the test measures, I never understood how the CFP Board of Standards had bestowed its precious mark on some of the very best and very worst planners I know; the answer is that the exam is an incomplete gauge of an adviser's skills.

And that's why you use credentials as a starting point, and not as the Good Housekeeping Seal of Approval.

One key thing to remember in hiring financial help is that with the exception of lawyers, none of the rest of the members of your financial team truly are professional.

Most dictionaries define the word "profession" as a vocation or occupation that requires advanced training either in sciences or the liberal arts. You do not need an advanced degree to practice as a banker, insurance agent, real estate agent, stockbroker, financial planner, or accountant.

The standards vary for each role, with state or federal law dictating if practitioners must even be registered. Most states, for example, require that financial planners be registered, but they have no educational or experience standards to back it up; anyone can become a planner, so long as they register. You don't need a CFP credential, let along the Personal Financial Specialist, Chartered Mutual Fund Counselor, or any other designation.

In many instances the governing bodies that designate the criteria for a particular standard are warring with competing organizations touting a different standard. (For example, there are Chartered Mutual Fund Counselors and Certified Fund Specialists. In fact there are two different groups awarding a "CFS," one for mutual fund experts, the other for "certified factoring specialists.")

It makes evaluating credentials difficult, even if you are dealing with someone like H.D. Vest and his amazing wall of certificates.

Indeed there are some credentials for which you must have a minimum of experience or the ability to pass a test, and there are others that you can acquire for the cost of a membership or the work of a mediocre correspondence course. Some designations require continuing education; others simply encourage it (but won't kick out members who don't hit the books).

It is against this paucity of educational standards that every professional group that has initials wants to hand them out to members, and it is against that backdrop of credentialing that you must arm

yourself. You must also be wary of frauds, people who simply appropriate nice-sounding designations without doing a shred of the required work.

Later in this book, as it explores the way to choose each specialist,
there will be a breakdown of the professional designations you might
run across and the specifics that are supposed to come with the fancy
letters on the business card. (This book will stick to what I consider
meaningful and/or common credentials, so don't expect to find all 18
of Vest's affiliations back there.)

In the meantime, however, there are four questions to ask
when you interview an adviser who greets you with professional
credentials:

*1. What did it take to earn your stripes and why did you consider it
important to achieve this distinction?*
Some credentials require experience, knowledge, and the ability to
pass a test, others grandfather in old-time practitioners, and still others
are simply membership organizations. There are, for example, CFPs
who earned their mark before the Board of Standards developed the
test; on paper they look as if they have received every bit as much
training as any newly minted CFP, when in fact they qualified under
much looser standards.

That's why you want to know, specifically, how someone earned a
designation. When verifying credentials, you may want to double-
check the various things an adviser must do to earn the designation
and keep it current.

In addition you want to find out why the adviser went to the
trouble of getting the credential. Hopefully it was for more than mere
first impressions.

If a financial planner did the work to earn a "Chartered Financial
Analyst" designation, they would presumably want to tell you how
that will help them manage your money. (CFAs are held primarily by
stock analysts and institutional money managers, and a planner who
earns one would likely tell you that it makes them a better stock/
mutual fund picker.) Conversely, if they are simply an "registered
investment adviser," they have paid a modest fee and submitted certain filings to the Securities and Exchange Commission; their "credential" is not likely to help you one whit.

*2. Are there continuing education credits—and if so describe what you
have been doing to meet them?*

Ask for a list of the courses your prospective adviser has taken to stay current on the credential, and ask how that education might help them work with you. These days the courses tend to run the gamut, from nuts-and-bolts practice-management classes to specific ideas on how to help clients get more from their money.

You are looking to make sure that the adviser takes the curriculum seriously, and that they are concerned with building expertise as it relates to you (and not simply in figuring out a way to get more profits from each client, the kind of course work that some organizations consider suitable continuing education). Rules and laws governing money management change so quickly that anyone who stays out of the loop for over a year may never be able to get back to it.

3. Can you get the number for the sanctioning body?
No adviser should be afraid of you calling the group that issues the credentials to make sure everything is on the up and up.

Because most consumers don't do their homework and make appropriate background checks, there are plenty of crooks who pretend to have credentials they never have earned. In addition most sanctioning groups will kick out people who run afoul of bylaws or codes of ethics, so someone who has a credential up on their office wall may not necessarily be entitled to continue using it.

If they work with the sanctioning group—and the addresses and phone numbers for those groups appear later in this book—they should have the phone number and should not fear what would happen if they give it to you.

If they act insulted when you want to check on them or can't come up with a valid telephone number, you should get very nervous. If they give you the phone number, call it. (The numbers for most accrediting agencies are listed later in the book, in chapters covering the selection of specific advisers.) If credentials play any role in your decision-making process, it pays to make sure everything is in order.

4. Does the designation mean anything unique in the service?
In tax preparers, for example, an enrolled agent can represent you at an audit; the return-preparer at the corner fast-food tax joint can't.

An accountant who also has a law degree, meanwhile, may be adept at trust and estate planning work. The same could be said for a financial planner with a law degree.

The new F-O or "fee-only" credential is expected to be used in several financial disciplines. It relates only to an adviser's method of compensation—signifying that the adviser works only on some type of fee-for-service basis—and has no bearing on the adviser's expertise. In fact the National Association of Personal Financial Advisors, which created the designation, has some of the strictest educational requirements in the business for its members; the F-O does not require membership, however, and the consumer who reads something into it is making a mistake.

In every specialty there are credentials that have meaning and can be helpful, and there are others that are self-serving and worthy of being ignored.

One thing you can assume, however, is that the letters after an adviser's name mean something to you in terms of the price, as in "the more credentials, the bigger the bill." If that turns out to be true—and it usually does—then be sure you need, and get, what you are paying for.

You don't want to be paying for expertise you don't need. You may decide that you don't need a certified public accountant to do an ordinary tax return, for example. At the same time you might prefer hiring a lawyer who has taken specialized classes in elder law.

By making the adviser spell out the benefits you get from their expertise, you go a long way toward defining what you expect to get from the relationship.

Once you have answered those basic questions about an adviser's credentials—and that could take hours if you are interviewing H.D. Vest himself—you can go about the rest of the interview process with an eye toward whether the person is good at what they do or merely proficient in doing what it takes to add some initials to a business card.

10 *They're smarter than I am; how do I keep control?*

Journalism students hoping to become great investigative reporters—or even serviceable writers on the police beat—operate under a hackneyed journalistic standard:

"If your mother says she loves you, check it out."

You are building a team of so-called "trusted advisers," and while it may seem disingenuous to start from a base of distrust, that's exactly the place to begin.

No matter how well recommended the adviser or how many of their satisfied customers you talk to or know personally, the whole process of hiring financial help is designed to give you control over your financial future—and not to give someone else control over you.

If you don't check out an adviser and then establish firm control of the relationship—be it with a broker, planner, accountant, lawyer, banker, real estate, or insurance agent—you could be headed for unpleasant surprises.

In writing the chapters on selecting the individual experts, I noticed one thing: in relating stories of how a client-adviser relationship gets into trouble, how a consumer gets taken, and what concerns you should have, I worried that maybe I was overstating the problems.

After all, I know countless financial planners and only one or two have had so much as a serious arbitration dispute over the last ten years.

Clearly the rogues and scoundrels out there are in the distinct minority.

There are, however, plenty of advisers who are honest but not very good at what they do.

For you to have successful relationships with your financial helpers, you will need to avoid both of those groups of people.

The fear of being drawn to bad advice is all too real for most people; an adviser dresses well and talks in a language that is all at once confusing, mysterious, and alluring. It is very easy to give them the proverbial keys and to let them drive the relationship.

To both protect yourself from scams and to not be overwhelmed by the ideas passed along by multiple advisers, you must be in control from the very beginning. That starts with the first interview, and it gets tricky right off the bat.

You want to choose counselors who want to "hire" you every bit as much as you want to hire them. If they do not value your business, you will not get the level of service you desire.

But in proving your worth to an adviser, it is absolutely essential that you maintain control of the relationship, that you do not become part of the flock with the adviser the shepherd. (Remember, the person who follows the herd steps in a lot of cow pies; you need to follow a path that is correct for you.)

The person across the desk from you is the hired gun, the expert whose help and guidance you are seeking. They may or may not talk in terms that are over your head—in which case some people mistakenly play along as if they understand every word—but their typical emphasis is on getting information out of a client or potential customer and then making business decisions.

You need to provide them the information they need to make judgments and give you options, but then rein them in so that the relationship moves at your pace.

If you are assembling a financial team of experts—and you will over the course of your lifetime—you must start by repeating a mantra until you are ready to live it:

"I'm the boss."

Your advisers are partners in your financial success, but you have the most at stake and therefore run the show.

As such, you are entitled from the very beginning of the relationship to ask about anything you want, from why a recommendation was made to why something cost more than you expected. Just as important, you are to be treated like the boss. Some advisers treat customers shabbily if the client does not follow proffered advice; this kind of reaction should function as an instant warning sign that the adviser respects their own position more than yours—and has put their own interests (and possibly their pocketbooks) ahead of yours.

It does not matter who is smarter or who knows more; your financial advisers are being hired in order to help YOU make the best decisions possible for managing your affairs.

As you go about managing your advisers, there are a few things to remember:

Never sacrifice control

Sign away control of your assets to someone else only in the event you are incapacitated.

We've all heard stories of the sports or movie star who turned a large fortune into a small one by letting an agent or financial planner "handle the money." They let someone else do the investing and money management, never used their own judgment as an appropriate balance, and got wiped out for their naivete.

It doesn't have to be someone who is out there trying to rip customers off. They simply need to exercise bad judgment.

One example is S. Jay Goldinger, who was a nationally recognized expert in bonds, a syndicated columnist and all-around big wheel, whose trading practices backfired and virtually wiped out his own firm—taking client money in the process. By all indications Goldinger didn't get rich while the ship was sinking; instead, he went down with the ship.

But that doesn't make it any better for the investors who were lost at sea with him.

There are advisers who do very well taking over control for their clients, who do not "churn" accounts—a practice of trading heavily to generate commissions—and who have earned the trust of their customers. But as far as I am concerned, surrendering control of your investments is an invitation to trouble. You want the adviser to believe that they must do a reasonable job of representing your interests in order to remain on the team; if they know that decisions must be run past you—and that they may have to justify choices—they are less likely to take actions that would jeopardize the relationship.

Never abdicate your responsibility

It may sound like a semantic difference from "never lose control," but it's more than that. Just because you haven't signed control over to someone else does not mean you have lived up to your role in running your affairs.

No matter who you hire to do any number of your financial chores, you retain a basic responsibility for managing your affairs, whether that is reviewing statements, reading a mutual fund prospectus, asking for alternative investment selections, and so on.

Delegating authority is great, surrendering it isn't.

A successful manager or coach offers adequate supervision, tells the players what is expected of them, and reviews the progress and asks questions before being satisfied with the results. This is your job in overseeing your financial helpers.

You can't just pick experts and expect the rest of your financial life to run itself.

Plenty of mutual fund investors, for example, don't look at their underlying paperwork. A conservative investor, for example, might tell a financial adviser to help select bond funds with a high rating from an independent service such as Morningstar Inc., which compiles risk-reward performance measures of fund returns.

If you made that request in the late 1980s, however, the highly rated bond funds as measured by Morningstar almost certainly would have been invested in junk bonds. (This has to do with the complicated risk-versus-reward measuring system Morningstar employs, but there are times when that system favors one type of hot investment —like junk bonds in the late 1980s—over others.) Since many financial advisers refuse to sell any funds that don't carry one of Morningstar's top two ratings, you could have found yourself unwittingly being sold a junk bond fund in the guise of a safe, conservative investment.

Sadly there are a lot of financial advisers who don't necessarily recognize junk, but see instead a "high-yield" vehicle that has a good rating. Or the adviser might believe in the bonds and buy into a safe-and-sound, Morningstar-says-so sales pitch. Attentive investors, however, might feel differently.

A quick read of the prospectus would provide enough information to avoid this kind of mistake. Even if you don't understand the Martian language that fund companies tend to use in their documents, you probably could get enough clues to question your adviser.

Similarly, just because you pay a tax preparer to put together your return doesn't mean you shouldn't read it before signing. If the preparer messed up—either in your favor or against—you are swearing to the information and making yourself liable, an action that demands a few minutes of your attention.

One very simple example of how this plays out comes in brokerage confirmation statements. If you work with a full-service broker, trading confirmation sheets—the tickets that describe the transaction you have made and detail any monies owed—show you whether the brokerage firm is a "market-maker" in a stock. Market-makers, in a nutshell, maintain an inventory in specific issues—which typically means more profits for the firm. Firms routinely plug stocks they make a market in, and may give brokers additional compensation for trading in those shares.

If your broker continually recommends stocks in which the firm is a market-maker—to the exclusion of outside selections—it is fair to wonder whether the broker is receiving incentives for selling issues from the company's hot list. Without either asking the question or reviewing the confirmation slips, however, you might never know.

Acknowledge your smarts and your shortcomings; make your advisers talk to that level of sophistication, and tell them when and why you have reservations and explain that feeling in your gut that tells you not to follow their suggestions. If an adviser does not respect those things and your judgment, they don't respect you, and you may need to reconsider the relationship.

Never do anything you don't understand

The job of an adviser is to be your expert and convince you to follow the plan of action they devise. A good expert can explain financial situations down to the level of a novice, and doesn't lose patience when asked dumb questions.

Your adviser should want—and be able—to provide simple answers.

The moment you agree to a financial decision you do not understand, you surrender control to the adviser. You are at their mercy, in that you will only understand what they explain to you—and a lot of unscrupulous advisers can really put the shine on the sewage and make a bad investment sound like a good one right up to the moment when you are out of money.

Make sure you ask whatever questions you have. No adviser should make you feel like this is a bother. You need sufficient information to feel comfortable, and if that forces the adviser to work a bit harder explaining things to you, so be it.

Do not feign knowledge; if an adviser spews out a bunch of statistics and jargon and you nod your head knowingly, they may assume you know more than you really do. This will only encourage them to speed up the discussions, let more terms go unexplained and—through very little fault of their own—confuse you further.

Always be forthcoming with information

You do not control advisers by giving them only a smattering of information. They need to know everything relative to their specialty in order to advise you successfully.

By making sure they know as much about your situation as you do, they become an extension of you. Withholding information does not make you smarter or more knowledgeable than the adviser, nor does it give you control over the situation.

Instead, it leads to advice that is incorrect. Worse yet, you can't adequately judge an adviser's work when you haven't supplied enough information to allow for good decision-making. The best advisory relationships occur only when the counselor and client are on the same wavelength and reviewing the same information.

Set the ground rules up front: Make sure your adviser knows his or her role

Before engaging an adviser—no matter the specialty—you should know what to expect.

By spelling out your expectations up front and repeating them at crucial times—"I thought we agreed we would go over the plan together rather than by phone"—you keep the relationship on your terms. This is particularly important when you pursue a big-name adviser because many of the top players in each specialty are so busy that clients sometimes get short shrift. It may be great to sign up a marquee name for your team—a planner featured regularly in your local paper, an accountant who heads the local CPA group, or the lawyer who has done estate plans for the biggest families in your town—but only if you can get them on your terms.

Just as important is that you let each adviser know their role on the team. There are plenty of insurance agents who double as financial planners—and visa versa—or accountants who are qualified attorneys, bankers who now offer financial advice, and more. Define the role you want for each player—the banker handles your borrowing needs, for example, but should leave the financial planning to another adviser on the team—and make sure they feel comfortable with you as a client on those terms.

You may want to have an adviser play dual roles—such as an accountant whose tax knowledge and legal degree make them appropriate to set up an estate plan—but you should qualify them separately for each job before giving them two hats to wear. You'll read more about that in chapter 26.

Never do anything with an adviser you can't meet face to face

You may do the bulk of your business by phone, fax, e-mail, and the postal system, but the ability to have a face-to-face sit-down is reassuring.

But hiring financial help is not the same as buying a product. The insurance policy or the mutual fund is a product, but you are paying for—and trusting in—advice.

It is perfectly acceptable to have an investment adviser, tax preparer or any type of adviser who is thousands of miles away (so long as they are licensed or registered to do business in the state in which you live). Just make sure that you can come down and see the operation and visit the adviser whenever you want.

Anyone who would not be comfortable accepting your check—or discussing your situation—in person is not worth trusting.

Consult with other experts and advisers

I hate talk-show radio advice, where someone calls into a station, gives a two-minute snippet of information and is told by an expert that their adviser has led them astray.

The radio host has an incomplete picture of your finances and little information to go on.

The same goes for most on-line chat rooms and other places where the average person can turn for a second opinion.

But if your adviser has made a suggestion that makes you nervous, you may want to consult with someone. It may be other financial advisers—your accountant or tax preparer knows your finances well and may know enough about financial planning to comment on whether they believe you are getting sound advice. If you have multiple advisers, their areas of expertise will overlap, and you should always consult your lead expert on any particular subject.

I have heard far too many horror stories of investors who went to redeem a bank certificate of deposit and had their banker sell them a mutual fund or some other investment that was inappropriate or simply a bad choice. On the one hand, the investor trusted their adviser, the banker in this case; on the other, they did not consult with their financial planner who is their primary adviser on investment selection.

This again is part of making advisers work within their defined roles.

Make sure that you take enough time to get this consultation; it's not that every tidbit of advice heard on the radio or sprayed across the Internet is inappropriate, but rather that you want to make sure that the person giving your second opinion knows enough—about you and your finances—to make a qualified judgment.

In addition to experts, consider huddling with friends or family, even if those people are not the most knowledgeable about financial matters. This forces you to explain—in plain language—what is going on. If you hear yourself talking, and it sounds like a sales pitch and one that you would be embarrassed to make to this friend or family member, then you have a pretty good idea that it is not right for you.

Do not avoid confrontations

Repeat after me: "I'm the boss."

If your broker or financial planner is dragging his or her feet issuing statements, processing your redemptions, or simply in meeting your expectations, demand satisfaction now.

These situations do not get better on their own; do not let the problem fester, or you will have a mess that almost certainly can't be solved without replacing a key member of your advisory board—or, worse yet, without hiring a lawyer and filing suit.

The opportunity for confrontations are few, but you should always let an adviser know when they have let you down—when their reaction to your decision not to buy the hot fund they are selling meets with a less-than-enthusiastic reaction, or when they bill you for a five-minute phone call that you thought would be free.

Many advisers will let a relationship start on your terms, and then move it to their own—because they are comfortable dealing with all clients in a cookie-cutter fashion. Don't let this happen—or prepare to make a change if the tenor of the relationship is changing and you cannot put it back onto your terms.

By making it clear that you will stand up for your rights and demand that your expectations are met, you are much less likely to be taken advantage of. If something doesn't seem right, get an explanation immediately; if a satisfactory one is not forthcoming, get ready to move on.

In the end you can always retain control of advisory relationships by making decisions with your feet.

11 Getting blood from a stone; how to get good answers from references

There's a men's store in the Northeast that uses the slogan "A satisfied customer is our best advertising."

Management is encouraging customers who don't believe the prices or the quality of the clothes to get some references before shopping.

And that's for a suit, something that would be worth anywhere from one to three hours worth of time with most high-quality lawyers, accountants, or financial planners.

But in financial services, references are tricky business. While plenty of advisers will volunteer names when asked, others will put up an apparent stone wall to keep you from getting to their customers.

First off, there are confidentiality issues. While most people simply do not want the specifics of their work blurted out to other prospective clients; others don't want anyone to know whom they work with. An adviser will tell you that he or she is protecting that interest, and doesn't want strangers prying into their customers' business.

That's a good excuse for not giving a reference, and one that will put off many customers.

It's also lame.

The vast majority of satisfied customers would be happy, if asked, to vouch for their adviser. Some volunteer their praise, but even those who don't raise their hand to accept this chore will acquiesce if the adviser places a phone call. When an adviser refuses to work with you on something as simple as a consumer referral—as opposed to the name of another type of adviser with whom they work—you should question whether you will ever be able to get the relationship onto your terms.

Then, as discussed in a previous chapter, there are the inherent conflicts of interest that are part of any referral/reference situation.

If you ask an adviser for references, chances are they will not simply give you the last five people who walked through the door—a measure that might provide some objectivity—but rather will give you the names of some good customers, or their volunteer praise-singers.

If they are giving the names of professional references—other advisers with whom they work and who can speak somewhat knowledgeably about the business—the list of people will include folks with whom the adviser likely has a business connection. Most likely it will be other specialists to whom your prospective adviser makes referrals when affairs go beyond the scope of his or her knowledge.

That person won't want to give a bad reference because doing so could stop the gravy train.

So when you want to do reference checks, you can assume that you are getting the names of people who are on the side of the adviser and who are satisfied customers.

Some advisers include that assumption in their reasons for not offering references. They will argue that a prospective client doesn't have much to gain, while their existing client supposedly loses both confidentiality and valuable time. Since they expect your conversation with a reference to consist of nothing more than an endorsement, they may even have letters of recommendation from customers; otherwise, they may simply try to pooh-pooh the whole process, pointing out that you may already have *de facto* references, namely the people who gave you a referral in the first place.

(As the chapter on dealing with referrals noted, it will be important to question them the way you would a reference given by the adviser. It's equally important to remember that some referral services are nothing more than paid advertising, and simply offer the names of advisers in your area rather than offering a particular recommendation.)

Those are valid points if your interview with a reference boiled down to asking "Would you hire the adviser again today?" That's a good question if you are a boss checking with a prospective employee's current supervisor, but it's kind of moot in checking real-life references for financial advisers.

If that was the type of question you were going to ask, then references would be unnecessary.

So be prepared that an adviser might not want to give you references or may even tell you that it is their policy not to provide names, citing the confidentiality and inconvenience issues.

Politely explain to the counselor that, despite the inherent biases, there are questions that a reference can answer that an adviser can't, notably dealing with the tenor and tone of the advisory relationship. The counselor can say how they intend to work with you, but only another client can give you an idea of how they actually do that work.

The trick is for you to be able to draw those comments out from a reference, and to listen carefully to what is being said. Then you can picture yourself walking the proverbial mile in the other client's shoes and deciding how they fit.

If necessary, show the adviser this book and explain that it will help you ask the right questions (although I do not recommend sharing the questions with the adviser because it might color their choice of which clients to offer you). Note that professional references really don't work because another adviser cannot shed light on the way you work with a client and make a customer feel; only a customer can do that.

In addition explain to the adviser that you only intend to call references as a final check, as the last piece in your decision-making process so that you will not bother the references of an adviser until you are close to making your selection.

And be sure to stress that your questions will not be invasive, that you will not be asking how much money the adviser is managing for the client or how big the client's profits have been. Those questions are personal and should not factor into your decision, so there is no loss in giving an adviser your assurance that the interview will not delve deep into the most private parts—the numbers—of the financial relationship.

If the adviser still will not give you the names of customers—rather than other professionals—you will have to decide whether to keep them in the selection process.

"In choosing someone to work with, I would want to talk to a customer and I would be suspicious or nervous if someone just flatly refused to provide me with a client contact," says Robert N. Veres, publisher of *Inside Information*, a trade newsletter about and for the financial planning industry. "I understand why people wouldn't to have their clients bothered and I understand the confidentiality issue. I still want the contact.

"While there is nothing unethical about someone not giving you the names of referrals—and not just professional referrals because those aren't worth much—I might prefer to go to the next person. It's going to be hard to get very comfortable with a person who won't do something this basic for you."

In chapters 12 through 23 on hiring each type of adviser, there are questions that may be specific to a particular specialty. But no matter which kind of adviser you are hiring—and whether the reference's name was given willingly or through cajoling—here are the general questions you will want to ask references.

How did you come to work with the adviser? How long have you been working together?

Just because you picked up this book and learned the details that help ensure a good selection is no guarantee that other clients did. Get the story on how this person found out about the adviser and what kind of work they put into qualifying the person before hiring, since it will go a long way to coloring the rest of what you hear from this person, whether they are someone who is detail oriented or leaves things to chance.

The more you determine about the background of the reference, the more easily you can evaluate what you hear and whether what makes a good relationship to them will measure up to your standards.

Obviously you want to know how long the reference and adviser have worked together. If it is a situation where there is no ongoing relationship—many references for real estate agents and lawyers are people who have no continuing tie to the adviser because they do not have a current need for services. In that case find out how long ago the person worked with the adviser; you would prefer a recent client to someone who worked with the adviser years ago, when the practice presumably was smaller.

How often do you hear from the adviser? Who initiates contact and what are most of those calls about?

A big part of every successful advisory relationship is communication. That doesn't necessarily mean a phone call every week, but it does mean that an adviser should show appropriate concern.

For an insurance agent, for example, it may be when policies are up for renewal. In the case of real estate agents and lawyers working on a case, it may be at regular weekly intervals of whenever there is any action you need to know about. For brokers and financial planners, the amount of contact will vary depending on the scope of the relationship.

The rule of thumb is that the bigger percentage of your assets you entrust with someone, the more often you want to hear from them.

If the adviser initiates all contact, but the calls are made only when there is a sale to be made—a hot stock tip, a change in the recommended mutual fund portfolio, or a new insurance product that might generate a commission, that would be a sign that the adviser is more interested in doing transactions than building a relationship, even if their happy client/reference hasn't figured it out yet.

Does the adviser always return your calls promptly? Does he or she give you the time necessary to answer questions?

You can never overemphasize communication. While you can't expect an adviser to take an hour in the middle of their day to take an unsolicited phone call that rambles over various points of your financial situation (and maybe onto how the kids are doing, etc.), you have a right to expect that each phone call will be taken seriously.

Find out, too, how the adviser reacts to what might be considered dumb questions. Even if you never ask one, you want to feel like you can without being made to feel stupid.

(There are no dumb questions, only things that people would be embarrassed to ask; you should never be embarrassed if you have a good working relationship with your adviser.)

Does the adviser include your spouse—or parents or children—in discussions and meetings?

Every good adviser gets to know the family, at least in the beginning. After that, however, many deal exclusively with the decision-maker.

There's nothing terrible about that. In my household, for example, my broker, insurance agent, and tax preparer all deal with me. Susan is included in important meetings and has enough of a relationship with each adviser to feel comfortable if anything should happen to me.

But if you and your partner make all decisions jointly, you want to make sure the adviser is happy explaining things to you as a couple, and has the patience to wait for both of you instead of pressing for an instant decision before the household can get together to discuss the issues involved.

How does the adviser react when you raise questions or come in with suggestions?

Many advisers try to make all clients fit into the same basic circle of reference. Accountants, for example, decide which types of deductions they like to pursue and may focus on those, lawyers have certain feelings about which way to proceed with a case, insurance agents and financial planners have their favorite products, and so on.

If you ask questions, rather than immediately accepting the advice as gospel, or if you bring suggestions to the table ("I read about a tax deduction for this situation and think I might be eligible ..."), you want to make sure the adviser won't give you the brush-off.

Have you ever decided not to take your counselor's advice? If so, how did they react?

Just because the reference is happy with the adviser's service does not mean they have taken all advice blindly. You want to find out what suggestions the adviser may have made that the client didn't like—why did the client decide they were not appropriate?—and how the adviser responded when their recommended course of action was not taken.

Have you ever had any pricing/billing problems? (If so, how were they resolved?)

You always ask an adviser about how they charge for their work. Presumably their client asked the same things—or had it explained by the adviser even if they never asked for an explanation of how the adviser gets paid for services.

That said, there should be no surprises on your bill—or on those of the reference.

If there were, you will want to know how things were settled (and you may want to rehash billing procedures with the adviser before making your hiring decision).

Has anything about the relationship surprised you?

This is a good way to find out if the relationship has lived up to, or exceeded, expectations.

Has the adviser's service ever disappointed you and, if so, what did you do about it?

Many times a client working with an adviser does not recognize problems or disappointments until they are asked to think about them. Problems then may come into sharper focus.

A reference's disappointments may not bother you—perhaps they wanted more face-to-face contact and you don't care about that issue —but it's important to find out if they had any.

Have you ever worked with any other advisers? If so, why did you make a change—and what does this adviser do better than the last one?

In chapter 1, Robert Clark, editor-in-chief at *Dow Jones Investment Advisor* magazine, noted that many people bounce from one adviser to the next, rather than picking one adviser with whom they can work comfortably for a lifetime.

If the reference has worked with other advisers, their experience may be valuable. Presumably the old relationship was lacking in some way, and the new one doesn't have the same problem.

Again, this helps qualify what the reference wants from the relationship—and how it compares with your desires—as well as how well those needs are being met.

What do you think this adviser does the best?

Hopefully what an adviser does best is something that you particularly value as a prospective client.

Remember Jim, the stockbroker in chapter 5 who was supposed to be the best broker in town but wound up losing the stock-picking contest by using the same miserable advice he was giving clients? What he did best, apparently, was schmooze customers and make them feel important.

No one knows better than you what you want out of an advisory relationship, whether that is hand-holding, financial acumen, the emotional discipline to stay the course, or whatever. You are looking for an adviser whose strong points fit your needs.

Is there any area where you wish the adviser would give you even more attention?

This is a logical follow-up to the previous question. Again, it helps you determine whether your expectations for the relationship are in line with the reference's and helps you decide if the adviser can meet your specific needs.

***How long do you anticipate working with the adviser? (Or, in the
case of advisers generally hired on a case-by-case basis, Do you
anticipate working with the adviser again?)***

You are looking for financial relationships that can last a lifetime, or
close to it.

Yes, a reference is going to be biased and say nice things about
their counselors. But if they can't see working with that adviser for
a lifetime (or again, if they hired the person because of a one-time
need), then you need to find out why they might hire someone else.
Indeed you might want to hire someone else too.

12   *Hiring a financial planner*

People hire financial planners because they need service; they fire them because they don't like the investment returns.

That's the right way to hire a helper, but not the right expectation.

Don't hire an investment manager to "beat the market."

Hire a financial planner to provide you with security and to make sure that you can reach long-term goals regardless of what the market does.

Remember, the stock market does not know when your next mortgage or tuition payment is due, nor does it understand your current financial needs.

An adviser should only attempt to develop a strategy that beats the market if that is what your personal circumstances call for. Otherwise, they should be focused on your long-term goals.

If the idea of managing your money is to never run out, and to live out your life comfortably, then that is the benchmark you should shoot for. Everything else is noise.

Financial planning is a wide-ranging topic, and it can be hard to find the right match of skill and service to meet your needs. But if you enter the relationship with the right expectations—that you want someone to offer you service, as opposed to merely picking winners—you are likely to come away with an adviser you can trust for a lifetime.

Here are the questions you will want to answer as you go about selecting and working with a financial planner.

Can I do this myself?

As Dwight D. Eisenhower once noted, "Plans are nothing, planning is everything."

So it goes with your financial situation. Everyone has plans for what they want their money to achieve, but not many people are reaching their goals comfortably.

No one actually needs to hire a financial planner or investment counselor, unless all they have on their own is a plan.

The average individual investor can manage a lifetime of savings and investment in no-load mutual funds and no-commission Treasury bonds.

What a financial planner brings to the table is what I like to call "emotional discipline." It is their job to make sure that plans are not just drawn up in your mind but that planning is done to reach those goals. When the market gets queasy, their job is to reassure you and to help you stay the course toward your long-term investment goals.

If you do not have the emotional discipline to invest regularly, in a fashion aggressive enough to reach your goals but without excessive risk and with the confidence to let your money ride when the market heads south, then chances are that you can't do your financial planning successfully, without at least a modicum of financial assistance.

What is a planner's role and responsibility to me?

This is what you will be defining through the interview process. You may just want an adviser to give you a fiscal physical, a snapshot of where you are now and what your long-term goals ought to be, or you may want to hire a money manager to plot a specific investment course for your money.

Whether you are going to a planner for periodic checkups—plenty of planning clients see their adviser once every two years after an initial consultation that set them on the course toward their goals— or having them play an active day-to-day role in managing your money, the planner should be able to play a role as adviser to you and to any other financial helpers you have hired.

Legally, planners have a responsibility to make sure that their advice is suitable for each client. "Unsuitable advice" is inappropriately risky, such as a super-aggressive small-company stock funds for a postretirement age, low-income investor. It may also have hidden costs or charges that the adviser could have avoided by making more savvy choices.

Picking investments that do not appreciate is not automatically considered inappropriate counsel. Suitability has less to do with real performance numbers than with the process that led to making an investment in the first place.

Truth be told, actual investment selection should be a small part of an adviser's role; if the only reason you want to hire an adviser is to get the names of some good mutual funds that you will feel comfortable investing with, chances are you will be headed for a poor relationship with a planner because you will balk at many suggestions.

Worse yet, an adviser whose role is defined as picking investments for you can be made obsolete by any number of computer software programs, none of which should cost more than about $50, or by a magazine subscription.

Am I better off having my insurance agent or accountant or stockbroker function as my overall financial planner?

You may already have an adviser with financial planning credentials and a background in advising customers. But, as you will see in the chapter on hiring utility infielders, you may want to limit your advisers to one job on your financial team.

Because the planner may be the quarterback of your entire financial team, the position is too important to simply hand over to an adviser, even one with whom you already have a successful relationship.

That being the case, if an adviser says they can handle your financial planning needs, start asking questions and make sure they pass muster in an interview. If they aren't as good or better, in your mind, than every other adviser you talk to, they should get no consideration toward playing two positions on your advisory team.

How are planners paid?

The entire financial planning community has been moving away from traditional methods of payment over the last few years.

Instead of traditional commission-based sales, a growing number of advisers get paid either on a flat hourly rate or as a percentage of assets under management.

Fee-only advocates would like us to believe that there is one of their brethren for every potential customer; that's just not true. It is hard for low-net-worth clients to find a fee-only adviser; instead, they wind up working on a commission basis that, essentially, allows them to pay for the specific services they need at the time they need them.

Despite the fee-only trend, or perhaps because of it, it is more important than ever not to assume how the counselor exacts their fee.

Be sure to find out if costs are associated with products or with overall services, and be careful of times when those lines are blurry.

For example, some advisers claim to be fee-only, but the moniker applies only to their investment products. The minute they are selling you insurance, they are back on commission. Likewise advisers may get a piece of the action for helping to keep you in certain mutual funds. A "12b-1 fee," for example, is a marketing charge that some funds apply to accounts every year. Essentially the fund takes as much as 1 percent of your account balance to pay for "marketing and distribution costs" and then pays a portion of the fee to your broker. This charge is in addition to the ongoing management fees charged by the fund itself.

The payment options boil down to fee-only, commission only, "fee-offset"—in which commissions reduce a fee for planning so that a client knows the maximum amount they can pay for advice in a year—and fee-plus-commission.

If you move your account from one adviser to another, make sure that any applicable marketing fees or "trailing commissions" get credited to the new adviser. This encourages your new helper to retain those holdings that are appropriate, rather than gutting the entire portfolio (a move you are likely willing to make if you have switched advisers) to get entirely new choices.

Last, your planner may offer you an investment management account with something called a "wrap fee," which combines management and brokerage fees. These fees can run as high as 3 percent of the assets under management, which is pretty steep. Something closer to 1.5 percent or 2 percent is about average for a stock wrap account; 1.0 to 1.5 percent is the norm with mutual fund wraps.

A wrap fee lets you know in advance what you will pay a money manager, but it will only be worthwhile if the manager trades actively and if you have a significant amount of cash—at least $25,000 and preferably $100,000 or above—to commit to the program; if you and the manager employ a buy-and-hold strategy, run the numbers to make sure that you aren't just better off with straight commission.

What credentials are important?

More than any other advisory role, financial planners are going to trot out their credentials, only some of which are truly meaningful.

It is important to know that financial advisers typically have to register with the state in which they work, but they do not need any credentials or designations to practice. Anyone who thinks they have an idea of what financial planning is all about can become registered to help others simply by filling out some paperwork and paying a small fee.

That said, you will probably want to hire an adviser who has some type of advanced credential. Here are the ones you are most likely to run across.

The Certified Financial Planner (CFP) mark has become the backbone of many searches for a financial adviser, and many experts consider this to be the minimum credential needed to make a planner worth considering. Essentially the CFP program is a self-study course —although many advisers now earn their designation taking classes at regional colleges and universities that have developed programs about financial planning. Advisers must have a minimum of three years of practice experience, plus the course work, and must successfully complete a two-day exam covering everything from insurance to investments to estate planning to employee benefits, taxes, and more.

In addition the Certified Financial Planner Board of Standards, which maintains the licensing requirements, expects licensees to adhere to a strict code of ethical conduct.

Advisers who concentrate on investment selection may offer a Chartered Financial Analyst (CFA) designation, one of the most prestigious of all financial services credentials, awarded by the Association for Investment Management and Research (AIMR). The CFA mark requires several years of work experience, as well as passing a study course and exams in securities analysis, portfolio management, financial accounting, economics, and ethics. The designation is common among institutional money managers and Wall Street analysts; it is an ideal credential to look for if you have a lot of money that you want a planner to help allocate and choose investments for.

If an agent comes to financial planning from the life insurance specialty, they may offer a Chartered Financial Consultant (ChFC) designation. Like its sister designation, the Chartered Life Underwriter (CLU), the ChFC is awarded by the American College in Bryn Mawr, PA, and requires extensive educational training. Because the Society of CLUs and ChFCs specializes in insurance issues, so too do most of the counselors who have this mark. If you prefer to leave your insurance planning to an insurance agent, this credential may be less of a selling point than some of the others.

The Personal Financial Specialist (PFS) label goes to certified public accountants (CPAs) who concentrate on financial planning issues and meet rigorous educational requirements. Keeping this credential means retaining their membership status within the American Institute of Certified Public Accountants, completing their course work, and undergoing periodic peer reviews.

In looking for an adviser to captain a financial team, experts who are particularly good at mixing investment knowledge with tax expertise often prove to be the best candidates, but that does not limit you to the relatively small world of the CPA/PFS. There are many CPAs and enrolled agents who also have their CFP credential; those particular dual-designations (CPA/CFP or EA/CFP) strike me as an even stronger combination for a team leader.

Beyond those designations, there are a number of credentials that a financial planner might trot out to you. In alphabetical order, they include Accredited Asset Management Specialist (AAMS) which is awarded to investment advisers who have completed the Asset Management Program offered by the National Endowment for Financial Education; Accredited Estate Planners (AEP) who pass a test and meet minimum continuing education requirements set by the National Association of Estate Planners and Councils; Certified Employee Benefit Specialist (CEBS) which is offered by the International Foundation of Employee Benefit Plans for a ten-course, ten-exam program covering all areas of planning and administration related to benefit plans; Certified Fund Specialist (CFS), a relatively new designation given to advisers who pass a course and exam on mutual fund selection and portfolio management; Certified Investment Management Consultant (CIMC) which is awarded by the Institute for Investment Management Consultants for passing its study course; Chartered Mutual Fund Consultant (CMFC) which is the National Endowment for Financial Education's version of the Certified Fund Specialist designation (as someone who writes a weekly column about mutual funds, I find neither of these designations particularly crucial to a financial adviser but prefer the CMFC for an adviser who insists on a fund-management credential); Certified Trust and Financial Advisers (CTFA) work for a bank or trust company and have passed the Institute of Certified Bankers' course covering taxation, investments, personal finance, and fiduciary duty; and Registered Financial Consultants (RFC), who have at least four years of practical experience, a degree in business, economics, or law and a CFP, ChFC, CPA, or more to boot.

Even with all of those credentials, there are a few other initials an adviser might toss onto a resume or business card. One is membership in the National Association of Personal Financial Advisors (NAPFA), a group of fee-only planners that is almost militant in the way it views advisers who work on commission. The group has stepped up its membership requirements in terms of education and practice knowledge, but the basic standard remains that the adviser charges on a fee-only basis.

NAPFA has created a new designation, the F-O, for fee-only advisers, a credential that has no educational meaning whatsoever and, instead, focuses entirely on compensation. NAPFA is licensing the F-O to members and outsiders alike, meaning that planners who do not meet the group's tough educational standards can still pay a fee and get the F-O so long as they do not work on commission.

Since you are going to check on an adviser's method of compensation anyway, the F-O truly is a meaningless designation; don't let it confuse you into thinking an adviser automatically is a NAPFA member or even an educated adviser.

If an adviser tells you they are in "The Registry," they are using an outdated term that once stood for an elite group within the International Association of Financial Planning. The problem was that the group grandfathered a lot of old-line practitioners, some of whom weren't so up-to-date in their practices or course knowledge; Registry members were subsequently given CFP designations (without having to complete the course work), so any adviser who mentions the Registry should be asked whether they earned their CFP mark or simply inherited it.

International Association for Financial Planning (IAFP) membership is also something that an adviser might toss out at you. This is a trade group open to anyone in the financial services business; although membership requirements have tightened, the group once admitted a dog into membership (the owner simply wanted to see if "Bo Regard" met membership standards). While IAFP is an important agency within the industry, membership should not impress you; if an adviser lists this as their primary credential, ask them what else they have to show you.

The Licensed Independent Network of CPA Financial Planners (LINC) is a membership group of fee-only planners who also are licensed as CPAs. There is no exam required for membership.

All told, the credentials are a sign that someone is proficient in the nuts-and-bolts, number-crunching side of financial planning. But as discussed in chapter 9—on dealing with credentials—an adviser's service and manner (and not ability with a scientific calculator) generally make the difference in a successful relationship; virtually none of the class/exam time involved in earning any of these designations is spent on the human side of a financial planning relationship.

Where do I start my search?

With all of the credentials out there, it can be hard to determine a starting point for a search. Obviously friends and relatives can give you referrals, but that can be a particularly tough fit with financial planners. Your personal circumstances can be so much different than those of your loved ones, and planners tend to work best with a clientele that is similar in needs.

Beyond word of mouth, you might go to the referral lines offered by the credentialing and membership groups themselves.

You are going to interview several candidates before making your selection. I suggest that at least one of your candidates be someone who was not a word-of-mouth referral; this allows you to have something of a "control group," to see whether your judgment is colored by the advice of a friend. Many people who have tried this at my suggestion have found that the adviser with whom they had no connection came off as most knowledgeable and helpful; a big reason for the difference is that their loved one picked a financial planner by serendipity, rather than science. Here are several organizations that can supply names of financial planners in your area:

▪ The Institute of Certified Financial Planners will give you a list of up to three planners in your area, along with a brochure to help guide you through the selection process. All planners whose names are provided will have achieved the CFP credential. Call 1-800-282-7526 for information (hearing impaired call 1-800-438-9968).

▪ The International Association for Financial Planning gives a longer list of area planners, along with a *Consumer Guide to Comprehensive Financial Planning* and other informational materials. To be in this referral program, a planner must have a financial planning designation (CFA, CFP, ChFC, or CPA), a law or financial planning degree. Call 1-800-945-IAFP.

▪ The National Association of Personal Financial Advisors, whose members must be fee-only planners, will give you a list of members from around the state, along with a financial planner interview form and a disclosure form to help you illustrate how and how much the planner and planning firm will be paid if you sign on. Call 1-888-FEE-ONLY.

▪ The American Institute of Certified Public Accountants provides the names of members who have earned its Personal Financial Specialist (PFS) designation. Call 1-800-862-4272 to ask for CPA/PFS referrals in your area.

▪ The Investment Counsel Association of America provides its membership directory free of charge to interested investors. The directory lists firms and provides details about the size and type of investment practice, along with account minimums. Although you will find some of the member firms accepting accounts of as little as $90,000, the majority of these firms only work with investors whose assets exceed $500,000. Call 202-293-4222.

How do I check them out?

Check all brokers out in at least two places, starting with your state securities regulator—whose number is listed in chapter 14—and including the groups that have awarded any credentials important to your decision. (The phone numbers for most of those groups are the same ones you would have called to start your search; if the adviser uses a different credential to sell you on their services, ask them to provide the organization's name and phone number so you can do a background check.)

Most states register financial advisers and will be able to share with you an adviser's Form ADV, which includes disciplinary history. The adviser should give you this information too, but make the phone call to be sure that you are aware of current complaints and actions; many advisers have been known to hand out old registration paperwork, figuring it would buffalo a potential customer into not checking with the state.

There may be a nominal charge to get a copy of these forms from the securities administrator's office; if you intend to check out several advisers, bunch the requests together, for the state may be willing to reduce the total fee.

In addition to checking out the adviser, run the firm's name past the securities office too. You do not want to be dealing with the most reputable character at a disreputable firm.

If the financial planner also a registered representative and licensed to sell securities, you will want to get their Central Registration

Depository (CRD) number and make sure they have no problems on that side of their practice. (If they work as a planner now but sold them in the past, get their CRD number so you can make sure it was not disciplinary problems that led to the career change.)

Likewise, if you intend to use a planner for your insurance needs, make sure they are licensed with the state—you will need to call the insurance commissioner's office in that case (numbers listed in chapter 16)—to make sure they have a clean bill of health all around.

What should I ask during an interview?

The late Charles Wilson, one-time chairman of General Motors Corp. and a former U.S. Secretary of Defense, once said in a speech that "No one can prevent a stupid person from doing the wrong thing in the wrong place at the wrong time—but a good plan should keep a concentration from forming."

Your job in selecting an adviser is not to be stupid about it so that you can build a plan and never worry about making bad moves at the worst possible times.

To do that, you will want to cover all your bases and make sure that your financial planning relationship lives up to your expectations both from an interpersonal and financial standpoint.

Here is the ground you will want to cover with a planner before making a selection:

What is your educational and professional background?
Look at a planner's background to see if they have a stable employment history. You want an adviser who is going to be there for you in the years ahead, as well as one who is not moving from job to job because their work did not satisfy previous employers.

If an adviser has had more than two jobs in the last three years, or has a regular pattern of jobswitching, find out what's going on. It could be that a planner moved to a firm that offered better opportunities or that specializes in a field that is of particular interest to the adviser; then again, they might have moved because they burnt their bridges at the old firm. If necessary, call the previous employer for a reference check.

As for a planner's educational and pre–financial planning background, that can be interesting to know. Many planners come to the field as a second career, whose first interest may have been teaching, money management, or art. You can often learn a lot about an adviser—and get a feel for the human skills they bring to the job—by finding out what they did before becoming a planner.

What continuing education classes have you taken? What certifications, if any, do you have?

The section on credentials already established why you want this information. An adviser who gives you the name of a credential should also be willing to tell you how to make sure they really have it. Ask them to give you the group's phone number, if only so you can call to get a better explanation of what the credential means and what kinds of financial specialists earn it.

Can I have a copy of your form ADV, both Parts I and II?

As far as I'm concerned, this one is a deal-breaker, so ask it early and pay close attention to the response.

Form ADV is an adviser's registration form. By rule, the adviser must give the form to all new clients. *But*, by the same rule, the adviser must only give you Part II of the form.

The problem is that Part I is where all disciplinary actions are listed.

The adviser knows you can get this information on your own from the state securities office. Despite this, most firms only give out Part II unless you specifically ask for both sections of the form.

This is one of the few deal-breaker questions in all of financial services, so don't waste your time and save it for the end of an interview.

If a financial planner will not give you both parts of Form ADV—and cites the rules in doing so—the interview is over. Just walk away.

A planner who knows you intend to do a background check but refuses to help give you information you can get on your own certainly is acting as if they have something to hide. Don't risk it.

If a planner says he or she does not have a Form ADV, find out how they achieved some exception to the registration rules and tread very carefully; unless you want an adviser for whom providing investment advice is *not* a key component of the service, an unregistered planner probably is someone to stay away from.

Who is your typical client?

If the average client looks like you and has concerns like yours, then chances are the adviser has already dealt with whatever situation your personal finances can dish up. In addition planners put the bulk of their educational time toward figuring out how to better serve their client base, which means learning about things that will benefit their average client.

Make sure the planner's answer doesn't focus solely on age, income, and size of portfolio. If you are a union worker with a particular type of pension plan, you want someone who understands the workings of those plans, as opposed to a consultant whose clients are largely self-employed and setting up their own retirement plans.

If you resemble an adviser's average client, there is a good chance they will want you as a customer because they will feel comfortable that they can deliver the services you want and need.

How—and how much—do you get paid?

You might recall the recent hit movie *Jerry Maguire*, in which a sports star tells his agent to "Show me the money!" Make your prospective adviser do the same, in terms of the money it is going to cost you for their services.

Remember, straight commission sales are not always worse for the client than a management fee; it will depend on your needs and the amount of buying or selling you do. Make an adviser discuss all payment options and show you the math.

The adviser also discloses how they are compensated in Part II of the ADV, so make sure the paperwork and the explanation you get in the office are in sync. Many advisers claim the fee-only label but then charge commissions on insurance products; you would want to know that before purchasing a policy that way.

Remember too that there are thousands of financial planners out there; if you can't afford the services of one, there will be others whom you can hire without breaking your bank.

What service will I get?

You might recall from chapter 8, which dealt with your first meeting with an adviser, how one of my colleagues once met and hired a financial planner in the same day, only to be disappointed when he received—by mail—an action plan that was full of strategy but devoid of investment selections and specific suggestions on where to make financial moves to improve cash flow and cut debt, along with a bill that was for more than he anticipated having to pay.

This question tries to avert that kind of situation.

You have just asked about how the planner will get paid, now find out specifically what you will get for your money. Ask to look at samples of what existing clients receive for the same level of service.

Make the adviser spell out precisely what to expect.

You want to know if an adviser will provide advice on any or all of the following: cash management and budgeting, tax planning, investment review and planning, estate planning, insurance needs, and retirement planning.

You want to make sure that you get a written review of your goals and a written analysis of your situation and what steps you should take next.

In addition you will want to know if the adviser offers ongoing counsel, periodic reviews, or both, and which they would recommend for you.

How often will I hear from you, and what will prompt your calls?

This question covers both phone calls and statements. You should find out how often you will get a statement of your account, as well as when you might expect a phone call from the planner.

Some financial planners do a lot of hand-holding, stroking their clients to preserve the emotional discipline necessary to be a long-term investor. Others call only when there is a need or an investment recommendation to make.

Good planners talk about a lot of things besides immediate sales. In addition they work with your other advisers to make sure you have adequate counsel in all areas of your financial life; make sure your financial planner is willing to work with other members of your financial team.

How many active clients do you work with at one time?

There are only so many hours in the work week. If a planner promises regular attention, but then tells you they have 200 clients, something doesn't add up. Either they palm off a lot of work on subordinates, or they don't live up to their promises.

Many of the top financial planners in the country work with no more than 60 clients at any one time. When their calendar is full, they simply stop taking new customers.

An adviser is not necessarily doing you a favor by squeezing you into their datebook, particularly if you aren't going to be satisfied with the attention they can offer you.

*Why do you want to hire me as a client? What kinds of people do you **not** want as clients?*

Presumably the answer to this question gets back to the fact that you are within the adviser's target client range, with a situation they find appealing. But if an adviser tells you what kinds of people they turn away, and they are describing you—but just don't know it because this is a first interview—you will be better off going elsewhere for your financial help.

Do you have an area in which you specialize?

Some planners are generalists; others are highly focused.

Obviously educational credentials will go a long way toward showing you someone's expertise, but you still want to find out how much time the adviser spends working on situations like yours. It is always best to work within the adviser's specialty.

Do you give financial advice only, or do you execute the transactions?

Anyone who executes the trades may have a conflict of interest, but in any event you will want to know how you will go about implementing the strategy you are paying so much money for.

What is your investment philosophy?

What criteria do you use before deciding what to buy?

Under what conditions do you sell?

Sure, you are hiring an expert, but the logic they put into their investment choices has to be something you agree with. If they tell you that astrology plays a key role in their decisions, for example—and I know a few brokers and planners who do a star chart for all new clients—you may decide to hit the road.

The reason to find out how a planner selects investments is because that criteria will be the basis for all recommendations made to you. If it doesn't sound good now, imagine how nervous it will make you when there is money on the line.

Can I review sample plans and statements?

You are paying to get a report on your finances and advice on where to go next.

Having reviewed literally hundreds of financial plans, I can tell you that some of the world's most respected financial advisers can't put a plan into plain English. They may be among the brightest minds in the field, but they can't communicate that knowledge to anyone but the most knowledgeable clients.

Conversely, I have seen plans that, in my opinion, talked down to even the most clueless of customers.

Advisers can black out or alter the names and addresses of clients in order to show you samples of their work. I know of several big firms that will give you real plans where the names and occupations have been fictionalized to everything from Prince Charming to Zeus.

As for a sample statement, go over the form with the adviser to make sure you understand everything. It will be your responsibility to monitor these forms and guard against fraud, so you want to make sure you can read a statement before you become a customer.

Can I get the names of a few clients to act as references?

Just because you have seen work samples doesn't mean you don't want to check with real live people. Ask clients about the character of their advisory relationship, and try to determine if the planner works with customers in a manner that you will be comfortable with.

Do you take possession of, or have access to, my assets?

Do you have discretion to change my investments without my approval?

If a financial planner wants you to sign a discretionary account agreement—which gives them the right to manage your money in accordance with your wishes (but without direct approval of each maneuver)—you should balk. This is a form of abdicating control; if you have picked a rogue planner (or just a stupid one) giving them discretion over your money could be a costly mistake.

There are rare circumstances under which an adviser might hold assets—or be able to access them at will—but these are extremely rare. Some financial advisers ask for "limited discretionary powers," especially if they are managing money in accounts at mutual fund supermarkets, like those offered by Fidelity, Charles Schwab, and others; make sure you understand the limits you are agreeing to.

The rule of thumb in these situations is to walk away from any financial adviser who pressures you for too much control over your assets.

Will anyone else be working with me?

Financial planning firms come in all shapes and sizes. I know of one prominent planner who functions largely as a rainmaker, bringing clients into the firm where they get passed on to subordinates; the big guy does the initial meeting and dispenses the advice, but he is little more than a puppet for the back-room personnel that does the grassroots work of strategizing.

If you are told that someone besides the planner you are meeting will work on your account, find out why. Then find out who; arrange to meet that person and, at the very least, get both parts of their ADV.

If an adviser promises to work with you but consistently lets you deal with an assistant, the relationship is in trouble.

Do you personally research the products you recommend?

If an adviser relies entirely on someone else's research, that should make you nervous. It means they are simply selling product, rather than necessarily believing in it themselves.

Good advisers know how to analyze financial products, know which investment analysts they trust, and make decisions that are based on their own experience and intuition, rather than on something they got in the firm's sales manual or a recommendation from a service they subscribe to.

If an adviser does not do their own research, ask whether they put their own money into the products they recommend.

How will we resolve complaints if I am dissatisfied?

Chances are you will sign an agreement that says you agree to try arbitration before turning to the courts; some arbitration agreements —the good ones—do not take away your right to pursue action in court, they merely attempt to settle things using lower-cost, faster-working arbitration.

Before you get to that, however, you want to know what would happen if there is a problem in your account, how the adviser would handle it—whether it is a technical glitch or a transaction you don't recall making.

Many planners try to reassure you that this stuff never happens. Make them guide you through the complaint process anyway.

And if the planner works for a large firm, get an introduction to either the office manager or the firm's compliance officer, the first people you are likely to be dealing with if there is a problem. Get business cards from these people, and keep their numbers handy.

All of these actions tell the planner that you will not stand for any shenanigans; a diligent customer is the best deterrent to fraud.

How can I terminate this relationship if I am not satisfied?

An advisory agreement should favor you, not the planner. That means it should come equipped with some sort of ejector seat. Most advisory contracts can be terminated with a month's notice—with fees pro-rated monthly—at any time.

Still, you will want to know how to open your escape hatch before you climb into the cockpit.

Have you ever had complaints filed against you by customers? How have those complaints been resolved?

The planner knows you are going to check their record with the state; this is when they get a chance to come clean and explain what, if anything, you will find in their records or to explain what they handed you in Part I of the ADV.

You want the adviser's side of the story, whether the complaint was the result of miscommunication, unrealistic expectations, or whatever.

If the broker tells you they have never had these kinds of problems and the state tells you something different, the game is over and you will turn elsewhere for financial help. If a planner tries sleight of hand when they know you are looking, what will they do when you have an established relationship and your guard is down?

Keep in mind that even the best financial planners sometimes run into bad relationships, people who believe they were entitled to buy investments that only increased in value or whose demands were simply unrealistic. You want to know why these problems happened so that you can ask:

How do we make sure that I will not have similar problems?

If the adviser has learned anything from their troubled clients, it is that they don't want to have these hassles again. Find out what they intend to do to make sure you do not become their next problem client.

What should I ask before making any individual transactions?

How much commission will you and your firm earn on this trade?

You should always find out what a transaction will cost you; remember, even fee-only advisers sometimes charge commissions on certain transactions (and may accept 12b-1 fees and other investment-related charges in addition to their proscribed fee).

What is your rationale for picking this specific product?

How does it suit my needs and risk tolerances?

What standard will we set for performance, and how will we monitor progress?
A planner should be able to justify their decisions and mesh their advice into your personal circumstances. If they can't, then you are getting off-the-rack counsel, even though you thought you were paying for a custom tailor.

After all fees are paid, how much does this investment have to gain in value before I break even?
Again, this looks at the cost of making an investment, showing you in dramatic fashion whether a trade puts you at a financial disadvantage. If costs are high, an investment may have to outperform the averages to generate the returns you want. With above-average performance potential comes above-average risk; make sure that's something you want to get involved in.

Will this sale help you win any prizes or sales contests?
Financial advisers often have incentives to sell you something, even if it doesn't show up in their compensation. I have friends in the planning business who have won trips all over the world, literally, as a result of being a top producer.

If the financial product meets your needs, there is nothing wrong with that—although I want the conflict of interest disclosed. More often, however, contests lead advisers to give cookie-cutter plans, putting all of their clients into one basket because it delivers the incentive and yet passing the service off as being individualized.

How long do you expect me to hold this investment? Why?
Most financial planners pursue a buy-and-hold strategy. Commission-based sales encourage trading, as does a fee-only adviser's participation in a "no-transaction fee" discount brokerage network such as Schwab's OneSource or Fidelity's FundsNet. (With no costs and only tax consequences to pay, critics argue that these mutual fund supermarkets encourage treating a long-term asset—a mutual fund—like a

short-term investment, trading whenever something else looks even a bit more promising.)

Unless someone can successfully time the market over a long period of time—and the vast majority of Wall Street's top experts get it wrong, so there is no reason to believe your planner has been touched by genius—constant portfolio turnover is likely to reduce returns.

Make a written record of how long a planner suggests you will hold a security. There's nothing wrong with holding on longer, but if they come back and suggest selling in a few months—unless there is a significant change in the investment's status that warrants a move—you can give them a wake-up call that they are going away from their original plan.

Can I get out of this investment quickly?

This is not a strange question, even in light of the last query about how long you would hold an investment.

No financial planner should sell you something without saying if it is hard or costly to unload. There may not be many buyers for an individual municipal bond, for example.

Other investments, such as annuities or mutual funds, may be easy to get out of but could carry steep penalties or surrender charges.

You've told me what it costs to buy this investment; how much would I get if I were to sell it today?

This is about "spread," which you may face if you use a planner to buy stocks and bonds.

Think of it like a new car, where you pay the sticker price but could not sell it back to the dealer at the same price the second after you drive it off the lot.

What is the worst-case outcome for this investment?

Before buying any investment or following any financial strategy, find out what the worst possible outcome for your investment could be.

What should I never do in working with a planner?

- If you are buying an investment, never make the check out to the representative.

The money goes to the firm (or the company offering a particular investment product, like a variable annuity) and is to be invested in your account. The firm will pay the commission and use the rest in accordance with you instructions. If you make a check payable to the planner, you just might find that they have left with your money.

- Never send money to any address but that of the firm or of an operation designated in the prospectus (such as a transfer agent).

Again, this avoids a rogue planner diverting money into their own pocket.

- Never allow transaction confirmations and account statements to be sent to your adviser instead of you.

These are your record of what is happening in the account; without them, you don't have the paper trail necessary to build a strong case when things go wrong. If an adviser wants confirmations and statements, they can help you arrange for duplicates.

How can I develop and build the relationship?

Whether an adviser is a regular partner in your financial decisions, or just someone you turn to for a checkup and fine-tuning of your own investment strategy, you will want to build a relationship.

This means calling with questions and concerns, arranging the occasional lunch when there is no business to transact, and integrating their services into your own financial planning agenda. In addition, involving a planner when you work with your other financial advisers is a wise idea (although you will always want to know whether you are being charged for any of these phone calls or ancillary meetings).

At the same time busy planners don't have a lot of time to kibbitz. Spend a few minutes planning your call to a financial adviser so that—if they have other business to do—you can be efficient and get the information you want without tying them up. Not only will they appreciate that approach, but they will be happy to take and return your calls.

What are the danger signs that the relationship is not working?

Beyond pushing upon you the things you should never do with a planner, other signs of trouble include:

- Paperwork you don't understand.

If you are ever asked to sign any agreement that does not make sense to you or does not seem in keeping with what you and the planner have arranged for, get nervous. Some planners pass discretionary agreements in front of customers as a matter of course; the authorizations make it much easier for the broker to mismanage your money, so don't sign unless you intend to.

▪ Statements that don't arrive on time, or no statements at all from anyone but the adviser.

You should receive regular statements from the investment or insurance companies with whom your planner works. If all you get is a statement from the planner, something is amiss.

Be prepared to follow up directly with the company if something is wrong with your statement; if an adviser is mismanaging your money, you almost certainly will have to go around him or her and go direct to the investment company in order to get copies of your statement that show how much of your investments have actually made it to where they were supposed to go.

▪ "It's just a computer error."

Glitches are extremely rare; when they happen, they should be corrected in a snap.

Do not tolerate this excuse if something shows up on your statement that does not belong there. If it is not corrected immediately, you have a problem.

▪ The only products being offered are run by the house.

This is a bad sign for two different reasons. First off, planners sometimes get more compensation for selling products developed by their firm.

Just as important, however, is that you want a free thinker, someone who does not give you formulaic, one-size-fits-all planning.

You are paying for expertise, and that involves more than just picking any old product to fill your financial voids.

▪ Significant declines in investment value for which you were not prepared.

There should never be any surprises in your investment portfolio. Products may decline in value or be hard to liquidate, but you should be aware of all of that.

If you aren't, it's a sign of poor communication.

There may be nothing illegal going on, but no adviser worth their salt would let a client get bushwhacked by bad news.

▪ The planner does not return you calls promptly.

To be an active partner in your financial life, a planner has to be interested in you and your case. When they don't return you calls promptly or answer your questions at their first convenience, they have lost interest in you.

Once you sense that lack of interest, you should start the search for someone who can serve you better.

What if my adviser changes firms?

There are many legitimate reasons why a planner would switch firms.

Whenever it happens, however, you will want to know the reasons for the change and should do a background check on the new employer.

If you decide to follow the planner, find out if he or she gets a bonus for bringing over new customers. Also find out who pays any transfer fees involved, or whether you might incur taxes because you'd be forced to sell some investments to follow along (which is likely to happen if your financial planner works for a brokerage firm and sells you the house funds).

If you choose not to follow your adviser, you will have to start the interview and background-check process over again, starting with a new adviser who works for the old firm who will serve as an interim replacement. You can then decide whether this planner merits consideration as a permanent replacement, or you can start shopping for an adviser all over again.

How do I complain or seek restitution if there is a problem?

The complaint problem always starts with the individual planner, but it can escalate quickly.

Most advisers have an agreement that puts disputes into arbitration or mediation before it allows you to take them to court; make sure you do not waive your rights to seek restitution in the legal system.

If the problem is operational—such as failure to deliver securities or checks due to you—and the planner is not helping to solve the situation, put your complaint in writing and seek a higher-up. If the planner is a sole practitioner, you should go immediately to the state securities office.

At the same time you are making this case in arbitration or court—and it generally takes between eight and twelve months for an arbitration case to go from your filing to a hearing—pursue the matter with state and federal securities regulators. They generally do not have the power to get your money back, but they do have the power to lean on an adviser—who knows what a black mark on their record might do to future business—and may be able to help speed a settlement.

In addition your complaint will dissuade others from repeating your mistakes.

Don't let a complaint sit around unfiled; the statute of limitations on these issues varies, but the general rule is to file the paperwork as soon as you recognize there is a problem that is not being solved amicably.

13 *Hiring a broker*

Oscar Wilde, the playwright and novelist, once noted that "with an evening coat and white tie, anybody—even a stockbroker—can gain a reputation for being civilized."

Brokers gained a reputation for being less-than-civilized because, for decades, the stock market was a mysterious place that most individuals couldn't get a handle on. It was the Wild West, where the good guys and bad guys were hard to tell apart, but impossible to avoid because they were the only ones with access to both information and data and the markets themselves.

In addition those brokers were, until recent years, always paid on a commission basis, meaning that many encouraged selling and trading in order to generate their own income at the customer's expense.

Actions like that caused people to think that the reason someone is called a "broker" is because that's what you are after dealing with one.

These days, however, brokers are reinventing themselves, offering more and different services, acting more like financial planners than mere sellers of investments and charging for their services in different ways.

The reasons for this evolution have to do with changes in the rest of the financial services industry. With the explosion of mutual funds, more people than ever before are participating in the stock market but not using a broker to do it. They purchase funds direct from the company or invest in companies that sell stock directly to the public and eliminate the middleman.

Many financial advisers suggest that individuals get their stock market exposure through mutual funds and not individual stocks, a move that forced traditional brokers to adapt or face being cut off from a big percentage of the market. And the development and growth of discount brokerage services, coupled with the explosion of available stock market information, has created price and research competition that forces a full-service broker to justify his or her existence.

While the changes were designed to make things easier and more straightforward for consumers, all they really have done is made things more complex. Commission, although fraught with conflict of interest, is at least easy to understand. Today a consumer shopping for a broker has more options that sound good and more confusion about how to get the best representation.

As with all financial advisers, the key to finding a good broker is having a good idea of what you want, and knowing how to look for it.

Here are the questions you will want to consider in selecting and developing a relationship with a broker.

Can I do this myself?

No one actually "needs" a broker. The average individual investor can take care of a lifetime's worth of investment needs by purchasing no-load mutual funds and stocks—and the number of stocks that are being made available to the public on a commission-free, no-broker basis has grown to the point that you can assemble a nice portfolio that way. Treasury bonds too are available on a no-commission basis, direct from the government.

Likewise anyone working with a financial planner, investment adviser, money manager, or the trust department of a bank could find a broker's services redundant and unnecessary.

But if you intend to invest in municipal or corporate bonds or want stocks beyond the universe of the few hundred that currently sell shares directly to the public—or if you can't live with the rules and restrictions that may accompany direct-purchase shares—you will want to at least work with a broker.

In fact you may want to work with several, each one specializing in meeting a specific need, charging a certain way for their services or handling a particular type of transaction. With that in mind, you will want to know:

What are the different types of brokers?

The typical picture of a broker is what is known as the "full-service broker." As the name implies, this is someone who can handle all manner of transaction and provide advice and information to help you make investment choices.

These days, full-service brokers often go by other titles, notably "investment consultants" or "asset managers." No matter what you call them, however, the job is the same—to identify investment opportunities and put investors together with appropriate choices.

Unfortunately, millions of customers pay the full-service rate without getting full service.

Linked to various news services and agencies that track every conceivable bit of data about public companies and bond issuers, a relationship with a full-service broker should be part guidance, part research, and part execution. In an ideal relationship the broker gathers information, passes it to you, outlining each prospect and supporting it with analyst recommendations, research reports, and other data. Once you have made your decision, the broker makes the trade.

Discount brokers, by comparison, generally offer a stripped-down version of that service (which is why a full-service client should get what they pay for). Typically a discount broker will not offer the investment guidance or its own research reports but will pony up the research of others and make the trade.

Still, as much as the name implies that they are cheaper than their full-service clientele, there is a lot to watch out for. Sometimes, those research reports come at an additional cost. Other times, there are account fees that can be costly.

And unless you plan to trade regularly, you may not work with anyone at a discount brokerage firm on a regular basis. Instead, you will get the broker who is available to process your trade, a far cry from the comfort and assurance you can get from developing a long-term relationship with a full-service broker.

So-called deep-discount brokers offer no-frills, ultra-cheap service for anyone strictly looking to execute trades. Some do virtually all of their business by telephone; as with ordinary discount brokers, be careful of fees and expenses. Otherwise, you could wind up actually paying for the firm to mail you annual reports and other shareholder materials from the companies you invest in.

If you are a buy-and-hold investor, price is less important than getting the service you want. It's more important to do business where you feel comfortable and people take the time to service your account properly than to save a few dollars on the trade.

Two other points to consider regarding full-service brokers: (1) Many will discount their commissions, particularly for good customers or on big-dollar trades, so don't be bashful about asking; (2) on very small trades, generally those under $2,000, the flat-fee charged by a discounter may actually wind up being more than the percentage commission taken by a full-service firm. Be sure to do the math.

Many people use more than one broker, hiring a full-service broker for advice and research but using a discounter when they come up with ideas on their own. Some people use a full-service firm to buy but redeem their shares at a discount firm.

Some brokers (and financial planners, for that matter) actually work as "money managers." Effectively they function like the manager of a mutual fund, buying and selling stocks and bonds to meet a particular investment objective, except with a personal touch.

Managers often take a fee of as much as 3 percent of the money they manage each year (the average mutual fund takes about 1 to 1.5 percent). In addition money managers want a lot of money to manage; that may mean opening an account for $25,000, although minimums of ten times that much or more are fairly common.

Unlike someone functioning as your broker—unless you have given them discretion over your account—a money manager will not call you to confirm trades or request your approval, so you must have tremendous confidence in their abilities. Don't be fooled into thinking that any old broker can manage your money in this fashion, however; giving up control of your funds is one of the easiest ways to be scammed. Typically a financial planner or one of your other advisers will make an introduction to a money manager; the money manager does not do the routine daily chores handled by most brokers. If they talk like a money manager but look like a broker to you, be doubly cautious.

What is a broker's role and responsibility to me?

The broker functions like a salesman but, unlike someone pushing vacuum cleaners or refrigerators, simply persuading you to write a check does not legally constitute doing their job.

Brokers have a legal responsibility to make sure that each and every recommendation they make is suitable for you, your financial circumstances, goals and objectives, and level of understanding. Anything less than that, whether done out of greed for a commission or mere stupidity, leaves the broker liable for resulting losses.

An "unsuitable investment" is one that is inappropriately risky, such as junk bonds for a conservative retiree. It may also be something that is inappropriate, such as a costly insurance product like a variable annuity with a "life insurance kicker" sold to someone with no real need for the insurance feature; if the insurance tie-in significantly erodes the client's investment—and those things can happen—then the investment was unsuitable.

What is suitable therefore is defined by you and not necessarily the broker.

(Unsuitable, by the way, does not necessarily mean selling investments that lose money; a broker is not liable for losses that are a normal part of investment ups and downs, so long as they clearly explained in advance the possibilities and circumstances that could lead to losses.)

An interesting anecdote about that involves my father, who a few years back was working with a broker who suggested what amounted to a high-cost, high-risk regional bank mutual fund. My father asked for my thoughts, and I told him the investment was inappropriate, given my father's extremely conservative nature, his outlook, and his needs.

When my father called the broker to say he would not be investing, the broker went off, asking whether my father thought that he knew more about investments than the broker did.

My father explained that the broker knew more about investments, but not enough about my father. (He subsequently stopped doing business with the broker.)

While you want a broker to present you with opportunities and reasons why you should—or should not—buy or sell a stock, bond or mutual fund, the broker's job is to get to know you well enough to only present you with opportunities that meet your needs.

If you broker doesn't know you—if they have just called on the phone, for example—and they do not ask a number of detailed questions, you should wonder whether they have enough knowledge to adequately do their job.

Am I better off with someone from a nationally known firm?

Truth be told, it is more important to have a broker who is expert at what he or she does than to have someone who is affiliated with a national wirehouse like Merrill Lynch, Dean Witter, Prudential Securities, and the rest of the big names.

Yes, the big names have access to more of their own research and may sell products that they developed on their own—offering you the house mutual funds instead of, say, an independent mutual fund.

But there are few other operational differences between the two, in that both should be equipped with the latest technology. And I have heard cases of "selling pressures"—brokers feeling management's push to reach certain sales quotas from both types of firm, so there is no consistent way to say whether a broker from one type of firm is more likely to face heat if they can't convince people to buy.

The additional research is important, but the fact is that you want a broker who does his or her own research, rather than relying solely on the firm's reports. In fact you want a broker who is not unafraid to do things that are out-of-step with the firm, advising you to stay away from industries or companies that make them nervous even if the brokerage house analysts don't share those fears.

How are brokers paid?

Unless they charge an asset-management fee—in which they take a slice of the assets they manage each year—brokers get paid on commission.

That said, it's not always easy to figure out just how much commission a broker is getting or how they are paid for each type of product they sell.

With stocks, for example, smaller trades and low trading volume generally results in higher commissions per share. If you buy just a few shares of stock, for instance, you may pay 50 cents per share, whereas the cost can decline to as little as 5 cents per share on a big-volume order placed with a discounter.

On mutual funds, brokers will be paid a "sales load" that can either be taken off the top as a front-end charge, or paid in the form of higher expenses over several years of owning the fund. While front-end loads run as high as 8.5 percent, 3.0 to 5.5 percent is more common. Back-end loads—sold as Class B or Class C shares of a fund—will charge you a high fee if you sell within the first few years of the investment; during that time, they tend to charge higher expenses in order to compensate the broker.

When it comes to bonds, there usually is no explicit commission. The broker buys the bond at one price and sells to you at another; the "spread"—the difference between the two prices—represents the commission. As in stocks, the more bonds you buy, the smaller the spread.

Then there are other products, ranging from limited partnerships to annuities, life insurance, new stock and bond issues, and more. Commissions can get as high as 10 percent in these cases.

The rule of thumb on these types of financial products is that the more complicated and harder to sell they are, the bigger commission the broker will get for convincing you to buy it.

In addition to up-front commissions, brokers sometime get on-going fees from your investments, such as a "12b-1 fee," which is essentially a marketing charge that some mutual funds apply to accounts every year. The fund takes as much as 1 percent of your account balance each year to pay for "marketing and distribution costs," and then pays a portion of the fee to your broker. This charge is in addition to the ongoing management fees charged by the fund itself.

Annuity companies and partnerships often charge similar ongoing fees.

Because these ongoing fees are removed painlessly, as opposed to getting a bill or confirmation statement in the mail that lays out the exact cost, they are easy to forget about. Don't. If you should decide to change brokers, make sure that any and all ongoing fees are transferred to the new broker; if you do not specify the change, the broker (or firm, if the broker has changed firms or left the business) will continue to receive these ongoing payments in perpetuity, without providing you with one shred of the ongoing service you are actually paying for.

Last, if your broker is functioning as a money manager—namely developing and executing an investment strategy on your behalf—they may charge something called a "wrap fee," which combines management and brokerage fees. These fees can run as high as 3 percent of the assets under management, which is pretty steep. Something closer to 1.5 or 2 percent is about average for a stock wrap account; 1.0 to 1.5 percent is the norm with mutual fund wraps. A wrap fee lets you know in advance what you will pay a money manager, but it will only be worthwhile if you have a significant amount of money—at least $25,000—to commit to the program, and the manager trades actively; if you and the manager employ a buy-and-hold strategy, run the numbers to make sure that you aren't just better off with straight commission.

What credentials are important?

Brokers sometimes pursue the same credentials as a financial planner. Like a planner, however, no credentials are necessary. A broker, however, must pass exams in order to practice, the basic tests being known as "Series 6" and "Series 7" exams.

Those will not necessarily be much help, since the typical licensing review course takes only two or three days. Moreover the exams are more concerned with a broker's technical proficiency—understanding of investment issues, legal and regulatory requirements—than with developing a real-world understanding of the various forms of risk or what makes for a suitable investment.

Research from the National Endowment for Financial Education showed that rookie brokers have been trained without a significant emphasis on "understanding a client's overall financial picture and assimilating the role of individual investments within that picture."

Until recently brokers did not have to even undergo continuing education to retain their license, although it is now required at certain anniversaries of licensing.

That means that you want a broker who either has some form of advanced credentials or who has been in the business long enough to develop an understanding of what it takes to help a client (instead of one who knows only how to sell the product).

To make themselves look like they have better credentials, a broker may inform you that they are a registered representative, a Registered Investment Adviser (RIA), or both.

The former is a fancy way of saying that someone has passed the exams needed to sell the products they represent (Series 2 or 6 for variable annuities or mutual funds, Series 7 for general securities).

The RIA, meanwhile, was aptly described by Worth magazine, as "Not really a credential, it simply means an individual or a firm has submitted certain filings to the [Securities and Exchange Commission] and paid a modest fee."

Brokers may work to earn their Certified Financial Planner, Certified Fund Specialist, Chartered Mutual Fund Consultant, or other designations that are described in the preceding chapter among the credentials common to financial planners.

But if an investment adviser focuses predominately on investment analysis, they may pursue a Chartered Financial Analyst (CFA) designation, one of the most prestigious of all financial services credentials, awarded by the Association for Investment Management and Research (AIMR).

Earning the CFA mark requires several years of work experience, as well as passing a study course and exams in securities analysis, portfolio management, financial accounting, economics, and ethics.

The designation is common among institutional money managers and Wall Street analysts; it is held in high regard in those circles, so if you find a local stock-picker with a CFA, they may merit strong consideration in your selection process.

What should I ask during an interview?

With brokers, you have an initial interview and, if you should do business, regular subsequent mini-interviews each time you are discussing a particular investment. The first interview should define the relationship and establish your comfort level with the broker; the other is part of ongoing maintenance and is designed not only to keep the broker honest but to keep you informed and aware of what is happening with your account.

When you first meet a broker, start with these questions:

What is your educational and professional background?
A broker's background will provide you with clues about their competence.

If they have been jumping around from one firm to the next, there could be trouble ahead. Many firms don't fire brokers, but simply encourage them to leave before they get the axe; when that happens, a poor performer simply packs up and moves to the next firm.

Good brokers sometimes jump ship, too, especially if they have been lured by bonuses and improved commission schedules.

If you find someone who appears knowledgeable and experienced but who has moved several times in recent years, be prepared to call the broker's previous employer for a reference. Ask the manager of the old office whether they would hire the broker again and whether there were any discipline problems; some office managers will feel constrained by confidentiality rules not to tell you, but most will warn you away if there were real problems. (After all, if they warn you away from the adviser, they may also be able to capture your business.)

What continuing education classes have you taken? What certifications, if any, do you have?

Classes aren't a necessity, but they do show a commitment to staying on top of available products and laws. This is particularly important if you plan to have a broker advise you on more than just plain-vanilla, pick-a-stock/fund/bond issues.

What is your CRD number?

This is one of the few deal-breaker questions in all of financial services, so don't waste your time and save it for the end of an interview.

CRD stands for Central Registration Depository, and it is the centralized clearinghouse used by regulators for filing complaints against brokers. When a broker passes the exams and gets a license to sell securities, they get a CRD number.

When there are complaints filed against them—even if they are cleared of wrongdoing—they go into a file listed by that number.

In performing a background check, having the CRD number—or the broker's Social Security number as a backup—guarantees that your state securities administrator will open the correct file. This is particularly important if the broker has a common name, as asking the state regulators or the National Association of Securities Dealers to find "Michael Johnson in Massachusetts" could lead to them pulling the wrong file.

It's not that you can't do a background check without the CRD number, but having it makes the work easier and faster. It also sends a message to the broker that you intend to do your homework.

Brokers may not know their own CRD number. Chances are they have never been asked and may not have it handy. That's an honest excuse, but it can be overcome. The broker's social security number also is on the CRD file and ensures that you get the right adviser when you tap into the CRD for a background check.

If a broker will not give you either his or her CRD number or social security number, end the interview immediately. No kidding, just walk away.

Think of it like a walking into a room and finding your children with something in their hands; as soon as they see you, they put their hands behind their back. Presumably they are hiding something.

When a broker knows you intend to do your checks and refuses to help you check their background, they must have some idea of what you are going to find in their CRD file. Don't take chances.

Who is your typical client?

As with all forms of financial adviser, you want a broker whose aver-age client looks like you and has concerns akin to yours. Typically brokers look for good investments and then try to match those selections with good candidates from within their clientele.

If the bulk of a broker's clientele is singles and young couples, chances are that she will spend the bulk of her time looking for more aggressive stocks and, possibly, high-grade zero-coupon bonds to fund education. If you are nearing retirement age, that broker is not likely to bring you a bevy of suitable options because you are out of the mainstream; they are looking largely for investments suited to someone else.

In getting the answer to this question, don't focus solely on age, income, and size of portfolio issues. Look instead at what the typical client wants to buy. This will give you an idea of whether the broker has a particular specialty. Remember that just because a broker is adept at picking stocks does not make them ideal for picking corporate bonds; make sure they will be able to meet your needs or be prepared to split your business between a few different specialists.

How do you get paid?

Always ask about the money, especially because it can lead to dis-cussions of your payment options. If the broker can act as a financial consultant and get paid a percentage of the assets you give them to manage, you may be better off than paying straight commission.

Can I get a copy of the firm's commission schedule? Is it negotiable?

Discount brokers will give you their fee schedule in a flash, because it is a major selling point that they have lower prices than a full-service shop.

Full-service brokers may not be so willing, hemming and hawing about how the schedule is not really fixed and how the commission can vary on each trade.

If at all possible, get the commission schedule, even if it means going to the office manager. With the schedule in hand, don't be afraid to negotiate for a discount; it may be a blanket price cut—brokers have discretion to lower the fees they charge—or you may negotiate price breaks on a case-by-case basis. Find out what, if any-thing, a broker is willing to do for you.

What service will I get for the commissions I pay?

If all you get from a broker is processing the trades—with no measure of portfolio management, investment research and suitability analysis—you might as well go with a deep-discount broker.

Keep in mind that "full-service" means different things to different people. To some people, it's an occasional phone call, to others it means twice-daily faxes. "Discount" varies in meaning too. Find out what these terms mean to your prospective broker and make sure their definition meshes with your own; if not, you either have to let the adviser know that you are raising the bar and want more attention than the average client, or you will have to find a broker who is willing to meet your needs.

Will I pay account management fees?

It would be a simple world if brokerage houses earned all of their money on commissions.

They don't.

Some will nickel-and-dime you at every turn, for everything from failing to maintain a certain balance to not generating a proscribed amount in commissions every year. Others offer "cash management accounts," which may charge you high fees for the convenience of check-writing and credit card privileges.

You may even pay a fee for opening and closing your account.

Fees like this add up—especially at the discount firms—so make sure you know about all potential ancillary charges before you sign up.

Are there any contests right now for signing up new clients? Do you get anything special if I decide to do business with you?

You may have gotten a cold call because you were the next name in the phone book or because a friend gave out your name; you broker might also be working to sign up new clients in order to get some sort of prize from the firm.

It's not that signing you up during a contest period is necessarily bad, but make sure that you believe that the broker's interest in you extends beyond the potential prize for bringing you into the fold.

How often will I hear from you, and what will prompt your calls?

This is a good question because it helps set expectations for the relationship and allows you to direct the broker on the right way to work with you. If you don't want a call every week pressuring you to invest, this would be the time to speak up.

At the same time, if the broker promises to call weekly and those calls become more sporadic, you will know immediately that you have a "loss-of-interest" problem.

You want to know why the broker will call because you may not want continual sales pitches. Good brokers call to talk about a lot of things besides immediate sales. They act as emotional disciplinarians to help clients stay the course when the markets turn volatile; they notify clients of changes in tax laws, talk about how their opinions concerning certain market segments are changing and more. If a broker only plans to call when they believe they have something appropriate for you, you will eventually have the problem my father encountered, namely a broker who values your contact only for the commission it can generate.

How many active clients do you work with at one time?

Because their job involves finding investments that fit any number of their clients, brokers can work with a fairly large number of people on an ongoing basis. Once they find the right investment, they may spend the whole day just culling the Rolodex looking for prospective sales.

But if you want guidance, then you want someone who is going to take the time to do more than a sales pitch.

Do the math. You know how often to expect the broker to call because you have asked. If the broker has a huge clientele and calls the average client once a week for five minutes, you will find out quickly that they are spending more than half of their time selling instead of researching investments.

The broker is not just supposed to be a conduit for trading, so make sure the size of their practice allows them to have the time to adequately research and come to conclusions about investments and how they fit in with your needs.

The broker who was upset when my father didn't buy on a particular suggestion, for example, was pushing a product rather than making sure that he had a good fit for his clients.

What criteria do you use before deciding what to buy? What makes something a sell?

It's time to figure out how the broker puts expertise to work. You want to know how they pick the stocks and mutual funds that they recommend to customers, and how do they match different types of funds to the individual needs of an investor.

If a broker can't tell you in plain English what gets them excited about an investment, then all you are getting is a practiced sales pitch rather than the benefit of knowledge accumulated from years in practice.

You also want to know up front why a broker buys or sells securities to make sure those conditions hold up later in the relationship. If you have been working with a broker and he or she suddenly changes stripes and starts recommending buys and sells that are out of character, you will recognize immediately that something is wrong and that the broker appears to be pushing trades—which generate commissions—that go against their own philosophy.

Can I get the names of a few clients to act as references?

You will want to check with references to determine the character of the broker-client relationship and decide if the broker works with people in a way that you expect to be comfortable with.

Can I review the papers you want me to sign when I open an account? Can I review and get a copy of my "new account form?"

Some brokers have clients routinely sign up for margin accounts or options agreements. Some also push discretionary agreements, which give the broker control over the trading activity in the account.

Don't do it.

In addition brokers fill out new account forms whenever they get a new client. These forms include information on your net worth, income, and investment objectives; they get filed away and are never seen—let alone signed—by customers.

Rogue brokers, however, fictionalize these forms, putting incorrect information in so that it looks like you want commission-generating activity. (Some brokers may tell you they have a great investment that they can't sell to you unless the forms say your net worth exceeds $250,000; if you fudge the paperwork to get in on the deal, you might be killing yourself in arbitration if/when things go wrong.)

Help the broker fill out the form, coming up with a definition for your investment objectives, and get a copy of the new account form for your own records. It could come in handy if there is ever a problem with how the broker managed your account.

(Lawyers at arbitration cases put tremendous value on "pre-dispute correspondence," written instructions about goals and objectives. If the broker will not let you participate in the new account form, put your investment circumstances in writing in a letter to both your broker and the office manager. If a dispute ever arises, this letter will go a long way to helping your case.)

Who will hold the securities? Why?

Most brokerage firms prefer to hold securities "in street name," which means that they keep the shares registered in their name but in an account registered to you. This makes it easy to buy and sell and to complete trades (rules provide that transactions must be closed—the money or shares turned over—within three days of after the trading date). They also like this because safekeeping the shares means you will likely use them when the time comes to sell, instead of redeeming shares through a discounter.

The majority of investment customers keep their shares in street name, so there is nothing wrong with that. But make sure your broker explains the process, and tells you how you can get your stocks or bonds if you want them, either to move to another firm or to hold on your own. Many brokerage houses now charge a fee for issuing stock certificates, a charge that is overblown—it does not cost a firm any $15 to handle issuing certificates, since all they do is push around some papers—but which may be unavoidable.

Make sure you understand how and why the broker explains the benefits of keeping your shares before agreeing to it. And if you prefer to hold all shares yourself, explain to the broker that this is how you do business; no broker worth their salt would let this be a deal-breaker.

How frequently will I get statements; will you go over a sample statement with me?

It's not the broker's fault if the firm has statements that are hard to read; it is the broker's fault if they don't prepare you on how to read them.

Get a look at the firm's statements, find out whether you will get them at regular intervals or only after there is activity in your account, and make sure you understand how to read them.

Will anyone else be working with me?

Some brokers have so many clients that they have sales assistants. These people call you on the broker's behalf. Very often the assistants get the clients who are less likely to make a trade. (In my father's case, when he decided to think for himself and not take the broker's tip, the broker threatened him with having to work with an assistant in the future.)

Sales assistants generally have a sales license, but they may not have the expertise and may not be particularly familiar with your situation. That could make it tougher for them to answer your questions.

If you will ever field calls from someone in the firm besides your broker, find out why. Then find out who; arrange to meet that person and, at the very least, get their CRD number.

If a broker promises to work with you but consistently lets you deal with the sales assistant, chances are that you have a transaction-oriented salesperson who is more interested in generating commissions than in developing a good long-term relationship.

Who will control the decision-making in my account?

If you sign a "discretionary agreement," you are giving up control of your investments. For your own financial safety, this is a bad idea.

Make sure that trades will not be made in your account without your approval. As obvious as it seems, make sure the broker acknowledges that this is your wish, and that they promise to contact you and get your authorization before moving your money.

How will we resolve complaints if I am dissatisfied?

The firm will probably have you sign an agreement that says you agree to try arbitration before turning to the courts; you would prefer not to lose your right to pursue action in court, keeping arbitration as a lower-cost, faster-working means to an end.

Before you get to that, however, you want to know what would happen if there is a problem in your account, how the broker would handle it—whether it is a technical glitch or a trade that you don't recall authorizing.

The broker may laugh off the likelihood of this happening. Make them humor you and walk you through the complaint resolution process.

In addition make the broker introduce you to the office manager or the firm's compliance officer, the first people you are likely to be dealing with if there is a problem. Get business cards from these people, and keep their numbers handy.

All of these actions serve notice to the broker that you will not tolerate trouble with the account.

How can I terminate this relationship if I am not satisfied?

Never enter any financial arrangement without knowing how to get out of it.

Have you ever had complaints filed against you by customers? How have those complaints been resolved?

The broker knows you are going to check their record in the Central Registration Depository. This is fess-up time. Complaints that require outside help in order to be settled—even if they clear the broker of wrongdoing—will be in the CRD file.

Essentially you are asking the broker for his or her side of the story about whatever you are likely to find in the CRD (although don't describe it this way because you wouldn't mind hearing about troubles that were resolved before hitting the file).

If the broker tells you they have never had these kinds of problems and the CRD report shows something different, call it off. Learning from past mistakes is important stuff, and if a broker tries to slip one past you when they know you are looking, what will they do when you have an established relationship and your guard is down?

Over time even the best brokers run into a customer who sues over the loss of principal, even though they understood that their stock portfolio might decline in value. What you want to hear is why these problems happened so that you can ask:

How do we make sure that I will not have similar problems?

The broker does not want you to become his or her next problem client. If they have learned from what went wrong the first time, they will explain it to you and say what they would do differently to make sure the problems would not occur again.

You will want this remedy—which may boil down to something as simple as improved communication—to be a part of your relationship with the broker.

Is your firm a member of the Securities Investor Protection Corp. (SIPC)?

SIPC provides limited protection to customers if a brokerage firm becomes insolvent or tries to shut down in the face of its financial responsibilities. SIPC does not insure against losses created by a decline in the market value of your securities.

In addition to SIPC protection, ask whether the firm has other insurance that carries over beyond the SIPC limits. Most good firms do provide this extra insurance; chances are that you will never need it, but it's a comfort if you are the type of investor who worries that your brokerage firm will disappear overnight.

(For further information, you can contact the Securities Investor Protection Corp. at 805 15th Street NW, Suite 800, Washington, DC 20005-2207, or call 202-371-8300.)

If a brokerage firm is not a SIPC member, don't do business with them—no matter what excuses or additional coverage you are presented with. It's simply not worth the risk.

What should I ask before making any individual transactions?

How much commission will you and your firm earn on this trade?

Yes, you asked about commissions and asked for the schedule during the initial interview, but you still need to check it out again with each and every trade.

At most firms a broker can get extra commissions—sometimes as much as 50 cents per share—for selling stock that the firm wants to get out of inventory. The firm may also offer extra money whenever it is a "market-maker" in a stock, meaning that is buys and sells a certain issue out of its own inventory.

Your confirmation slip should tell you whenever the firm is a market-maker, but by then it is too late; you already have paid the commission.

Similarly brokers may get a commission boost when they sell the house mutual funds.

By asking, you get a chance to maybe get some of that commission back, in the form of a discount. In general, brokers have the authority to cut commissions by anywhere from 20 to 60 percent, although your chances of getting that discount probably depend on just how good a customer you are.

Just as important as getting a discount is asking a related question: "Would your recommendation be the same if you weren't getting paid more?" If you question the sincerity of the broker's answer to that one, make them justify the decision by comparing the investment to similar choices on which the commission would be lower.

After all fees are paid, how much does this investment have to gain in value before I break even?

This is another way of getting at the costs involved in the trade, but it helps you see in dramatic fashion just how big a hurdle trading costs can be. If trading costs are a big nut to crack, it will make it harder for an investment to deliver real, after-expenses returns that meet your expectations.

Will this sale help you win any prizes or sales contests?

Yes, you asked something similar during the initial interview, but that was a bit different. Contests to sign up new clients aren't bad because there is no inherent conflict; if you need brokerage services, there is no real conflict between your interest and those of the broker.

But if the broker is being paid to sell you an investment—whether they receive a health club membership, a fancy dinner, or some bigger incentive—that's a problem. If the broker is selling all of his clients the same product to win a product, he does not have the clients' individual needs at heart.

The National Association of Securities Dealers is cracking down on contests and limiting what is allowable. That should wipe out the worst abuses, but you should still find out whether the broker is involved in a sales contest. If the broker's advice doesn't feel to you like it's a great fit and you then find out there is a contest involved, you probably can develop enough of a gut feeling to decide whether or not to do the trade; without the knowledge of the contest, you might shrug off your uneasiness and assume the broker knows better than you do.

How long do you expect me to hold this investment? Why?

Most investors are better off pursuing a buy-and-hold strategy, but commission-based sales encourage trading. Unless a security shoots up in value, short-term profits may be swallowed by the costs of the trade.

Make a written record—which you may want to confirm with the broker—of how long they suggest you will want to hold a security. In that way, if they come back and suggest selling in a few months—unless there is a significant change in the company's status that warrants a move—you can give them a wake-up call that they are going away from their original plan.

If that doesn't work, you may be making a wake-up call to the office manager (where your written record could come in handy).

Can I get out of this investment quickly?

This may seem a strange request given the previous question, but there is a difference.

The broker should tell you, before you invest, whether a product is hard or costly to unload. There may not be many buyers for an individual municipal bond, for example.

Other investments, such as annuities or mutual funds with a back-end load, are easy to get out of but carry steep penalties. Make sure you know about these charges in advance too.

Are there other available share classes or any cheaper ways to pay for this?

Sometimes the broker has payment options, such as Class A, B, or C shares for mutual funds, each of which charges a different load/fee structure. Make sure the broker does the math and shows you how the costs vary over the life of the investment. One share type will be less expensive in the short run, another over ten years, so mesh the answer to this question with the answer on how long the broker expects to hold the security.

You've told me what it costs to buy this stock (or bond or mutual fund); how much would I get if I were to sell it today?

This is not just a commission issue but one of "spread" and market value. Think of it like a new car, where you buy the car at the sticker price but could not sell it back to the dealer at the same price, even if you had not driven it off the lot.

If the spread is too big here, you should get an explanation as to why, and you may decide that the investment is not worth it.

What is the worst-case outcome for this investment?

Not every investment makes money or hits its target. Before purchasing any security, you need to understand the most dire circumstances you could face.

If a broker "guarantees" something, make sure they are offering your money back—and that you know how to get it and have it in writing—and that they are not just using an expression that shows they are confident a security will make money.

Is this in keeping with my investment strategy?

This question applies only in those cases when the broker is providing investment counsel or portfolio management services. A full-service adviser should always be able to explain how an investment choice fits into the overall scheme of your portfolio. If they can't answer this question, chances are that you have not done enough work together for them to know exactly what is a suitable investment for you.

You will want to be aware of a broker whose selections represent a drastic shift in your portfolio, such as the regional bank mutual fund that was an oddball choice for my father's investment portfolio. If the investment raises a red flag, be sure to know what the broker is basing his or her selection on.

What should I never do in working with a broker?

- Never send money based entirely on a telephone sales pitch.

You can work with a deep discounter over the telephone—although many people are not comfortable with the idea—because you will be the one initiating those contacts; the broker will not be trying to sell anything but merely processing trades.

Convincing you to buy over the phone is a different matter altogether. If you can't go to the broker's office and meet them in person—after checking out a license—forget about it.

- Never make a check out to the representative.

The money goes to the firm to be invested in your account. The firm will pay the commission and use the rest in accordance with your instructions. If you make a check payable to the broker, the broker just might cash it and leave you high and dry.

- Never send money to any address but that of the firm or of an operation designated in the prospectus (such as a transfer agent).

Again, this avoids schemes where an unscrupulous broker diverts money from a brokerage account and into their own pocket.

- Never allow transaction confirmations and account statements to be sent to your broker instead of you.

These are your record of what is happening in the account; without them, you don't have the paper trail necessary to build a strong case when things go wrong.

If a broker asks you to do any of these four things, contact the firm's office manager or compliance officer immediately. Chances are you will want to end a relationship in these circumstances because any broker who asks for these things—even if they have not taken any of your money yet—is playing fast-and-loose with the rules.

You would be asking for trouble if you stayed with a broker who asked for these concessions from you.

Where do I start my search?

Brokerage services tend to be a word-of-mouth business. Whether you meet a broker as the result of a cold call or on a tip from a friend, however, the important thing is that you gauge their skill and practice knowledge.

All of the best brokers once started out making cold calls; it's a fact of life in the business. So you need not shy away from cold calls if you happen to be looking for a broker, but you will want to mix that selection with advice from friends.

In addition many brokers hold local seminars, designed to educate consumers and, then, draw them in as clients. Don't be bashful about attending these seminars, which usually are free. Just remember that the fact that someone can fill an auditorium or a fancy restaurant does not make them the right broker for you.

How do I check them out?

Check all brokers out in at least two places, starting with the National Association of Securities Dealers and extending to include your state securities regulator.

Armed with the broker's CRD number, these checks will be easy (the phone numbers for the agencies are included in chapter 24).

In addition check with any agency from which the broker claims to have credentials or professional designations. The numbers for these agencies also are listed in chapter 24.

How can I develop and build the relationship?

There's an old saying that the best way to get good market information is to "take a broker to lunch." It's not far from the truth.

The best way to develop a relationship with a broker is to be able to talk about money and investing when there is no commission on the line and no sale to be made. The more you learn about your broker and his or her attitudes toward money and the markets, the better your working relationship is going to be.

These meetings don't have to be regular, just often enough to get a feel for how the broker operates and to give the broker a better understanding of who you are and how you tick. It takes more than an initial interview and subsequent phone calls to do that.

At the same time a busy broker doesn't have all day to schmooze. When you have questions, spend a few minutes planning your call to the broker so that—if they have other business to do—you can be efficient and get the information you want without tying them up. Not only will they appreciate that approach, but they will be happy to take and return your calls.

What are the danger signs to a bad trade? What are warnings that something is amiss in my dealings with a broker?

It's not important whether a stockbroker wins or loses; it's where they place the blame.

That's not just a clever play on words for a famous maxim, it's a true statement.

When things go wrong, listen carefully to the explanation, as it will speak volumes as to whether the relationship is in trouble.

Beyond pushing upon you the things you should never do with a broker, there are other signs of trouble, such as:

- "Happiness letters." That sounds pretty innocuous, which is the problem. What these really are is "activity letters," where the brokerage firm has spotted a lot of trading in your account. You get a letter from the office manager, sounding like an introduction, recognizing your trading activity and wanting to make sure you are "happy" with the firm and offering you the chance to sit down and discuss more opportunities there.

If the trading continues, you may get another one of these.

This is a hint that perhaps your trading pattern is not normal. The firm is trying to alert you without making you unduly alarmed.

At the same time this letter is designed to give the brokerage firm proof that they warned you of the abnormal activity in your account.

If you get a happiness letter, review your account statements immediately.

The second or third happiness letter may ask for you to sign the document and return it to the firm; the broker may even tell you that they need for you to sign or they could get in trouble.

Don't do it, at least not until you have completed reviewing your records and made sure everything is in order. You may even want to get another opinion.

If you sign a happiness letter and later have problems with the account, your signature will be the first thing trotted out before the arbitration panel. Remember, too, that a broker cannot make you sign these acknowledgements; the worst that can happen is that failing to sign, you may force the firm to refuse further activity in your account, which might not be such a bad thing.

- Paperwork you don't understand.

Just because the broker says you will have control of investment choices doesn't mean that they won't pass a discretionary agreement or a form to allow them to trade in options in front of you. Some ask all clients to sign these agreements as a matter of course, but the authorizations make it much easier for the broker to mismanage your money.

- "It's just a computer error."

If there is an unauthorized trade in your account and the broker tells you not to worry because it's just a computer glitch, you should get very nervous. As time goes by and the error is not corrected, it will become harder and harder to get a problem straightened out.

These days, technology is so good that there are virtually no computer errors in brokerage statements. It is the proverbial needle in a haystack.

If there is a problem in your account and it's a "computer error," see the office manager. They should be able to get it straightened out immediately.

- Inside information, allegedly confidential stuff, an upcoming research report, merger rumors, or "dynamic new products."

Hot trades like this tend to have bigger commissions. They may also be excessively risky, and you may not have a good shot at capturing the kinds of profits that attract you in the first place. Hot new-issue stocks are distributed to brokerages and firms, and chances are that your broker is not among the lucky few. That's just the way it is; a deal that sounds too good to be true probably is.

- Being treated like "quota bait." Generally this means the broker is trying to increase a monthly paycheck or reach sales goals, all about five days ahead of the end of a billing cycle. That would be around the 19th of the month.

If that is the only time you hear from your broker—and all they want to do is talk sales and not strategy—you should question whether they are interested in you as a client or merely as a commission.

- "The deal is done," "It's too late," or "You have no choice" on a trade you did not authorize or understand completely.

Just because the broker says something is a done deal does not make it so. Sometimes there are errors and trade disputes, and the broker knows that anything you do to set things straight is going to cost the broker some money.

If there is a problem and your broker throws this line at you, see the office manager.

▪ The only products being offered are run by the house or are stocks in which the firm is a market-maker.

This is a bad sign for two different reasons. As mentioned previously, the broker tends to make more money in these trades.

But just as important, you want a broker who is a free thinker, who makes his or her own evaluations and does not rely entirely on the firm's research. Brokers know which analysts in the firm are the most on-target, whose judgment they trust the most, and they should be able to sort out the firm's recommendations for what to sell all customers from what is right to sell you.

Remember, you are paying for expertise, and not just for executing a trade or bringing you the brokerage firm's latest tip.

▪ Significant declines in investment value for which you were not prepared.

The new generation of brokers has not lived through any significant, lengthy market declines.

There may be nothing illegal going on here, but the truth is that—short of a market crash that brings everyone down—no broker who respects a client would let them be ambushed by a huge decline in portfolio value. There should be no surprises in your relationship with a broker.

"Many of today's brokers have no idea markets can decline," says Mary Calhoun, a former broker who is now a securities arbitration consultant in Watertown, MA. "They believe it is only a question of how long before something goes up.

"It's a broker's job to explain the possible downside of your investment. It's not that losses are the broker's fault, it's that you should never be shocked by what happens in your account."

What if my broker changes firms?

As discussed previously, there are many legitimate reasons why a broker would switch firms. Make sure that your broker has one of those reasons when they maker a change.

I recently spoke with a couple whose broker was changing firms for the second time in three years, moving from a national firm to a regional one. They feared working with the new firm, but wanted to keep the broker.

Whenever a broker changes companies, do a background check on both the new firm and the broker. A broker's record can be sullied pretty quickly, so be sure to get the details. Just because the broker was clean when you started working with them doesn't mean things have stayed that way.

The couple had never done a background check on their broker. He explained that he had left the big firm for a pay raise and less sales pressure. A check of his background uncovered some other problems, notably a number of complaints concerning the suitability of his choices for older couples. That was enough to convince the couple not to follow the broker, even though the broker's new firm checked out fine.

If you decide to follow the broker, find out if he or she gets a bonus for bringing over new customers. Also find out who pays any transfer fees for the securities, or whether you might incur taxes because you'd be forced to sell investments to follow the broker.

If you choose not to follow the broker, you will have to start the interview and background-check process over again with a new adviser who works for the old firm.

How do I complain or seek restitution if there is a problem?

If the problem is operational—such as failure to deliver checks promptly or to correct an error—start with the broker. If he or she can not immediately rectify the problem, contact the branch manager, and follow up your initial complaint with a letter.

A written record of your complaint is important, so write letters detailing your dispute and how it is not being resolved.

If the manager is not responsive, contact the state securities administrator's office.

The same path applies to misconduct on the part of the broker. Keep all records—provide copies only to the office manager—and be prepared to pursue an arbitration or court case if necessary. Most brokerage agreements state that disputes will be settled in arbitration whenever possible.

At the same time you are making this case in arbitration or court— and it generally takes between eight and twelve months from an arbitration case to go from your filing to a hearing—pursue the matter with state and federal securities regulators. The complaint will eventually hit the CRD and help dissuade others from repeating your mistakes.

Don't let a complaint fester; the statute of limitations on these issues varies, but the general rule is to file the paperwork as soon as you recognize there is a problem that the broker, office manager, and firm are not able to resolve to your satisfaction.

Remember, there's no limit to the promises stockbrokers can make, only to the promises they can keep.

14 *Where to check the background of a broker/financial planner, where to file complaints*

Checking the background of a broker or planner

You will want to make two phone calls to find out whether the person you are dealing with—or their firm—has a history of complaints and client troubles. Over a career, a problem or two is not uncommon, more than that should be a big red flag.

Start with your state securities administrator. You will find the addresses and phone numbers listed below. Most can send you background materials on your adviser—all of which the adviser could also provide you directly—and can tell you about any pending or prior cases or disciplinary actions against both the adviser and the firm. Requests may take a few days to process, and there may be a nominal charge for copies of records.

The state securities administrators—along with those from Mexico and the provinces of Canada—all are part of the North American Securities Administrators Association. If you have trouble getting data from your state securities administrator—offices frequently are overwhelmed with requests for information—you might contact NASAA at Suite 310, One Massachusetts Avenue NW, Washington, DC 20001. Phone 202-737-0900.

When you have finished with the state agency, put in a precautionary call to the National Association of Securities Dealers public disclosure phone center, 1-800-289-9999, which can tell you whether the NASD if the agency has any complaints or cases pending against member broker-dealers. This is a very quick double-check, which may be helpful if a broker previously worked in another state or has operations in more than one area. Stockbrokers generally are NASD members, many financial planners are not.

You can also check with the Securities and Exchange Commission to find out if a company is legitimate or why the agency took action against a broker or firm for wrongdoing (actions that the state securities administrator should have notified you about). The laws concerning which agency has oversight on investment advisers have been changing. Today the SEC retains oversight only on large investment adviser firms, those with more than $25 million in assets under management. State securities administrators oversee the rest of the firms, about two-thirds of the 23,500 firms that were registered with the SEC prior to the rules changes.

SEC officials acknowledge that state officials are likely to have more background information in almost all cases. Still, since both the SEC and the states can bring enforcement actions for violations of antifraud laws, a precautionary phone call is worth the effort.

In addition the SEC should always be notified in the event of a complaint. You will find the address and phone number of the nearest SEC regional office at the end of this chapter.

State and provincial securities administrators

Alabama

Securities Commission
770 Washington Avenue,
Suite 570
Montgomery, 36130-4700
205-242-2984

Alaska

Department of Commerce and
Economic Development
Division of Banking, Securities
and Corporations
333 Willoughby
9th Floor
Juneau, 99811-0807
907-465-2521

Alberta

Securities Commission
300 5th Avenue SW
4th Floor
Calgary, Alberta
T2P 3C4 Canada
403-297-4277

Arizona

Securities Division
1300 West Washington
3rd Floor
Phoenix, 85007
602-542-4242

Arkansas

Securities Department
Heritage West Building
200 East Markham
3rd Floor
Little Rock, 72201
501-324-9260

British Columbia

Securities Commission
1100-865 Hornby
11th Floor
Vancouver, British Columbia
V6Z 2H4 Canada
604-660-4800

California

Department of Corporations
3700 Wilshire Boulevard
Suite 600
Los Angeles, 90010
213-736-2741

Colorado

Division of Securities
1580 Lincoln, Suite 420
Denver, 80203
303-894-2320

Connecticut

Department of Banking
Division of Securities
260 Constitution Plaza
Hartford, 06103
860-240-8230

Delaware

Division of Securities
State Office Building
820 North French Street
8th Floor
Wilmington, 19801
302-577-2515

District of Columbia

Director of Securities
Public Service Commission
450 Fifth Street NW, Suite 821
Washington, 20001
202-626-5105

Florida

Office of Comptroller
Department of Banking and
Finance
Plaza Level, The Capitol
Tallahassee, 32399-0350
904-488-9805

Georgia

Office of the Secretary of State
Division of Business Services and
Regulation
2 Martin Luther King Jr. Drive
Suite 315, West Tower
Atlanta, 30334
404-656-2894

Hawaii

Commissioner of Securities
Department of Commerce and
Consumer Affairs

1010 Richards Street
Honolulu, 96810
808-586-2744

Idaho

Department of Finance
Securities Bureau
700 West State Street
Boise, 83720-2700
208-334-3684

Illinois

Securities Department
520 South Second Street
Suite 200, Lincoln Tower
Springfield, 62701
217-782-2256

Indiana

Office of the Secretary of State
Securities Division
302 West Washington
Room E-111
Indianapolis, 46204
317-232-6681

Iowa

Securities Bureau
Lucas State Office Building
Des Moines, 50319
515-281-4441

Kansas

Office of Securities Commissioner
618 South Kansas Avenue
2nd Floor
Topeka, 66603-3804

Kentucky

Department of Financial
Institutions
Division of Securities
477 Versailles Road
Frankfort, 40601
502-573-3390

Louisiana

Securities Commission
Energy Centre
1100 Poydras Street, Suite 2250
New Orleans, 70163
504-568-5515

Maine

Department of Professional and
Financial Regulation
Securities Division
State House Station 121
Augusta, 04333
207-624-8551

Manitoba

Securities Commission
1128-405 Broadway Avenue
Winnipeg, Manitoba
R3C 3L6 Canada
204-945-2548

Maryland

Office of the Attorney General
Division of Securities
200 St. Paul Place
20th Floor
Baltimore, 21202-2020

Massachusetts

Secretary of the Commonwealth
Securities Division
One Ashburton Place
Room 1701
Boston, 02108
617-727-3548

Mexico

Comision Nacional de Valores
Av. Insurgentes Sur 1971
Torre Sur, Piso 10
Col. Guadalupe Inn CP 01020
Mexico, DF
011(525)661-5483

Michigan

Department of Commerce
Corporation and Securities
Bureau
6546 Mercantile Way
Lansing, 48910
517-334-6212

Minnesota

Department of Commerce
133 East Seventh Street
St. Paul, 55101
612-296-4026

Mississippi

Office of the Secretary of State
Securities Division
202 North Congress Street
Suite 601
Jackson, 39205
601-359-6371

Missouri

Securities Commissioner
Office of the Secretary of State
600 West Main Street
Jefferson City, 65101
573-761-4136

Montana

Office of the State Auditor
Securities Department
126 North Sanders, Room 270
Helena, 59604
406-444-2040

Nebraska

Department of Banking and
Finance
Division of Securities
1200 N Street, Suite 311
Lincoln, 68509-5006
402-471-3445

Nevada

Office of the Secretary of State
Securities Division
555 East Washington Avenue
5th Floor
Las Vegas, 89101
702-486-2440

New Brunswick

Securities Branch
77 Germain Street, Suite 102
St. John, New Brunswick
E2L 4Y9 Canada
506-658-3060

Newfoundland

Director of Securities
Department of Justice
PO Box 8700
St. Johns, Newfoundland
A1B 4J6 Canada
709-729-4189

New Hampshire

Bureau of Securities Regulation
Department of State
State House, Room 204
Concord, 03301-4989

New Jersey

Bureau of Securities
Department of Law and Public
Safety
153 Halsey Street
Newark, 07101
201-504-3600

New Mexico

Regulation and Licensing
Department
Securities Division
725 St. Michaels Drive
Santa Fe, 87501
505-827-7140

New York

Department of Law
Bureau of Investor Protection
and Securities
120 Broadway
23rd Floor

New York, 10271
212-416-8200

North Carolina

Department of the Secretary of
State
Securities Division
300 North Salisbury Street
Suite 100
Raleigh 27603-5909
919-733-3924

North Dakota

Office of the Securities
Commissioner
600 East Boulevard
The Capitol, 5th Floor
Bismarck, 58505
701-328-2910

Northwest Territories

Registrar of Securities
Government of the Northwest
Territories
4903-49th Street
Yellowknife, Northwest
Territories
X1A 2L9 Canada
403-873-7490

Nova Scotia

Securities Commission
1690 Hollis Street
Joseph Howe Building, 2nd Floor
Halifax, Nova Scotia
B3J 3J9 Canada
902-424-7768

Ohio

Office of the Attorney General
Securities Section
PO Box 11549
Columbus, 29211-1549
614-644-7381

Oklahoma

Department of Securities
120 North Robinson, Suite 860
Oklahoma City 73102
405-235-0230

Ontario

Securities Commission
200 Queen Street West
Suite 1800
Toronto, Ontario
M5H 3S8 Canada
416-597-0681

Oregon

Department of Insurance and
Finance
Securities Section
21 Labor and Industries Building
Salem, 97310
503-378-4387

Pennsylvania

Securities Commission
Eastgate Office Building
1010 North Seventh Street
2nd Floor
Harrisburg, 17102-1410
717-787-8061

Prince Edward Island

Department of Justice
Securities Office
105 Rochford Street
Charlottetown, Prince Edward
Island
C1A 7N8 Canada
902-368-4550

Puerto Rico

Office of the Commissioner of
Finance
1492 Ponce de Leon Avenue
Centro Europa Building
Suite 600
San Juan, 00918
809-723-8403

Quebec

Commission des Valeurs,
Mobilieres de Quebec
800 Square Victoria
17th Floor
Montreal, Quebec
H4Z 1G3 Canada
514-873-5326

Rhode Island

Department of Business
Regulation
Securities Division
233 Richmond Street, Suite 232
Providence, 02903-4232
401-277-3048

Saskatchewan

Securities Commission
1914 Hamilton Street, #850
Regina, Saskatchewan
S4P 3V7 Canada
306-787-5645

South Carolina

Office of the Attorney General
Securities Division
PO Box 11549
Columbia, 29211-1549
803-734-1087

South Dakota

Division of Securities
118 West Capitol Avenue
Pierre, 57501-2080
605-773-4823

Tennessee

Department of Commerce and
Insurance
Securities Division
500 James Robertson Parkway
Volunteer Plaza, Suite 680
Nashville, 37243-0485
615-741-2947

Texas

State Securities Board
200 East 10th Street
5th Floor
Austin, 78711-3167
512-305-8300

Utah

Department of Commerce
Securities Division
160 East 300 South
Salt Lake City, 84111
801-530-6600

Vermont

Department of Banking,
Insurance and Securities
89 Main Street, Drawer 20
Montpelier, 05620-3101
802-828-3420

Virginia

State Corporation Commission
Division of Securities and Retail
Franchising
130 East Main Street
9th Floor
Richmond, 23219
804-371-9051

Washington

Department of Financial
Institutions
Securities Division
210 11th Street SW
3rd Floor West
Olympia, 98504
360-902-8760

West Virginia

State Auditor's Office
Securities Division
1900 Kanawha Boulevard East
Room W-118
Charleston, 25305

Wisconsin

Office of the Commissioner of
Securities
101 East Wilson Street
Madison, 53702
608-266-3431

Wyoming

Secretary of State
Securities Division
State Capitol Building
Cheyenne, 82002
307-777-7370

Yukon Territory

Department of Justice
Justice Services Division,
Corporate Affairs
1230 Second Avenue
Whitehorse, Yukon Territories
Y1A 2C6 Canada
403-667-5005

If you need to complain about your adviser

You will want to involve both the state securities administrator and the Securities and Exchange Commission. Start at the state level, not only because you already have those addresses and phone numbers but because they receive a much smaller volume of complaints and may be able to take action more quickly.

As you are making the state contacts, however, you will want to send copies of your complaint to the SEC.

Typically the SEC processes a complaint by reviewing it and deciding if it needs to go to the Division of Enforcement or some other office for review; that can take up to thirty days.

The SEC may then send a copy of your complaint to the broker, planner, or firm involved, asking for a report on what happened; the firm should respond to this request in writing, sending you a response. This often takes up to six weeks.

While firms often settle these disputes, the SEC cannot force a company to resolve your complaint, so this is no substitute for pursuing the company on your own (many firms ask you to agree to resolve disputes through arbitration). You must file that action within a year of discovering any wrongdoing or within three years from the date when the actual problem occurred.

Remember, your complaint becomes an important part of an adviser's record, and will help dissuade future investors from making a mistake in selecting an adviser. For that reason, notify the state and federal securities groups even if you are pursuing action on your own.

To reach the SEC
Office of Investor Education and
Assistance
U.S. Securities and Exchange
Commission
Mail Stop 11-2
450 Fifth Street NW
Washington, DC 20549
202-942-9634
E-mail: help@sec.gov or
enforcement@sec.gov

District offices
Atlanta District Office
Securities and Exchange
Commission
3475 Lenox Road NE, Suite 1000
Atlanta, GA 30326-1232
404-842-7600

Boston District Office
Securities and Exchange
Commission
73 Tremont Street, Suite 600
Boston, MA 02108-3912
617-424-5900

Central Regional Office
Securities and Exchange
Commission
1801 California Street, Suite 4800
Denver, CO 80202-2648
303-844-1000

Fort Worth District Office
Securities and Exchange
Commission
801 Cherry Street, Suite 1900

Fort Worth, TX 76102
817-978-3821

Midwest Regional Office
Securities and Exchange
Commission
Citicorp Center
500 West Madison Street
Suite 1400
Chicago, IL 60661-2511
312-353-7390

Northeast Regional Office
Securities and Exchange
Commission
7 World Trade Center, Suite 1300
New York, NY 10048
212-748-8000

Pacific Regional Office
Securities and Exchange
Commission
5670 Wilshire Boulevard, 11th
Floor
Los Angeles, CA 90036-3648
213-965-3998

Philadelphia District Office
Securities and Exchange
Commission
The Curtis Center, Suite 1005E
601 Walnut Street
Philadelphia, PA 19106-3322
215-597-3100

Salt Lake District Office
Securities and Exchange
Commission

500 Key Bank Tower
50 South Main Street, Suite 500
Box 79
Salt Lake City, UT 84144-0402
801-524-5796

Southeast Regional Office
Securities and Exchange
Commission
1401 Brickell Avenue, Suite 200

Miami, FL 33131
305-536-4700

San Francisco District Office
Securities and Exchange
Commission
44 Montgomery Street
Suite 1100
San Francisco, CA 94140
415-705-2500

To find help pursuing a complaint against a broker or financial planner, consider hiring a lawyer who specializes in such claims. In addition to the references mentioned in chapters 18 and 19 on hiring lawyers, contact the Public Investors Arbitration Bar Association, whose members specialize in representing individual investors in arbitration and other cases.

You can reach PIABA at 3490 Piedmont Road NE, Suite 900, Atlanta, GA 30305. Phone 404-365-0150.

15   *Hiring an insurance agent*

For many people, insurance coverage is the leaky roof of financial products.

When it's raining, it's too late to fix it.

When it's sunny, it works as well as any other roof.

An insurance agent therefore is like a roofer, building shelter for clients by providing coverage that protects against storms that cannot be weathered alone.

But in insurance as in homes, there are a lot of ways to build or fix that roof. It can be plain asphalt shingles or fancy wooden ones, old covers can be ripped off or simply covered up and improved. It can be designed to last a few years or a lifetime.

And the quality of the roofer who builds it will go a long way to determining your happiness with the product.

Enter the insurance agent, roof builder to your financial house.

The basic idea behind insurance is simple: protect those things you cannot afford to replace yourself, and cover yourself for outcomes you cannot otherwise afford to pay for.

That means, for example, that you might want insurance to replace a new car, but you might not carry collision protection on an old clunker. In both cases, however, you would carry liability insurance, so that your bill resulting from an auto accident would be limited to a manageable deductible.

In financial services circles the saying is that insurance is a product that is always sold, never bought, meaning that no one would purchase protection unless they either were required to or received a convincing sales pitch. That's not far from the truth, in large measure because of the subject matter involved in purchasing insurance.

You have to be convinced that something terrible might happen to you, or you have to consider your own mortality, neither of which is particularly pleasant. From a financial standpoint, you have to be willing to part with current disposable income to protect yourself against something that may never happen—or where you or your family will see the benefits many years from now.

The other reason that insurance products are sold is that they often involve complex jargon and, in the case of life insurance, illustrations.

The combination of stomach-turning topics and mind-numbing words is a real turnoff. As one friend of mine put it: "Every time I talk to my insurance agent, I have a headache by the end of the phone call. That's why I don't talk with him as often as I probably should."

But in putting off the selection of an insurance agent, many people fall victim to the very sales process they disdain. They delay the process until the day they get a cold call or bump into an insurance agent at a party, and take it as a sign that the time has come to pay for protection. The agent with the lucky timing becomes the adviser, and has a client who is ready to accept an active sales pitch.

The best way to avoid that problem is to tackle insurance head-on, hiring an agent early and working with them to develop, upgrade, and maintain a program of financial protection that will always keep a roof over your head, and the heads of your family.

To select that agent, you will want to answer the following questions:

Can I do this myself?

There are two ways to look at this question, in terms of insurance and the agent selling it to you.

If you have no insurance, you are doing this yourself, it's called "self-insurance." If something happens tomorrow, however, you will be liable for all costs associated with the problem.

If your home is burglarized and a television is stolen, that might not be so bad, just as you might prefer to pay to repair a fender-bender rather than report the accident to your insurer.

But if you lose all your possessions to a fire or suffer a major disability for which you have no coverage, you will find out quickly just how inadequate your resources are.

If you want insurance, but don't want an agent, you are looking at the low-load insurance market, where an insurer sells directly to the public. This is an emerging business, one that has tremendous potential but not a huge number of participants with a long-term track record. Still it's worth looking around to see if there are no-load options available. At the very least, that information will come in handy for comparison purposes.

What kind of insurance agent do I want?

There are two basic choices for agents, independent agents and exclusive or "captive" agents.

Independent agents represent any number of companies and may change the firms whose lines they carry depending on whether they are satisfied with price and service. In theory, independent agents offer you more choices because they have more companies to work with and those firms are competing for your insurance dollar; in practice, they may only show you the options that bring them the most money.

Captive agents, as the name implies, work with only one insurer. The good news is that they will know the provisions of their policies better than an independent agent because they only work with the one company and, over time, will learn how its policies work inside and out. The independent has too many insurers to deal with to become that well-acquainted with the product.

The rest of the good news is that exclusive agents tend to earn lower commissions than their independent counterparts; the bad news is that those commissions may still be every bit as costly as what you can get from an independent agent, and the coverage you are shown will represent the only choice offered, with no low-cost competition to speak of.

Do I need an agent, or can someone else help me?

The answer to this question depends on your circumstances, the type of insurance you are purchasing and the state in which you live.

As mentioned previously, low-load insurers sell policies direct to the public—although their service may not be available in all states, and they don't offer all kinds of coverage. You may be able to purchase life and auto insurance from low-load companies, for example, but not a disability policy.

Insurance quote services may sound like a direct-purchase choice, but they are not. The telephone quote services, which promise the best available rates on simple policies such as term life, effectively are independent insurance agencies representing many companies. By doing a bulk business, they can cut costs and offer basic policies at a slight discount.

Effectively you are buying coverage through an agent, without the benefit of the service you might expect from hiring someone local. In addition the great prices don't always turn out to be any better than you can get from an agent in town because the quote services may offer bare-bones "teaser" policies designed to get you interested. You may not qualify for the policy—your health isn't good enough or you fall outside of certain age restrictions—or the agent does a needs analysis that shows you need coverage beyond the basics and suddenly you are looking at a higher-priced policy that is no better than what you could have gotten from your local seller.

Insurance brokers, they prefer to be called advisers, may be a better alternative to the quote hotlines. Their job is to analyze a policy on your behalf, but unlike an agent who works both for you and the company, they work only for you.

Life insurance advisers can help you obtain coverage at wholesale rates or through the direct-sellers. For their services an insurance adviser collects a flat fee, usually based on the amount of insurance you will need to purchase. The easiest way to find qualified insurance advisers is to call one of two organizations, the Life Insurance Advisers Association (800-521-4578) or the Fee Insurance Alliance (800-874-5662).

What credentials am I looking for?

Credentials are not necessary. but they are one way good agents distinguish themselves. With insurers setting prices uniformly, you won't be able to play one adviser off against the next—unless the second agent can come in with a different insurer who can deliver the same product for less—so you might as well choose someone with a high degree of professional achievement, where their expertise might help you find ways to make your coverage more efficient.

The other reason to pursue a credential is the codes of conduct that generally go along with membership in these groups. Insurance agents are dual agents, working for both you and the insurer, they are supposed to serve in the best interest of both masters. Professional standards will help them accomplish that difficult goal.

For life insurance agents—and that is where you will want to focus your search, since state insurance commissioners set acceptable premium levels for many other types of coverage—consider the Chartered Financial Consultant (ChFC) and Chartered Life Underwriter (CLU) marks. Both are awarded by the American College in Bryn Mawr, PA, with the CLU generally considered the top credential for life insurance agent and the ChFC a financial-planning addendum.

Agents who achieve one or both of these designations—and a CLU generally takes between three and five years to complete—agree to abide by the college's code of ethics and conduct.

A Chartered Property Casualty Underwriter (CPCU) is someone who has completed property and liability coverage education requirements. Awarded by the American Institute for Chartered Property Casualty Underwriters, a CPCU also agrees to conform to a code of professional ethics.

You may also prefer to work with an agent who is a member of the National Association of Life Underwriters (NALU), a sort of umbrella group for life insurance agents. While membership does not require the kind of training of the other programs, there is a code of conduct and ethics that members must follow.

Beyond insurance credentials, insurance agents may pursue financial planning designations, such as the Certified Financial Planner (CFP) mark. This is helpful, but you need to make sure that the agent understands the role you expect them to play, and that you may already have engaged a financial planner to oversee your general money-management needs.

Other designations, such as "Member of the Million-Dollar Round Table," are essentially nothing more than sales awards. Someone who can sell a lot of insurance is a good salesperson, not necessarily a successful one in terms of the relationships they develop with customers.

If your prospective agent offers you credentials beyond these, find out what it took to earn them. The industry is churning out new designations quickly, and you will want to make sure the letters after an agent's name have meaning before you factor them into your hiring decision.

What kind of insurance do I want?

This applies, again, mostly to life insurance. It is not hard to figure out whether you need auto insurance—although you will want to get coverage that is most efficient—but the choices in life coverage can be confusing.

Because insurance is sold more often than it is purchased—if you call agents out of the blue to buy insurance, some will wonder if you have just flunked an annual physical—it helps to go in armed with some information. Otherwise, you will wind up being pitched products where you lack the basic understanding to make a distinction.

"Universal life, " variable life," and any number of similarly named types of coverage are designed to provide both life insurance and investment growth. The type of policy and the restrictions it carries will determine how the money grows; there will be strict rules for how you can access or borrow against the cash value of the policy.

"Term insurance" is designed to provide coverage over a certain period of time. It does not build any investment value but rather provides coverage for as long as you have a need; when the term ends—provided the policy is not converted into some other form of insurance—there are no premiums and nothing to cash in. Term is ideal for people who have a need for insurance, perhaps to pay off a mortgage or college education but who have no need for insurance once their family is grown and home is paid for.

Term policies carry lower premiums than cash-value policies, the idea being that holders will invest the difference on their own, hopefully providing greater returns than might be available saving through an insurance policy.

There are a great many arguments as to which type of policy is best, and for whom.

In my role as personal finance columnist at *The Boston Globe*, I have come to believe that insurance is best used to do what it is intended for, namely offer protection and not savings.

That said, there are plenty of people who would not save were it not for insurance, or for whom the peace-of-mind factor of having one big chunk of money that they absolutely will never touch is comforting. And I have heard a great many insurance sales pitches that make very convincing arguments.

The idea therefore is to find what is most comfortable for you, realizing that the cash-value policies will cost you more money and bring your agent a bigger commission. In addition remember that there generally is some flexibility in policies, such as term coverage that can be converted to cash-value if your needs (or opinions) change within a few years of signing for the policy.

How do insurance agents charge for their services?

Most agents are paid on commission, which is not surprising given the fact that most policies must be sold. Commissions can be pretty hefty, depending on the type of insurance, as much as 50 percent of some first-year premiums and 3 percent to 5 percent of annual commissions thereafter.

Commissions also depend on the quality of the insurer. A high-quality company does not pay as much in commissions as one that is in tougher financial straits because the good company's high ratings make its products easier to sell.

The commission structure is why the low-load and fee-only adviser options are becoming increasingly popular.

If there is good news on the commission front, it is that the differences between one company and the next are so minimal that good agents will simply bring you the best available policies; they aren't likely to gouge on commissions if it puts their reputation at risk for just a few dollars in extra take-home pay.

And while it is important to know how every financial adviser gets paid, it is less of a concern with insurance agents than with the other types of financial advisers. The reason for that is because you are looking at a product and can make apples-to apples comparison.

If an agent shows you two life policies with, say, $200 per month in annual premiums; both policies offer virtually identical coverage and are sufficient for your needs. If the price is identical, the commission is irrelevant; you are getting what you paid for at a price that is reasonable and nonnegotiable. Provided that your agent has done his or her job in finding the best policies in this kind of scenario, the cost of the overall policy is going to be more of a determining factor than how much of your premiums goes to compensate the salesperson.

Where do I start my search?

Nothing beats word of mouth, particularly if it comes from someone who has had claims experience with an agent. The best minds in the insurance business say the place to start is with friends, relatives, and coworkers to determine who they use as an insurer.

Beyond that you can try the national accreditation organizations for a list of their members in your area. You can find a Chartered Life

Underwriter in your area by calling the American College at 610-526-1000; you can find a CPCU by calling 800-644-2101.

Last, you might check with the independent insurance agent's association in your state, for which you will find addresses and phone numbers in the next chapter.

How do I check them out?

Always check with your state insurance commissioner's office to find out if there have been any complaints, disciplinary problems, or licensing actions taken against an insurance agent. You will find the insurance commissioner's office for your state listed in the next chapter.

In addition, if an agent shows you credentials such as the CLU or CPCU, call the issuing agency—whose phone numbers are included in the answer on where to start your search—to make sure the adviser is up to date, in good standing, and has no disciplinary history.

Finally check with the local Better Business Bureau for a report on the agent, firm, and insurer.

What should an agent ask me during an interview?

Regardless of the financial specialty, the adviser will have plenty of questions for you during an initial interview. But unlike the other specialties, the life insurance agent isn't doing his or her job if you don't hear certain queries.

An agent is not doing their job if they do not ask about your income, assets/net worth, the makeup of your investment portfolio, marital status and children to support, employment status, salary, insurance benefits offered by the company, and how much money your family needs to maintain its standard of living if you die.

An agent who has not gotten this basic information cannot adequately determine your needs.

With that in mind, save yourself time and energy if an agent starts talking about a policy's price or earning potential before they ask you for this information.

Once the agent has gone over your needs, they can show you the variety of ways to meet your needs and help you integrate insurance coverage into your financial plan. Until they have gone over your needs, they are strictly a salesperson.

What should I ask during an interview?

Once the agent is done interviewing you, it is back to your due diligence in selecting an adviser. That will mean asking most of the following:

Do you specialize in any particular area of insurance?

You want to find out if an agency is full-service or limited to specific lines and types of coverage. Some agencies specialize in high-risk drivers and securing coverage for those insured, others can sell boat, homeowners, automobile, life, health, and business insurance.

You may pick individual agents for each specialty, but that gets complicated and cumbersome. Generally you will want to pick one agent and go to a specialist only when the need arises, such as if you have one child who is a high-risk driver and who might not be insurable under the family policy (or whose coverage would cost a fortune).

If an agent is not full-service, you should not automatically disqualify them. Some agencies focus on property and casualty coverage for your home and cars and property, while others concentrate on life coverage. Picking one of each can be a perfect marriage. (In fact a property insurance specialist often makes for a good referral to a life insurance agent; ask them who their life insurance agent is.)

How long have you been involved in the insurance business?

How long with this particular agency?

Experience counts, but it's not everything. If an agent has bounced around from one firm to the next, there may be a reason. While there are many reasons why an agent would switch firms, anyone who has done it repeatedly—every two years or so—may have a problem.

At the very least you will have to question whether the agent will be there to service your long-term needs, or if they will be gone when you need an insurance checkup, leaving you with a policy that is in force but a surrogate agent to advise you on what to do next.

Like many financial services disputes, problem insurance agents can sometimes get off without a scratch to their record by settling cases and resolving complaints before the problem reaches the state insurance commissioner. The firm that employs the agent may not be so lenient, however.

If the agent has a checkerboard employment history, you may want the office manager at their previous firm to be a reference, answering whether or not they would hire your prospective agent back.

How many insurance companies do you represent and can you place my business with?

How long have you worked with each company?

The more insurers an agent represents, the more options they can present you with.

At the same time they may have a few favorites that they know well and prefer to work with. There are a lot of reasons why an insurer might drop an agent, not the least of which is state regulations that make the company decide not to participate in the market any more.

Still, if an agent has a long history in the business but a short time with each of their insurers, it should raise a concern that they have not been the kind of agent that these insurers want to keep. If there have been a lot of changes in their product line, find out why.

Which companies get most of your business and why?

Independent agencies are a great idea, but that doesn't mean they won't play favorites.

That's okay, so long as the insurer is a good one—and not just the one paying the highest commission.

The reason to ask this question in advance, however, has more to do with how you will size up an agent's advice. If they come back with several options but are recommending against their favorite company, you will want to know why. And if they come back picking their favorite, you will want them to convince you why it's a better policy than the others.

How are the companies you deal with rated?

Before buying an insurance policy, you are going to want to know about the financial strength of the company that is writing your policy. There are five major independent firms that rate the financial strength of insurers: A.M. Best, Duff & Phelps, Moody's Investors Service, Standard & Poor's Corp., and Weiss Research.

The ratings firms measure a company based on the depth of its reserves, the spread of its risks, profitability and investment income, the quality of management, and more. After this analysis each firm assigns a letter grade, although the scale varies from one company to the next. (Duff & Phelps and Standard & Poor's both make AAA their highest rating while Weiss Research offers a simple A as its top grade.)

Your agent should be willing to give you at least two ratings reports on any insurer you consider. If he or she can't deliver those reports, question whether they are hiding something.

Unless you have a special need—such as a hard-to-insure driver who has limited choices for securing auto insurance—you will want to deal with insurers whose ratings are excellent or superior. Your adviser should not only show you the ratings but explain to you how the grade system works.

What continuing education classes have you taken? What credentials, if any, do you have?

Insurance, like the other financial services specialties, is evolving; you want someone who is current on the law and on the best procedures to follow to maximize your insurance dollar. With pricing being less of an issue in insurance than most other specialties, expertise is at a premium, so to speak, and you will want to make sure your agent is an expert rather than merely a salesperson.

Can I have your insurance license number?

Ask this one early in the process and you could save some time. It's a deal-breaker.

You must be licensed by the state in order to sell insurance. Getting the license number will speed up your background check with the state insurance commissioner (although not having it won't stop you), and it sends a clear message to the agent that you intend to do a background check.

You can laugh it off as being precautionary, and being a waste of a phone call if that gets the agent to show you a license, but you should make it clear that you won't hire an agent who has not proved to you that they are currently licensed.

Some states give agents a card to show, others a certificate for the wall. It doesn't matter; ask for proof, look at the document, check the names and dates.

Refusal to give you the number—when they know you are going to check—is as good as an admission of trouble to me. Without trouble, there is nothing to hide.

If an agent balks at showing their license or letting you take the number, call the interview off.

How do you charge for your services?

Every financial adviser must be asked to spell out their cost structure. Despite the fact that, as described previously, that insurance is a product or commodity—like a vacuum cleaner—where the sales-person's commission is less important than the overall cost of the good, you still want to make sure there will be no surprises, partic-ularly if you intend to develop a relationship and get on the phone periodically seeking advice.

Insurance agents get paid a lot more for selling new policies than for maintaining older clients, and some try to recover this by adding hourly costs for offering ancillary financial planning services. If the adviser is going to put you on a clock when you call for advice, you want to know about it up front, especially if that kind of charge is in addition to the ongoing commissions from your insurance policies.

How much of my initial premium payment will go to commissions and fees, and how much of that commission do you get?

This is a big issue with life insurance products, where the agent is going to get a big cut out of what you spend up front to buy cover-age. A big chunk of your first premium payment is going to the adviser, no matter what, so be sure the agent has shown you several options and given you the information necessary to pick the best one for you. That won't necessarily be the policy that provides the agent with the biggest payday.

How can I reduce my costs?

In all types of insurance, there are plenty of ways to cut costs, jet-tisoning unnecessary coverages, consolidating policies under one insurer, qualifying for discounts, and more.

Ask for a list of all potential discounts. Insurers offer discounts for everything from people who stop smoking to those who enter a weight-loss program or get good grades.

In addition discuss any situation that is "abnormal."

Say you have a child who is covered by your auto insurance. The child goes to college for several months at a time and has no access to a car. During the time when the student is at school, you can remove them from your policy and save on the premiums.

Likewise, if you stop driving to work for a long stretch of time—such as a maternity or sick leave—if you leave a car in the garage while you travel for a long time, and so on, you may be able to stop coverages temporarily, saving on the cost of protection you don't need.

You should not be paying for any coverage you are not likely to use or need, and a good agent can unbundle standard policies to at least see if you are better off financially with a menu of services customized to your needs.

How does your firm operate?

When is it open? What about after-hours contacts?

How will claims reporting be handled?

These questions are the nuts-and-bolts of your relationship with an insurance adviser. There are plenty of reasons to get these answers long before you have to put the agent to the test.

Say you decide to go buy a car on a Saturday afternoon but don't know whether your current policy offers you sufficient protection for the new car. If you drive off the lot and get in an accident, you could be in for a heap of financial troubles; if your agent isn't available until Monday, you may not have any way of knowing whether you are sufficiently covered to protect the new car.

Likewise you have a car accident on the weekend and need to find out if you can rent a car and bill it to the insurer, or you have a fire in your home and want to know how quickly you can get people working to weatherproof the parts of your home that survived the fire.

And because insurance affects your spouse and family, you want to make sure they will know how to deal with the agent if something unexpected happens to you.

With all of those things in mind, you want to find out how an agent pursues claims—some walk customers through the process, others leave everything to adjusters—and make sure you are comfortable not only with the agent's sales pitch but with the level of service you can expect after the sale.

What is your philosophy on working with insurance companies and consumers in settling disputed claims?

This is one of those areas where an independent agent may have an edge.

If your agent believes the insurer was wrong in denying a claim, they should step in and lobby on your behalf. When an agent represents one company, they may not want to put up too big a fight or they could wind up being out of business. An independent agent, meanwhile, has the threat of moving the business to another company that he or she represents.

Under any circumstances you want to find out not only how an agent will help in the processing of claims but whether they will go to bat for you when a claim goes against you.

Who will have the primary responsibility for handling my account?

If an agency is big enough, the salesperson may only be the person who closes the deal. Subordinates or clerical staff do the actual paperwork and much of the research.

If that's the case, you are going to want to find out who will have responsibility over your account.

After the initial sale, when will I hear from you, and why?

If the agent is transaction-oriented, you will only get calls when there are other products to pitch, most likely at policy renewal time when there is a chance to convince you of the need for an upgrade.

If the adviser wants to pursue a relationship, they should call periodically, notably when they notice that a major life change is in the offing (kids getting ready to leave for college, mortgage debt almost retired, etc.)

Good agents can be good salespeople, but they earn that distinction by taking care of their clients first, and filling their sales ledger second. If you plan to have a long-term relationship with an adviser, make sure they are willing to work with your other financial advisers and that they will meet with you at times when there is no pressing need for service, just to do an insurance checkup and to make sure that you have not outgrown your financial safety net.

How involved are you in the local community?

If you have decided to hire a local agent, a big part of your reasoning will be that they offer better service than someone from outside the area or a person working on a quoteline.

Todd Muller, a vice president with the Independent Insurance Agents of America, notes that

"the more ingrained in the community an agency is, the more they have a very selfish reason to be serving customers to their utmost ability. Preservation of their reputation is exceedingly important because they can not just get up and move one day, because they are tied into the community.

"In the end, every agent has that conflict of working for you and for the company. If there is a conflict, you want someone who is working for you, and if the company is located somewhere across the country, a guy who is tied into your town is going to be thinking 'My customer lives here and I go to church with him or coach his son in Little League and, by golly, I am going to make sure the people in my town are taken care of.'"

Muller has a point. An agent tied into your town faces a lot of bad word-of-mouth if your house burns to the ground, and he or his company are seen to be the proverbial fiddlers orchestrating an unhappy settlement.

Could I get the names of a few recent clients who you have worked with?
At this point in the process, you are ready to get the names of some customers, preferably folks whose cases are similar to yours and who use the adviser for the same sorts of situations.

Have you ever been the subject of any complaints to the insurance commissioner or any lawsuits? If so, for what and how do we make sure that situation does not happen again?
By this time the adviser knows you are going to check them out. That makes it pretty senseless to lie because that would get them tossed from your list of candidates.

Still, if anything comes up, make sure the explanation jibes with what you find out in their disciplinary history, and that it sits well with you and does not give you the shakes. If you believe the action that landed them in trouble is unforgivable, move on.

How will we resolve complaints if I am dissatisfied?
Most times, real problems will wind up in mediation, but find out how the process works and which chain of command your complaint will follow. That way, if problems do arise in the relationship, you can pursue redress immediately.

How can I terminate this relationship? How do I get out from under these insurance contracts?
You may be able to walk away from the agent, but not the insurer. Your contract may specify a certain period of time during which your

policy is in force, and may have financial penalties for leaving early.

If you are satisfied with the coverage but not the insurer, you might call the company and ask for the names of other agents in your area; the insurer will be happy to oblige because it is less likely to lose your business.

As with any financial arrangement, however, it is important that you know ahead of time how you can get out if you are not satisfied with products, service, or performance.

What do I ask references?

The main thing you want from an insurance adviser is service. If all you cared about was price, it would not matter much who you picked.

With that in mind, ask not only the questions appropriate to all reference checks (as laid out in Chapter 11) but also find out what kind of claim experience a client has had, and how involved the agent was in helping them get a satisfactory resolution in their time of need.

What are the danger signs to a relationship gone sour?

Several year ago a few prominent insurance groups got together and drafted what they called the insurance consumer's bill of rights.

Essentially, as a customer, you have rights to protection, to be informed, to choose, to be heard, to redress, and to services.

If your rights are being violated, then you've got problems with your agent.

Let's examine each situation individually.

The right to protection. Obviously, you are paying in order to get adequate protection. If your policies do not meet your needs, or you find out through dealing with other financial advisers that your needs were not properly met, you have not received the guidance you were paying for.

The right to be informed. Insurance is a mysterious business, cloaked as it is in jargon and with so much of it being subjective and hard to assess. If you are not kept abreast of changes in your policy, in state or federal laws that affect you, of the basic assumptions being made in calculating your insurance needs, and of adjustments made to those assumptions over the years, you are operating in the dark. If you are not informed, then you will truly be one of those customers to whom insurance is sold.

The right to choose.   The choice may come down to finding another agent, but you should always have options. If an agent tells you that you have no choice and no options—remember, giving up a policy and paying surrender charges is an option, no matter how unattractive—something is wrong.

The right to be heard.   You should be the leading voice in any decisions that affect you, and you should be treated with the respect accorded the key decision-maker. That means prompt response from your agent and insurance company. If your agent is not listening to your concerns or keeps pushing something at you that is not in accordance with your wishes—or if your agent is not quick to resolve problems—the agent has stopped listening to you.

The right to redress.   If you have legitimate claims, they should be settled quickly. If not, and the agent isn't taking up your cause, get ready to pursue a case with your state insurance commissioner's office.

The right to service.   Chances are that the insurance salesperson knows a lot more about polices and coverage than you do. That doesn't change the fact that you are entitled to prompt, fair attention. An insurance agent should want to be a part of your financial team and should never be afraid that they can't justify your coverages to the other members of your advisory squad; if they can't show your other experts how they have served you well and acted in your best interests, something is amiss.

Beyond those basic rights, the other big sign that may underscore a problem in your relationship with an insurance agent is surprise.

The whole idea of insurance is protection. The catastrophe that forces you to make an insurance claim—whether it is an auto accident, a fire at your home, a death in the family, or whatever—is traumatic enough. If the coverage or service in those times of need does not live up to expectations, or if the protection you thought was sufficient turns out to be faulty, the relationship probably was based more on making a sale than protecting you as a client.

At that point the relationship probably is past sour because the agent will have a tough time regaining your trust.

If I have a complaint, where do I go?

If the agent is a sole practitioner, your first place to turn may be the insurance company to see if they are willing to intervene on your behalf, or to step in and correct a perceived wrong.

With an agent at a large firm, your complaints will start with a supervisor.

In both cases you may have signed an agreement agreeing to mediate any disputes between you and the adviser. Do not wait to start the ball rolling; if the agent's actions were so heinous that they cannot be adequately settled in mediation, you will want to pursue other remedies (lawsuits) before any statutes of limitation expire.

If your problem is severe enough to require a mediator, it also warrants a call to the state insurance commissioner's office, which has the power to frighten most agents into at least reviewing tough cases.

Don't stop there, however. The insurance agent's responsibility is to sell you products that are in your best interest and are suitable for your needs; if they have failed to do this, your remedy is likely to come in court.

How can I develop and build the relationship?

Like a will or an estate plan, insurance coverage must be reviewed periodically, particularly when there are major life changes.

Take the time to do this in person, to have an insurance checkup that brings the adviser up to date on your coverage, your needs, your desires, and how your financial picture has changed over the last few years.

Make sure the adviser knows you welcome their input to your financial team; most will want to work with you in that fashion— and to interact with your other advisers—because it provides a refreshing change from the routine, as well as a chance to make good contacts that can lead to future referrals.

State insurance regulators maintain oversight of insurers' solvency and market practices. They determine whether an insurance company meets the financial standards necessary to sell insurance in your state, and they monitor the activities of both insurers and agents.

Most state insurance commissioner's offices can provide consumer information about prices, products and the financial strength of the companies selling insurance within the state. Most insurance commissioner's offices have some form of consumer telephone service for answering inquiries, distributing information on the complaint history, financial ratings, and prices offered by individual insurance companies. Some also maintain databases of information on complaints about individual agents.

Here is a list of state insurance commissioner's offices:

Alabama

Insurance Commissioner's Office
135 South Union Street
Montgomery, 36130
334-269-3550

Alaska

Department of Commerce and
Economic Development
Division of Insurance
PO Box 110805
333 Willoughby Avenue
9th Floor
Juneau, 99801
907-465-2515

American Samoa

Office of the Governor
Pago Pago, 96799
011-684-633-4116

Arizona

Department of Insurance
2910 North 44th Street,
Suite 210
Phoenix, 85018-7256
602-912-8400

Arkansas

Department of Insurance
1200 West 3rd Street
Little Rock, 72201-1904
501-371-2600

California

Department of Insurance
300 Capitol Mall, Suite 1500
Sacramento, 95814
916-445-5544

Colorado

Division of Insurance
1560 Broadway, Suite 850
Denver, 80202
303-894-7499

Connecticut

Department of Insurance
PO Box 816
Hartford, 06142-0816
860-297-3802

Delaware

Department of Insurance
Rodney Building
841 Silver Lake Boulevard
PO Box 7007
Dover, 19903
302-739-4251

District of Columbia

Insurance Administration
District of Columbia

Government
441 Fourth Street NW
8th Floor North
Washington, 20001
202-727-8000 x3007

Florida

Department of Insurance
State Capitol
Southeastern Plaza, Level 11
Tallahassee, 32399-0300
904-922-3101

Georgia

Department of Insurance
Floyd Memorial Building
704 West Tower
2 Martin L. King, Jr. Drive
Atlanta, 30334
404-656-2056

Guam

Department of Revenue and
Taxation
Government of Guam
Building 13-1, 2nd Floor
Mariner Avenue
Tiyan, Barrigada, 96913
011-671-477-5106

Hawaii

Insurance Division
Department of Commerce and
Consumer Affairs
250 South King Street
5th Floor
Honolulu, 96813
808-586-2790

Idaho

Department of Insurance
700 West State Street
3rd Floor
Boise, 83720
208-334-4250

Illinois

Department of Insurance
320 West Washington Street
4th Floor
Springfield, 62767
217-785-0116

Indiana

Department of Insurance
311 West Washington Street
Suite 300
Indianapolis, 46204-2787
317-232-2385

Iowa

Division of Insurance
Lucas State Office Building
6th Floor
Des Moines, 50319
515-281-5705

Kansas

Department of Insurance
420 SW 9th Street
Topeka, 66612-1678
913-296-7801

Kentucky

Department of Insurance
215 West Main Street
Frankfort, 40602
502-564-6027

Louisiana

Department of Insurance
PO Box 94214
950 North 5th Street
Baton Rouge, 70801-9214
504-342-5423

Maine

Department of Professional and
Financial Regulation
Bureau of Insurance
State Office Building
State House
Station 34
Augusta, 04333

Maryland

Insurance Administration
510 St. Paul Place
Stanbalt Building
7th Floor South
Baltimore, 21202-2272
410-333-2521

Massachusetts

Division of Insurance
470 Atlantic Avenue
6th Floor
Boston, 02210-2223
617-521-7794

Michigan

Insurance Bureau
Department of Commerce
611 West Ottawa Street
2nd Floor North
Lansing, 48933
517-373-9273

Minnesota

Department of Commerce
133 East 7th Street
St. Paul, 55101
612-296-6848

Mississippi

Department of Insurance
1804 Walter Sillers Building
Jackson, 39205
601-359-3569

Missouri

Department of Insurance
6 North
301 West High Street
Jefferson City, 65101
573-751-4126

Montana

Department of Insurance
Mitchell Building, Room 270
126 North Sanders
Helena, 59601
406-444-2040

Nebraska

Department of Insurance
Terminal Building
Suite 400
941 O Street
Lincoln, 68508
402-471-2201

Nevada

Division of Insurance
Suite 152
1665 Hot Springs Road
Carson City, 89710
702-687-4270

New Hampshire

Department of Insurance
169 Manchester Street
Concord, 03301
603-271-2261

New Jersey

Department of Insurance
20 West State Street, CN325
Trenton, 08625
609-292-5363

New Mexico

Department of Insurance
PO Drawer 1269
Santa Fe, 87504-1269
505-827-4601

New York

Department of Insurance
Agency Building One
Empire State Plaza
Albany, 12257
518-474-6600

North Carolina

Department of Insurance
Dobbs Building
Suite 4140
430 North Salisbury Street
Raleigh, 27603
919-733-7349

North Dakota

Department of Insurance
600 East Boulevard
Bismarck, 58505-0321
701-328-2440

Ohio

Department of Insurance
2100 Stella Court
Columbus, 43215
614-644-2658

Oklahoma

Department of Insurance
PO Box 53408
Oklahoma City, 73152-3408
405-521-2686

Oregon

Department of Consumer and
Business Services
Room 200
350 Winter Street NE
Salem, 97310-0700
503-378-4271

Pennsylvania

Insurance Department
13th Floor
1326 Strawberry Square
Harrisburg, 17120
717-783-0442

Puerto Rico

Office of the Commissioner of
Insurance
Cobian's Plaza Building
1607 Ponce de Leon Avenue
Santurce, 00909
787-722-8686

Rhode Island

Insurance Division
233 Richmond Street, Suite 233
Providence, 02903-4233
401-277-2223

South Carolina

Department of Insurance
PO Box 100105
Columbia, 29202
803-737-6160

South Dakota

Division of Insurance
Department of Commerce and
Regulation
500 East Capitol
Pierre, 57501-3940
605-773-3563

Tennessee

Department of Commerce and
Insurance
Volunteer Plaza
500 James Robertson Parkway
Nashville, 37243-0565
615-741-2241

Texas

Department of Insurance
PO Box 149104
Austin, 78714-9104
512-463-6464

Utah

Department of Insurance
3110 State Office Building
Salt Lake City, 84114-1201
801-538-3800

Vermont

Division of Insurance
Department of Banking,
Insurance and Securities
Drawer 20
89 Main Street
Montpelier, 05620-3101
802-828-3301

Virgin Islands

Division of Banking and
Insurance
1131 King Street
St. Croix, 00820
809-773-6449

Virginia

Bureau of Insurance
State Corporation Commission
1300 East Main Street
Richmond, 23219
804-371-9694

Washington

Office of Insurance
Commissioner
Insurance Building—Capitol
Campus
PO Box 40255
Olympia, 98504
360-753-7301

West Virginia

Department of Insurance
1124 Smith Street
Charleston, 25301
304-558-3354

Wisconsin

Office of the Commissioner of
Insurance
121 East Wilson
Madison, 53702
608-266-0102

Wyoming

Department of Insurance
Herschler Building
122 West 25th Street
3rd Floor East
Cheyenne, 82002-0440
307-777-7401

If you are searching for an independent insurance agent—or trying to find out their disciplinary history—you might also check with the state association for independent agents. Most offer referral and disclosure services.

Alabama Independent Insurance
Agents
PO Box 320410
Birmingham, 35232
205-326-4129

Alaska Independent Insurance
Agents & Brokers
PO Box 203088
Anchorage, 99520-3088
907-349-2500

Independent Insurance Agents &
Brokers of Arizona
2828 North 36th Street, Suite C
Phoenix, 85008
602-956-1851

Independent Insurance Agents of
Arkansas
PO Box 24808
Little Rock, 72221
501-221-2444

Insurance Brokers & Agents of
the West (California)
101 Market Street, Suite 702

San Francisco, 94105
415-957-1212

Professional Independent
Insurance Agents of Colorado
801 East 17th Avenue
Denver, 80218
303-837-0627

Independent Insurance Agents of
Connecticut
30 Jordan Lane
Wethersfield, 06109
203-563-1950

Independent Insurance Agents of
Delaware
PO Box 1948
Dover, 19903-1948
302-736-2604

Metropolitan Washington
Association of Independent
Insurance Agents (District of
Columbia)
PO Box 25341
Alexandria, VA 22313
703-706-5446

Florida Association of Insurance
Agents
PO Box 12129
Tallahassee, 32317-2129
904-893-4155

Independent Insurance Agents of
Georgia
PO Box 48386
Atlanta, 30362
404-458-0093

Hawaii Independent Insurance
Agents Association
100 Bishop Street, Pacific Tower,
Suite 1350
Honolulu, 96813
808-531-3125

Independent Insurance Agents of
Idaho
595 South 14th
Boise, 83702
208-342-9326

Professional Independent
Insurance Agents of Illinois
2205 Wabash Avenue, Suite 206
Springfield, 62704
217-793-6660

Independent Insurance Agents of
Indiana
3435 West 96th Street
Indianapolis, 46268
317-824-3780

Independent Insurance Agents of
Iowa
4000 Westown Parkway
West Des Moines, 50265
515-223-6060

Kansas Association of Insurance
Agents
815 SW Topeka Avenue
Topeka, 66612
913-232-0561

Independent Insurance Agents of
Kentucky
1021 Linn Station Road
Louisville, 40223
502-426-0610

Independent Insurance Agents of
Louisiana
One American Place, Suite 2020
Baton Rouge, 70825
504-387-5149

The Independent Insurance
Agents Association (Maine)
432 Western Avenue
Augusta, 04330
207-623-1875

Independent Insurance Agents of
Maryland
2408 Peppermill Drive
Glen Burnie, 21061
410-766-0600

Professional Independent
Insurance Agents of
Massachusetts
137 Pennsylvania Avenue
Framingham, 01701
508-628-5452

Michigan Association of
Insurance Agents
PO Box 80620
Lansing, MI 48908-0620
517-323-9473

Minnesota Independent
Insurance Agents
7300 Metro Boulevard, Suite 605
Edina, 55439
800-864-3846

Independent Insurance Agents of
Mississippi
PO Box 22588
Jackson, 39205
601-354-4595

Missouri Association of Insurance
Agents
PO Box 1785
Jefferson City, 65102
314-893-4301

Independent Insurance Agents of
Montana
PO Box 5593
Helena, 59604
406-442-9555

Independent Insurance Agents of
Nebraska
PO Box 30716
Lincoln, 68503
402-476-2951

Nevada Independent Insurance
Agents
PO Box 645
Carson City, 89702
702-882-1366

Independent Insurance Agents of
New Hampshire
125 Airport Road
Concord, 03301
603-224-3965

Independent Insurance Agents of
New Jersey
PO Box 3230
Trenton, 08619-0230
609-587-4333

Independent Insurance Agents of
New Mexico
PO Box 25447
Albuquerque, 87125
505-843-7231

Independent Insurance Agents of
New York
109 Twin Oaks Drive
Syracuse, 13206
315-432-9111

Independent Insurance Agents of
North Carolina
PO Box 10097
Raleigh, 27605
919-828-4371

Independent Insurance Agents of
North Dakota
418 East Rosser Avenue
Bismarck, 58501-4085
701-258-4000

Independent Insurance Agents of
Ohio
PO Box 758
Columbus, 43216
614-464-3100

Oklahoma Association of
Insurance Agents
PO Box 18428
Oklahoma City, 73154
405-840-4426

Independent Insurance Agents of
Oregon
2701 NW Vaughn, Suite 760
Portland, 97210
503-274-4000

Independent Insurance Agents of
Pennsylvania
2807 North Front Street
Harrisburg, 17110
717-236-4427

Independent Insurance Agents of
Rhode Island
2400 Post Road
Warwick, 02886
401-732-2400

Independent Insurance Agents of
South Carolina
PO Box 210008
Columbia, 29221
803-731-9460

Independent Insurance Agents of
South Dakota
PO Box 327
Pierre, 57501
605-224-6234

Insurers of Tennessee
2500 Hillsboro Road
Nashville, 37212
615-385-1898

Texas Association of Insurance
Agents
PO Box 684488
Austin, 78767
512-476-6281

Independent Insurance Agents
Association of Utah
4885 South 900 East, Suite 302
Salt Lake City, 84117
801-269-1200

Independent Insurance Agents of
Vermont
PO Box 1387
Montpelier, 05601
802-229-5884

Independent Insurance Agents of
Virginia
8600 Maryland Drive
Richmond, 23229
804-747-9300

Independent Insurance Agents of
Washington
PO Box 6459
Bellevue, 98008
206-649-0102

Professional Independent
Insurance Agents of West
Virginia
PO Box 1226
Charleston, 25324
304-342-2440

Independent Insurance Agents of
Wisconsin
725 John Nolen Drive
Madison, 53713
608-256-4429

Independent Insurance Agents of
Wyoming
PO Box 711
Cheyenne, 82003
307-634-4299

17 Hiring an accountant or tax preparer/tax planner

Former U.S. Senator Edward Gurney once noted that the United States is the only country where "it takes more brains to figure your tax than to earn the money to pay it."

To be honest, that's not entirely true. It's only more complicated to pay your taxes if you earn a lot of money.

If you don't earn much or if you have a very simple situation—you are single and have no deductions—then navigating through the tax code is pretty easy (or EZ, in the words of the tax forms you will have to prepare).

Once things get complicated, however, you will need to decide whether you are the best-qualified person to represent yourself to the Internal Revenue Service. In addition there is a real value-of-your-time issue when it comes to preparing a tax return; if you spend five or ten hours gathering your materials, crunching the numbers, and reading the forms so that you file by the book, you might actually be better off turning the paperwork over to a preparer. The loss of more than five hours of your time—depending on how you value it—and the aggravation of trying to sort out what the Internal Revenue Service passes off as English may be more costly than the price of paying someone to help you.

To a lot of people, a tax preparer is merely someone who processes paperwork. That's a bit shortsighted, considering that whoever prepares your tax return will learn your deepest secrets, things not even your family may know about you, such as household income, investment returns, and more. It has to be someone who can draw out that information, be trusted to keep it confidential, and use it to your advantage while staying securely within the boundaries of the law.

And while most people engage a tax preparer for the current year, there is good reason to want someone who will be around to defend both their math and tax logic in the event that the IRS comes calling.

The challenge for an individual looking to hire a tax preparer is finding the right match of competence, expertise, price, and attitude toward dealing with the IRS.

That's not easy because, literally, anyone can be a tax preparer. By law, even you—feeling the need to hire help to do your own taxes—would be allowed to hang out a shingle and sell your services as a tax preparer.

Here are the questions you will want to answer as you search for a tax preparer or accountant who is right for you.

Can I do this myself?

Cowboy philosopher Will Rogers became an American legend in part for his salty comments about the government. Part of his attitude was shaped by his own experience.

Rogers once overpaid his income tax and had one heck of a time getting the money back.

He wrote letters and contacted officials, but never got answers—let alone a check for his overpayment.

When it next came time to file his taxes, Rogers reportedly tried to recapture his lost funds. On the form listing deductions, Rogers listed "Bad debt, U.S. Government—$40,000."

Everyone is entitled to prepare their own tax return, so no one actually needs to hire a preparer or accountant to do the work.

The question you must answer is whether taxation without representation is stupidity.

In every tax situation there are three solutions: the "right" way, the wrong way, and your way.

The right way gets every allowable deduction without stretching the truth or making you vulnerable to penalties or a problem if you get audited. It generally involves not only doing the paperwork necessary to complete a tax return, but occasional phone calls throughout the course of the year to allow for tax planning.

The right way is not necessarily letter-of-the-IRS tax advice because officials in that agency acknowledge that there are many ways to do the tax return. It depends on how aggressive you want to be in taking deductions and pursuing opportunities; go for too much and you get into trouble, pursue too few opportunities and the IRS gladly will accept the extra money you are paying.

Every year, for example, *Money* magazine has a number of tax preparers do the same sample returns, almost all of them coming up with different amounts for taxes due. The trick is to get as close as possible to the one ideal solution; few tax advisers ever hit that target.

The wrong way is slapdash and sloppy, thrown together to beat the deadline or simply to get out from under the pressure of the filing deadline. It may involve stretching the truth or trying to take deductions which you have reason to expect the IRS will disallow. It will cost you interest charges and penalty payments, or will simply result in paying more tax than you needed to pay (and would have paid had you done things the right way).

Then their is your way, which is probably somewhere between the other two. Like the *Money* magazine survey of tax preparers, you too will likely find that in aiming for the perfect tax return you are shooting at a moving target.

The result is that you will either want to prepare a return yourself— or work with an adviser who can do it for you—that comes as close as possible to the ideal return for someone in your particular situation.

It's not easy.

As Albert Einstein once noted, "The hardest thing in the world to understand is the income tax."

If you don't feel comfortable that you can understand it on your own—and Einstein's theory of relativity probably proves that he was capable of understanding complex things—then it's time to at least consider hiring help. The following questions will guide you toward choosing the appropriate tax specialist.

What kind of tax preparer do I want?

Tax preparation advice runs from free-and-simple to costly-and-complex.

Your selection will depend on your needs.

You can start by considering the IRS itself as a counselor, since the agency offers free advice on figuring out the right way to fill out your return forms. Sadly, free does not necessarily mean good, even when the IRS is the source of the data.

The IRS does not stand behind its preparers; if they give you the wrong information—and they do, sometimes—you will be responsible for any problems with your return. In addition the IRS offices and phone lines are swamped during tax season, so getting free help is better left to those people who only want a quick clarification or rules interpretation before finishing the work on their own.

The next level of guidance is the local tax preparation specialist. This can range from someone looking to earn extra money during the tax season to a real expert. The problem is that unless this prospective adviser has credentials, you will have very little to go on in making your decision. Worse yet, the most attractive thing many plain-vanilla preparers have to offer is the promise of a refund, a promise that is often kept by playing fast and loose with IRS rules.

Just because anyone is allowed to act as a tax preparer doesn't mean they are any good at it. If you are dealing with an individual who has no firm and no verifiable credentials—but who talks a good game—make sure that everything about the person and their operation (is it an office or a kitchen table?) strikes you as competent. If not, don't risk it.

The next step up the ladder is the national tax preparation chain, the H&R Blocks of the tax world. These firms have locations across the country and may have multiple offices within your area.

They process so many tax returns that they can do instant estimates on what yours is likely to cost, and they offer refund-anticipation loans, essentially an advance on your refund (for which you will pay an outrageously high rate of interest).

The national chains require their preparers to pass an annual course that covers the bulk of what they will see during the course of tax season. They may also hire advisers with more advanced credentials.

Each year my tax preparer—who is an enrolled agent, a credential we will get to in a moment—fills her calendar and makes a little extra money by working at a storefront return service, a regional equivalent of an H&R Block office. If you happen to walk into that shop in the middle of tax season and she is the next available preparer, you luck out and get a highly qualified, expert tax professional doing your work on the cheap.

Of course, if she is tied up, you might get the person at the next desk who, on any given winter's day, might be a high school dropout who slept through the company's annual tax-preparation class. Even if this person can do a decent tax return for you—and it's not that hard if your return is basic—they may not be able to do the best job for you, given their limited knowledge. And chances are they won't be around the next summer when you have a question on the tax treatment of one of your investments. (And they will be long gone by the time you get an audit notice from the IRS; if the firm promises you representation in an audit, they will offer someone else, not your actual tax preparer.)

And therein lies the problem with the walk-in tax preparation centers. To deal with the crush of people during the tax season, they may hire people who are inexperienced, who view tax preparation as a part-time job rather than a career opportunity.

Worse yet, many firms pay these preparers on the basis of how many returns they complete, which is an incentive to get you finished and out the door as quickly as possible. That is not conducive to sweating the details; since you pay the penalties and are responsible for all taxes due, even if your preparer was incompetent, *you* need to sweat those details and should want a preparer who is as fussy as you are.

If you are looking for more than the basics from a national firm, inquire about their "executive tax services," which typically function more like a traditional accountant's office than a walk-in center. You will need to make appointments, you will most likely be able to develop an ongoing relationship with an adviser who is available all year long, and you will pay about three times the going rate charged to walk-in clients. In other words, if you went to the national firm looking for a bargain but need to hire the executive-level preparers, you can probably kiss the brgain goodbye.

If you decide to kiss off the national firm at the same time, your next stop would be either an Accredited Tax Preparer (ATP) or Accredited Tax Advisor (ATA), credentials that signify that the adviser has completed a tax preparation course offered by the College of Financial Planning and passed an exam offered by the Accreditation Council for Accountancy and Taxation.

You should also consider "enrolled agents," possibly the most under-recognized specialist in any of the advisory fields.

Enrolled agents are former IRS workers, people with extensive dealings with the agency, or folks who have passed a comprehensive exam entitling them to represent clients before Uncle Sam. Most spent at least five years working for the IRS, then passed a two-day exam; in order to retain the designation, an enrolled agent must complete a required number of hours of college-level continuing education each year; many fulfill this requirement by pursuing a master's degree in taxation or accounting.

You can find enrolled agents, like mine, who work independently, but you will also find them working with accounting firms and law practices. Like a certified public accountant, an enrolled agent is trained to be expert in all areas of tax preparation; the difference is that they are not certified—which often translates into lower-cost services.

Enrolled agents don't sound as glamorous as certified public accountants, but they are no less qualified as tax advisers. While anyone can be a paid tax preparer, you can only be represented in an audit by an enrolled agent, certified public accountant, or tax attorney.

Certified public accountants (CPAs) must earn at least a bachelor's degree and pass a strict national exam, in addition to meeting several requirements for continuing education. CPAs may specialize in areas besides tax preparation, so the credential itself does not make someone right for you. (You should be aware that someone may be an "accountant" without being a CPA; in some states a licensed public accountant is considered the equivalent of a CPA, in others no one who has not qualified for the CPA can even say they provide "accounting services." If an adviser mentions accounting but is not saying they are a CPA licensee, ask enough questions to be sure you are getting the expertise you expect.)

CPAs should be a member of their state society of certified public accountants as well as the American Institute of Certified Public Accountants. As such, they are governed by a strict code of ethics, and their firm must undergo regular quality reviews conducted by peers. They also should be licensed to practice in your state.

Tax attorneys generally do not prepare returns themselves. In fact some tax attorneys don't even have anyone on staff who can handle that chore. Instead, the role of a tax attorney is to provide counsel in tricky areas of tax law, notably divorce, estate planning, and business issues. If you get into those arenas, or are embroiled in any sort of dispute that might put you at the mercy of the Tax Court, you may at least want to consult with a tax attorney (preferably with a master's degree in taxation or some other advanced credential) to be certain that you are on sure footing.

Picking between the various levels of expertise depends mostly on your individual situation. The more complex your needs, the higher up the scale you most likely will go to ensure qualified counsel. Be realistic in assessing your needs; you don't want to pay for a Rolls Royce when a Yugo can get you comfortably from here to there.

What can I expect to pay? How do tax preparers charge for their services?

There are no good numbers for what the average tax return costs, which is good reason to shop around before settling on the adviser you intend to work with.

Typically tax preparers charge either by the form or by the hour. Expect less-personalized service if you are being charged by the form because the preparer has an incentive to crank out the paperwork and move onto the next return; while this could also be an incentive to file more forms on your behalf, the only way an adviser can get away with that is if you have a tax situation that requires some sort of extra forms, like for a business-at-home expense.

On the hourly side, most preparers can give you an estimate of how much time your return will take by taking a look at what you filed last year and listening to whatever changes in circumstances you have gone through in the last twelve months.

Some preparers charge a flat fee per return completed. The problem is that flat rates put a premium on getting returns done quickly, not necessarily correctly or with the most favorable tax outcome.

You might save a few bucks now but owe big-time costs later; make sure any adviser who charges a flat rate per return tells you how they handle complex cases—in case yours falls into that gray area—and how much time they spend on the average return. Compare the number of hours they expect to spend per return to the hourly estimate you are given by other advisers and you may find out whether the flat-rate preparer spends too little time on the case (or the hourly adviser too much).

Remember, too, that you will pay less if you deliver your papers in good order, rather than dumping a cigar box worth of receipts on the preparer's desk.

Clearly pay scale is tied to expertise, but all enrolled agents aren't cheaper than all accountants, so shop around. And the national preparation services aren't always such a bargain either; my enrolled agent charges less in her individual practice than if you met her at the storefront practice because she has less overhead.

In addition find out how a tax adviser will bill you for time spent during the year that does not translate directly to what appears on your tax return. If, for example, you want tax advice before selling an investment, or want to make sure that another adviser's take on tax law is correct, you could pick up the phone to call your adviser in, say, June.

Find out up front how you will be billed for that time.

As you schedule interviews with a preparer, ask whether an initial get-to-know-you meeting is free. If you wait until tax time to find a preparer, you could be paying for their time, but the amount might be rebated if you hire them to do the tax return; at other times of the year, most tax advisers should be willing to schedule a how-do-you-do at no charge.

Where do I start my search?

As with all financial advisers, word-of-mouth recommendations carry a lot of weight. Still you should go beyond your circle of friends to make sure that you have gotten a good fit of expertise to needs.

The Accreditation Council for Accountancy and Taxation can give you a list of accredited tax preparers in your area—advisers who have earned the ATP or ATA credentials. Call 1-703-549-ACAT for a directory of preparers located near you.

Likewise the National Association of Enrolled Agents will send a list of qualified members in your area. The group's referral line is available at 1-800-424-4339.

For accountants, the best place to turn is your state CPA organization. Most state associations have referral services; a list of the state groups follows this chapter.

In all cases the referral services should not be perceived as endorsements. Depending on the group, it may simply offer an alphabetized list of practitioners in your area, or the referral service may be a fee-based service charged to members. In addition many practitioners take themselves off referral services when they are not actively seeking a rush of new clients, preferring to build their practice through word-of-mouth.

As one enrolled agent put it, "The people who can serve you when you call on April 1—right before your return is due—may be good preparers who simply have the ability to handle more clients, or they may be the folks who can't get clients any other way."

How do I check them out?

The very same organizations that you would call for a referral are the ones that you will contact to check out a tax preparer. Obviously, if you got the name from the referral service, you can assume the person is a member in good standing.

If you got their name from a friend or an advertisement, however, this is a call you will want to make.

If your adviser works for a firm—whether it is a major firm, a storefront preparation service, or a partnership with a friend—be sure to check on the reputation of both the individual and the company.

Sadly, there is no clearinghouse for you to call to get information on practitioner penalties, but ask after that data anyway. Some state CPA boards will check their database for complaints, disciplinary or licensing action. If you come across a CPA who has a licensing problem in their file, call the interview off, disciplinary actions and complaints are rare, but can be overlooked so long as the circumstances are explained to you and clarified by the adviser.

Last, check with your local Better Business Bureau (phone numbers for bureaus nationwide are included in chapter 24).

What should I ask during an interview?

Elvis Presley once noted that he "had no use for bodyguards. But I have a very special use for two highly trained certified public accountants."

How Presley determined the credentials of those advisers was never made clear in accounts about that quote. The best way for you to determine that your adviser—whether they are a CPA, enrolled agent, local preparer, or the college kid at the corner franchise—is qualified to meet your needs is to ask the following questions during an initial interview.

How long have you been preparing tax returns?
While tax law is always changing, experience counts for something. Think back to the first time you faced any given tax form and you'll understand why you don't want to be any preparer's test drive into a new area of the tax code.

"The first thing you want to know is how familiar the person is with your type of tax situation and whether they have done returns like this before," said Mike Snowdon, academic associate at the College for Financial Planning in Denver. "You don't want to be the guy's first shot at some form, or even the second. If they aren't used to doing a return like yours, find someone who is."

Looking at my return from last year, how do I compare to your average client? Am I more or less complex, or about the same?

You should bring previous tax returns to an initial interview so that the planner gets an idea of what is involved and can accurately forecast a cost.

By asking how you compare to a typical client, you should find out what concerns the adviser might have in preparing your returns. ("Well, most of my clients don't have self-employment income [or fill-in-the-blank unique need]" should raise a red flag.)

Make sure the adviser describes the average client to you, using specifics of age, family situation, average income, and so on. Their idea of what is average may come from the paperwork—a 1040 with Schedules A, B, D, and other standard forms—rather than the people. If you want them to be able to give you advice beyond merely filing returns, if they are going to become an asset to your financial team, you will need to resemble the average client in more than just the forms you fill out.

Another way of getting at this information is to ask for the range of forms the preparer filed the previous year. They may have done a lot of Schedule A and B forms but not a single Schedule SE, which affects people who are self-employed. If their range of forms experience is narrow, make sure your previous returns do not eclipse the adviser's comfort zone.

Are there any areas on which your practice is focused or in which you specialize?

Like most financial counselors, tax advisers can be generalists or specialists. They may focus on a particular clientele—small business owners, for example—or type of situation, such as cases of divorce.

Just because an adviser has a specialty doesn't mean they won't branch off into other arenas depending on a client's needs. If you are facing an adviser with a particular area of expertise, make sure your needs fall in the trunk area of the practice and not out in the tree limbs.

What continuing education classes have you taken? What credentials, if any, do you have?

As discussed previously, tax-preparation credentials require ongoing classes or certification exams. Find out what makes the preparer qualified to be your personal expert; you will find that many people with similar professional designations have different backgrounds, with some opting to do the minimum and others going back to school for master's degrees in taxation.

Regardless of credentials, your preparer must be current on the law, which changes almost daily. The IRS does not care if you—or your preparer—are unaware; ignorance is no defense for overzealous deductions or underpayment of taxes due, so be wary of advisers who haven't been to continuing education programs in more than a year. Remember, it's almost always going to be you who foots the bill if your adviser makes a mistake, even if the blunder was caused by not keeping current on the tax laws.

How many client do you work with?

Most of the year, this will not be a particular issue; you can almost always reach a tax preparer for advice over the summer.

This question looks at the crucial time of the year when your paperwork is due. There are about 600 working hours in a tax season, and a busy firm with an office staff may do 600 or more returns. A small practitioner with little or no office support can handle a few dozen.

Make sure the adviser is not too busy to give you their full attention. If they have a big clientele, ask how that affects your return, whether that changes when you must have paperwork ready, and so on.

Are you open for business all year?

It's not just the storefronts or the local preparers out to make an extra buck who may be gone when your audit notice arrives. There are some enrolled agents and accredited tax preparers who shut down when it's not tax time.

That said, this is not a dumb question. If you want more information on a return—say to challenge an IRS ruling on your deductions—or if you want tax planning and have ongoing questions, you will want someone who is in the business for the long haul.

What percentage of your clients file for an extension?

Some advisers file extensions for everyone, others make a habit of having all clients polished off by April 15.

An extension does not put off paying the IRS any taxes due, it simply gives you more time in which to file the paperwork.

If you are expecting a refund, it slows the process tremendously.

If an adviser has a lot of clients and files extensions as a matter of course—rather than need—you have a reason to question whether they have adequate time available to serve you.

How do you charge for your services? What do I get for my money?

Every financial adviser must be asked to spell out their cost structure. In addition you want to find out if paying for a tax return simply means getting the paperwork completed or whether you can call throughout the year when you have a tax question, and whether the meter will be running during those phone calls.

Get billing details up front too. For instance, find out when you will be expected to pay—when the return is ready? in advance?—and how detailed the bill will be.

What other costs might I incur?

Like any other sort of financial advice, the level of service included in the return varies. Some tax preparers may charge you for filing a tax return electronically; others may charge you copying costs for the copies you take home.

It's a miserable feeling to get the bill for services and feel like you have been squeezed for every extra penny, so ask ahead of time what you could pay for besides the time spent meeting with you or preparing a return.

In addition ask about research time. If a tax adviser needs to do research to prepare your return, will they bill you for that time. If so, make sure the research is specific to you, and that they are not double-billing, putting the research time needed to check out a fairly common issue on the bills of several clients. If the research was not required specifically by your circumstance—and if it is applicable to others—you shouldn't pay for it any more than you would pick up the tab on some continuing education classes.

How can I reduce my costs?

If you plan to take the shoebox and drop it on your adviser's desk, you are going to pay dearly to have someone go through your receipts and try to piece together your life. In fact many advisers won't agree to do it, particularly if you are hiring them well into tax season.

But even if you think you have done all of the math yourself, you may be coming to them with material that requires more preparation time than you might have expected. Find out from them what you can do to make to process more efficient without reducing the accuracy of the return.

Most advisers will be happy to give you this information because, even though it cuts into their take on your return, it makes the filing process a whole lot easier.

If an adviser has a certain way they like material organized and wants particular details in place before they work on your return, chances are you will cut your bill significantly if you can become the preparer's ideal client.

If you do not have the expertise to handle my return—or to advise me about the tax implications of financial moves that I may someday consider—where do you turn for help? Do you ever allow those other experts to take over a client?

This doesn't apply if your case is straightforward, but it is not uncommon for a tax situation to get sticky in a hurry. Inheritances, investment losses, and changes in career, family, or your health, for example, can take a simple tax return and make it a complicated mess overnight.

Find out where an adviser turns when situations get murky.

Will anyone else be working on my return?

You're the one paying the bill, so you should know what you are getting for your money.

If an accountant uses junior partners or enrolled agents to do tax returns, you will want to know. Not only will you want to be able to check out the subordinate's credentials, but you want to ask about the return-review process and find out whether the big shots double-check all work before asking you to sign it.

It's dumb to pay for a figurehead. Find out what, if anything, the involvement of others does to your projected costs; you should pay less if an accountant merely oversees your return than if they do the math and the work on their own.

What can I do to lower my taxes, both for this year and in the future?

Don't expect detailed advice in an initial interview, but rather try to get a feel for whether the adviser is content to have you stay the course or whether they believe that actively managing your tax situation could save you some dough.

If all they want to do is crunch the numbers, they might not be the right kind of adviser to help you over a lifetime.

What is your approach to deductions?

You are trying to find out just how aggressive a tax preparer intends to be. I once interviewed an enrolled agent, for example, who told me he would not file an office-at-home deduction because "those things wind up as a red flag that makes you more likely to be audited."

That would be great logic if I were worried about facing an audit and losing.

My office is a legitimate, meets-the-IRS-standard deduction, and a big one at that. Not taking it to avoid a potential audit would cost me thousands of dollars over the years; taking the deduction would not cost me in an audit because it's legitimate.

Clearly that tax adviser was too conservative for me.

I agree with the late American jurist, Learned Hand (yes, that was really his name), who said "There is nothing sinister in so arranging one's affairs as to keep taxes as low as possible."

What you are looking for in a tax adviser is someone who is as aggressive or conservative as you are. Are they unafraid of incurring questions from the IRS or do they take a conservative approach that is less risky but possibly more costly?

Ask how the preparer deals with the gray areas of the tax code. If the preparer wants to push the envelope of legality and you don't— and visa versa—you don't have a good match.

Remember, you will pay the extra tax if you are too conservative, or be responsible for the tax and penalties if the IRS quashes exuberant deductions made by your preparer. That's a reminder that there is a right way, a wrong way, and your way to do these things, and you will want to find a preparer who does things your way.

Will you guarantee me a tax refund?

The answer you are listening for is *no*.

Any adviser who says that they can always get you money back from Uncle Sam is prepared to bend the rules—particularly, if they haven't had a chance to dig into your files and see whether you (or previous advisers) have done well on your own.

What are the potential outcomes of my return?

From a basic description of your current circumstances and a perusal of last year's tax return, an adviser should be able to tell you whether you are looking at a refund or taxes due. What you want is a realistic assessment of where you stand now; you do not want the tax equivalent of a "yes man," telling you what you want to hear.

Even if you don't have the expertise to do your own taxes, you have enough knowledge to know the kind of shape you are in. You know whether your earnings have shot up, if you have withheld more of your salary, if you sold investments and realized capital gains, if you gained or lost deductions based on your marital status and circumstances surrounding your children and more.

Presumably the adviser should give you an answer that you expect, even if that's not the answer you would like to hear.

If you get this adviser's answer in a meeting held before tax season—which is always the best time to hire a tax planner—follow it up by asking:

Are you familiar with the laws of the states in which I am subject to tax?

Presumably every adviser knows the rules of the state in which they live.

But if you have financial interests in more than one state, you will want someone familiar with the rules in both places. This is particularly important for people who live in one state and work in another, who receive income from a partnership based in another state, or who have moved and owe taxes to two state governments.

What percentage of the returns you filed last year were audited?
What percentage of returns over the course of your career have been audited?

If it's an abnormally high number, above 1 percent or 2 percent, that warrants some explanation.

Periodically the IRS focuses on certain occupations and industries and niches; specializing in returns on this hit list—you have a clientele composed primarily of doctors and the IRS decides to take a better look at that profession, for example—can dramatically inflate a preparer's audit numbers.

If there are not those kinds of special circumstances, ask why the clients have been audited and what were the outcomes of most audits. Too many audits can be a sign that the IRS and the preparer don't see eye-to-eye in how certain rules are interpreted; the IRS generally wins those arguments.

Who will represent me in an audit?

You already know that only enrolled agents, CPAs, and tax attorneys can actually represent you if the IRS comes calling. That said, even some of those advisers do not handle audits themselves, leaving the work to partners or others with more audit experience. In the case of storefront preparation services, you want to find out who the firm will send with you and how you will contact the firm in the event of an audit (some storefront services set up locations that are open only during tax season; these temporary offices will be gone when the audit notice arrives, so you will want to find out who to call on).

If your adviser plans to be with you during an audit, ask how much experience they have in handling audits. On the one hand, you'd like some experience; on the other, too much is not a good sign.

Be sure also to ask about the cost of being represented in an audit. Just because an adviser can do it doesn't mean they will not charge you for it. Find out the costs involved, just in case; it may help you decide exactly how aggressive you want to be with those deductions.

If I am audited or notified of a problem with my return, who pays penalties and interest on the amount I owe?

There is no getting around the taxes; you are going to pay what the government determines you owe, as well as for any blunders that you are responsible for. That means that if you do not withhold enough money from your paycheck and owe Uncle Sam taxes and penalties on April 15, it's your responsibility. But say your adviser whiffed on a portion of the tax code and a deduction was disallowed; you will owe the taxes on the income that is no longer tax-deductible, but the adviser may agree to pay any penalties and interest due on the amount you owe.

Find out what the adviser will do for you if they miscalculate your return. Most will make good on punishments you incur because of their mistakes.

When will I hear from you, and why?

If all you want is someone who can ease your paperwork burden one time, this year, then this question is not important. The adviser could be out of business in six months—and many are—and it wouldn't matter to you.

If, however, you want to integrate a tax adviser into your financial team and work with someone you trust for many years, you will want an adviser who is interested in dealing with you all year long. Just as important, you will want to know what to expect from the relationship after he paperwork is filed.

There are four basic functions that you should expect from a tax adviser: suggesting tax strategies, preparing returns, minimizing tax exposure, and, if necessary, preparing you to meet tax authorities.

Find out whether an adviser will cover those bases. To do that, they are going to have to contact you periodically. It will not be enough to tell you to collect your paperwork and call you when it's over.

A relationship-oriented adviser will want to handle all of the four major functions plus review your estate planning, and help in managing investment and insurance decisions.

That may mean regular visits, phone calls when you plan to sell investments, end-of-the-year tax-reduction brainstorming, or more. In any event you want to find out how involved the adviser gets in helping clients prepare for the future. Armed with that information, you can decide whether this is the kind of person with whom you want a long-term professional relationship.

Could I get the names of a few recent clients who you have worked with?

At this point in the process, you are ready to get the names of some customers, preferably folks whose cases are similar to your and who use the adviser for the same sorts of situations, whether that is simply putting together a tax return or seeking long-term tax counsel.

Have you ever been subject to any practitioner penalties? If so, for what?

Tax advisers do not have to tell you if they have been subject to practitioner penalties, and there may not be a way for you to track down that information.

Ask anyway.

If a preparer reacts funny, use your intuition.

How will we resolve complaints if I am dissatisfied?

There is no standard procedure for solving problems in the preparation of a tax return. If you are dealing with a sole practitioner, for example, there is no boss to go to.

Still you want to find out what will happen if you are not satisfied with the work done on your behalf (and that means that you are displeased with the quality of the advice, not with the fact that you owe Uncle Sam some money).

A tax adviser may not have a great answer to this question; that tells you that your recourse may have to be some type of malpractice action.

How can I terminate this relationship if I am not satisfied?

Until you get to the level where you are hiring an accountant, there may be no formal agreement to sign. Termination may be as simple as walking away, although you may need to make sure you get all of your paperwork back.

Most accountants ask you to sign a "letter of engagement." Never enter any financial arrangement without knowing how to get out of it.

What do I ask references?

Aside from the questions you would ask any adviser, as described in chapter 11, there are several things you should learn about a tax adviser from a client's perspective. They include:

- Did the adviser seek deductions that might otherwise have been missed?

- Did the adviser suggest ways to lower taxes due?

- What kind of tax planning do you receive in midyear reviews?

- Does the preparer work to keep bills down by listing in advance the data they require?

- Has the adviser, in general, avoided nasty surprises so that even if the news was bad, you were prepared for all possible outcomes?

- If you have ever had to pay any tax penalties because of something the adviser forgot to do, did the adviser correct—and pay for—the mistake at no cost? (Remember, the adviser is likely to pay only for penalties and, possible, interest due; the actual tax liability always is the responsibility of the customer, even if it was the adviser who suggested, say, a deduction that was disallowed.)

What are the danger signs to a relationship gone sour?

Aside from guarantees, the biggest danger sign is some sort of surprise.

You may owe a monster tax bill, for example, but it should not be a surprise. You may have had to liquidate a retirement account and be facing major penalties, but that should not come as a shock; your adviser should have forewarned you about these things and even helped with the math.

Obviously, if a tax planner suggests moves that generate these bills—without warning you of the consequences—you have another problem, namely lack of communication.

A tax adviser should help you develop a strategy and work with you on implementing it; they should help you consider all of your options and the likely tax outcomes. Anything less than that and the relationship is headed for trouble, so don't let your adviser lose you in the tax code; make them explain everything necessary to your level so that you can avoid those surprises.

Failure to meet deadlines is another potential problem with tax advisers. You have asked in the interview about extensions; if you wind up filing one that you were not prepared for—or which should not be necessary because you have a simple return—you might question whether the adviser has taken on more clients than he or she can adequately handle on time.

Recurring annual problems can be another sign of trouble. A tax refund is not a bonus, it's a sign that you withheld too much money. It represents an interest-free loan to Uncle Sam; conversely, having significant tax bills due every April could be either a strategy, or a sign that you are headed for cash-flow problems.

A tax adviser should be able to tell you the correct amount to withhold or pay in estimated taxes so that, in any given year, you are as tax-efficient as possible, neither owing nor expecting a significant amount of money from the government. If an adviser can't get you on that even keel, either they don't have enough information from you, one (or both) of you is pursuing a particular tax strategy or they aren't working hard enough.

If I have a complaint, where do I go?

The answer to this question depends on what kind of adviser you are hiring. If you are working with a national tax preparation service, you will start with the office or regional manager. With an accountant or enrolled agent in a large firm, chances are that you will first pursue a complaint with the managing partner.

If you work with a CPA, your next step will be to approach the state society, to see if it can offer you any relief. At the very least, file a complaint in the hope that the group will make it available to others who call to check out the accountant's record.

If you cannot work out some form of settlement, contact an attorney. Accountants can be guilty of malpractice as much as lawyers, brokers, or doctors.

How can I develop and build the relationship?

The only way to turn a tax preparer into a tax planner is to seek out their counsel at other times of the year and to involve them in your other financial relationships.

It makes sense, for example, for a tax adviser to question whether you are taking advantage of individual retirement accounts. You may not be because of the availability of other savings vehicles. That does not make IRAs a poor option, however; if the adviser asks you a question that you can't answer, you will want them to work with your broker or financial planner to help determine a money management strategy that is both rewarding and tax-efficient.

No one gets tax planning in March or April. You get it the rest of the year, when there is still time to move money around and take advantage of your own personal tax circumstances. If you want to build a relationship with a tax adviser, make a regular appointment to sit down after tax season ends, and make it a point to call them for advice whenever taxes play a role in your other money-management decisions.

The idea, in this case, is to be like Elvis and find the special uses for your tax preparers.

Because anyone who wants to can hang out a sign and operate as a tax preparer, it is not always easy to check a tax preparer's background or expertise.

That being the case, you may decide to pursue an adviser with an advanced credential. Nationally you can check on advisers with the following agencies:

For enrolled agents:

The National Association of Enrolled Agents
200 Orchard Ridge Drive
Suite 302
Gaithersburg, MD 20878-1978
301-212-9608
800-984-4339 for referrals

For accredited tax preparers (ATP) or accredited tax advisors (ATA):

Accreditation Council for Accountancy and Taxation

1010 North Fairfax Street
Alexandria, VA 22314
703-549-6400

For certified public accountants (CPA):

American Institute of Certified Public Accountants
1121 Avenue of the Americas
New York, NY 10036-8775
800-862-4272

In most areas, however, checking with the state society of CPAs will yield more than you can get from the national organization. With that in mind, you are probably better off contacting the agency for your state, listed below:

Alabama Society of CPAs
PO Box 5000
Montgomery, 36103-5000
334-8340-7310

Alaska Society of CPAs
341 West Tudor, Suite 105
Anchorage, 99503
907-562-4334

Arizona Society of CPAs
432 North 44th Street, Suite 300
Phoenix, 85008-7602
602-273-0100

Arkansas Society of CPAs
415 North McKinley, Suite 970
Little Rock, 72205-3022
501-664-8739

California Society of CPAs
275 Shoreline Drive
Redwood City, 94065-1412
415-802-2600

Colorado Society of CPAs
7979 East Tufts Avenue
Suite 500
Denver, 80237-2843
303-773-2877

Connecticut Society of CPAs
179 Allyn Street, Suite 201
Hartford, 06103-1491
203-525-1153

Delaware Society of CPAs
28 The Commons
3520 Silverside Road
Wilmington, 19810
302-478-7442

District of Columbia Institute of CPAs
1023 15th Street NW
8th Floor
Washington, 20005-2602
202-789-1844

Florida Institute of CPAs
PO Box 5437
Tallahassee, 32314-5437
904-224-2727

Georgia Society of CPAs
3340 Peachtree Road NE
Suite 2750
Atlanta, 30326
404-231-8676

Guam Society of CPAs
361 South Marine Drive
Tamuning, 96911
671-646-3884

Hawaii Society of CPAs
PO Box 1754
Honolulu, 96806
808-537-9475

Idaho Society of CPAs
250 Bobwhite Court, Suite 240
Boise, 83706
208-344-6261

Illinois CPA Society
222 South Riverside Plaza
16th Floor
Chicago, 60606
312-993-0407

Indiana CPA Society
PO Box 40069
Indianapolis, 46240-0069
317-726-5000

Iowa Society of CPAs
950 Office Park Road, Suite 300
West Des Moines, 50265-2548
515-223-8161

Kansas Society of CPAs
PO Box 5654
Topeka, 66605-0654

Kentucky Society of CPAs
PO Box 436869
Louisville, 40253-6869
502-266-5272

Society of Louisiana CPAs
2400 Veterans Boulevard
Suite 500
Kenner, 70062
504-464-1040

Maine Society of CPAs
PO Box 7406
Portland, 04112-7406
207-772-9639

Maryland Association of CPAs
PO Box 4417
Luthersville, 21094-4417
410-296-6250

Massachusetts Society of CPAs
105 Chauncey Street
10th Floor
Boston, 02111
617-556-4000

Michigan Society of CPAs
PO Box 9054
Farmington Hills, 48333-9054
810-855-2288

Minnesota Society of CPAs
NW Financial Center, #1230
7900 Xerxes Avenue South
Minneapolis, 55431

Mississippi Society of CPAs
PO Box 16630
Jackson, 39236
601-366-3473

Missouri Society of CPAs
PO Box 419042
St. Louis, 63141-9042
314-997-7966

Montana Sociey of CPAs
PO Box 138
Helena, 59624-0138
406-442-7301

Nebraska Society of CPAs
635 South 14th Street, Suite 330
Lincoln, 68508
402-476-8482

Nevada Society of CPAs
5250 Neil Road, Suite 205
Reno, 89502
702-826-6800

New Hampshire Society of CPAs
3 Executive Park Drive
Bedford, 03110
603-622-1999

New Jersey Society of CPAs
425 Eagle Rock Avenue
Roseland, 07068
201-226-4494

New Mexico CPA Society
1650 University NE, Suite 450
Albuquerque, 87102
505-246-1699

New York State Society of CPAs
530 Fifth Avenue
5th Floor
New York, 10036-5101
212-719-8300

North Carolina Association of CPAs
PO Box 80188
Raleigh, 27623
919-469-1040

North Dakota Society of CPAs
2701 South Columbia Road
Grand Forks, 58201
701-775-7100

Ohio Society of CPAs
PO Box 1810
Dublin, 43017-7810
614-764-2727

Oklahoma Society of CPAs
50 Penn Place
1900 NW Expressway, #910
Oklahoma City, 73118
405-841-3800

Oregon Society of CPAs
PO Box 4555
Beaverton, 97076-4555
503-641-7200

Pennsylvania Institute of CPAs
1608 Walnut Street
3rd Floor
Philadelphia, 19103
215-735-2635

Colegio de Contadores Publicos Autorizados de Puerto Rico
Call Box 71352
San Juan, Puerto Rico 00936-1352
787-754-1950

Rhode Island Society of CPAs
One Franklin Square
Providence, 02903
401-331-5720

South Carolina Association of CPAs
570 Chris Drive
West Columbia, 29169
803-791-4181

South Dakota CPA Society
PO Box 1798
Sioux Falls, 57101-1798
605-334-3848

Tennessee Society of CPAs
Box 187
Brentwood, 37024-0187
615-377-3825

Texas Society of CPAs
1421 West Mockingbird Lane
Suite 100
Dallas, 75247-4957
214-689-6020

Utah Association of CPAs
455 East 400 South, Suite 202
Salt Lake City, 84111
801-359-3533

Vermont Society of CPAs
100 State Street
Montpelier, 05602
802-229-4939

Virgin Islands Society of CPAs
PO Box 3016
Christiansted
St. Croix, 08822-3016
809-773-4305

Virginia Society of CPAs
PO Box 4620
Glen Allen, 23058-4620
804-270-5344

Washington Society of CPAs
902 140th Avenue NE
Bellevue, 98005
206-644-4800

West Virginia Society of CPAs
PO Box 1142
Charleston, 25324
304-342-5461

Wisconsin Institute of CPAs
PO Box 1010
Brookfield, 53008-1010
414-785-0445

Wyoming Society of CPAs
1721 Warren Avenue
Cheyenne, 82001
307-634-7039

19 *Hiring a lawyer*

In investment circles, there is an old saying that goes like this:

Insurance salesmen profit on fear.
Stock brokers profit on greed.
Lawyers profit on everyone.

All jokes aside, there will come a day when you need a lawyer. In fact the likelihood is that over your lifetime you might need several lawyers, so no matter how loathsome you find the profession and how many vicious lawyer jokes you swap with friends, you will at least want to know how to contact and select an attorney who can answer your questions.

Most of financial planning comes down to creating a safety net, finding help for growing, tending, and protecting what you earn. Lawyers are a part of that safety net; just as insurance can protect you from accidents and catastrophes, so can lawyers protect you from trouble and help you retain your rights when something goes wrong.

In today's litigious society, the first thing you must do in any situation with legal ramifications is assess whether you need an attorney's special training. If the problem is complex enough that it could wind up in court, or if novice mistakes could cost you tons of money—as happens all the time with poorly drawn estate plans—it's probably time to consult with a lawyer.

There was a day when lawyers were almost a one-size-fits-all group, where the same guy who wrote your will also went to court with your cousin to defend against those reckless driving charges. It's the country-lawyer image portrayed in old movies and it's about as current as those black-and-white films; today law is highly specialized, and most attorneys concentrate in just a few areas.

That doesn't mean a lawyer won't take up almost any request that comes his or her way, but it puts the onus on you to gauge whether the lawyer has the skill to handle your specific needs. Since switching attorneys in the middle of a case is both complicated and costly, take the time to get comfortable with a lawyer before going forward as a client.

Here are the questions you will want to answer before hiring an attorney:

Can I do this myself?

The oldest axiom in legal circles is that the man who acts as his own lawyer has a fool for a client.

Of course it was lawyers who created that axiom, and they only make money when they have clients to represent.

Truth be told, there are plenty of situations where you may not need or want a lawyer. Almost every local community has some form of small claims court, where you can resolve disputes valued up to a few thousand dollars by representing yourself in informal proceedings (and with minimal court costs).

Likewise some situations can be resolved through arbitration, where an impartial arbitrator—generally former judges, current and former lawyers, and business people—settles your dispute in a binding situation. The ground rules for arbitration, including the maximum allowable monetary damages, are set when you agree to the process. The process is quick and the results are private, unlike a court hearing.

Mediation is similar, except that the neutral mediator only offers suggestions to resolve the dispute. There is no settlement unless you and your opponent come to terms.

Then there is the do-it-yourself segment of the legal business, which includes reference titles and software available at most bookstores. There are any numbers of books and computer programs designed to help individuals write their own wills, handle their own divorce, file for the protection of the bankruptcy court, establish various types of trusts, and write basic business contracts. All of them certainly meet the minimum standards for those legal documents but may not go far enough to cover your individual circumstances. Ironically the best way to make sure that these programs measure up to the current legal standard is to do the work yourself and, then, hire a lawyer to review it; it may drive your costs up—though it will be cheaper than having the documents drawn up by the attorney—but your efforts still will be rewarded with dramatically reduced legal bills.

Most lawyers I have talked to say that the decision to hire an attorney comes down to three factors:

1. How complicated is the situation? Complications can be due to the technicalities of the law, the number of parties involved in the suit (and the fact that some of them live out of state), or the complexities of the case.

Think of it this way: If the situation is complicated enough for the other side to have an attorney, chances are that you should too.

2. How much is at stake? That's not just a monetary question, since anything more serious than a traffic ticket could put your civil liberty at risk. Likewise you probably wouldn't want to go through a foreclosure proceeding without an attorney on your side.

Ask yourself "Is this really so important to me?" If it is, then you probably don't want to risk going to court without counsel.

3. Do I need someone to speak for me? This is a personal decision, but if you are in an emotional situation that could provoke anger or rage, you should consider getting a lawyer to act as your mouthpiece.

On the one hand, acting as your own lawyer allows you to vent your frustrations; on the other hand, such venting might cause more harm than good in the eyes of the court.

What is the lawyer's job?

Once you have decided not to represent yourself, only a lawyer can represent you in legal proceedings. All lawyers must pass a state bar exam and a character review in order to receive a license to practice law.

Because practicing law without a license is a crime in most states, lawyers are the only ones who can be your advocates, although paralegals, bankers, and others may help draw up your papers. (In some states paralegals who work directly under the supervision of lawyers may handle minor matters and even offer direct consultation in a few very limited areas.)

What a lawyer is supposed to bring to the table is knowledge of legal procedures and informed judgment. A good lawyer listens to your problem and searches for the best course of action, whether it be a recommendation on which type of trust to establish or whether a personal-injury case is worth pursuing.

What kind of lawyer do I need?

There are legal specialists for almost every situation imaginable. In alphabetical order, here are the major areas of legal practice and a short list of what each type of lawyer provides:

Business lawyers give advice on general corporate matters, from start-ups to mergers and acquisitions, business taxation, contract, and partnership issues.

Consumer lawyers represent their clients in disputes with stores and consumer products companies.

Criminal lawyers do the obvious, defending or prosecuting people accused of criminal wrongdoing.

Estate-planning lawyers write wills, set up trusts, establish powers of attorney, counsel clients on property management, inheritance, tax, and probate issues. Some will also act as the executor on a client's estate.

Family lawyers—more widely known as *divorce attorneys or domestic-relations lawyers*—handle cases of divorce, separation, annulment, child custody, and support. Many family lawyers (along with some estate-planning attorneys) also are specialists in "elder law," which are the rules and regulations that apply to the rights of the infirmed.

Governmental lawyers are generally considered an extension on business lawyers, helping clients comply with (or dispute) local, state and federal rulings, regulations, and statutes.

Immigration lawyers represent people in immigration and naturalization proceedings, helping them to become citizens or to avoid deportation.

Intellectual property lawyers, also known as "patent attorneys," advise their clients on issues involving copyrights, trademarks, and patents.

Labor lawyers cover a wide range of issues. They can represent employers, unions, or individuals in cases involving workplace safety, compliance with government regulations, and questions of allowable union activity but will also get involved in cases of discrimination (age, race, or sex) in the workplace.

Personal injury lawyers take on the cases of people who have been hurt through the intentional or negligent actions of a person or company. Many also specialize in workers compensation claims for people injured while on the job.

Real estate lawyers help their clients analyze real estate contracts, mortgage paperwork, disputes with brokers or agents and contractors, and process the paperwork involved in a closing. They can also get involved in neighbor disputes and other real estate issues.

Tax lawyers counsel individuals and businesses in federal, state, and local tax matters, interpreting the tax code when sticky situations arise. Most will not fill out your tax return, although some will be affiliated with accountants and others who handle the actual paperwork.

How is my lawyer going to be compensated?

Lord Henry Peter Brougham, a nineteenth-century British statesman and jurist, once noted that a lawyer is "a learned gentleman who rescues your estate from your enemies and keeps it for himself."

Indeed one reason many people fear hiring a lawyer is the cost.

There is a real fear that it's too expensive to hire a lawyer, or that the only way to get good legal representation is to pay a lot of money. Sometimes those fears turn out to be true.

Lawyers are paid in several different ways, sometimes more than one depending on what they are doing for you.

Flat fees or *fee-for-service payments* are common when the procedure is straightforward and generally requires a routine amount of time. Many lawyers quote a flat rate on simple wills, title searches, reviewing a real estate contract, and other common practices.

(Routine procedures are also perfect opportunities to use pre-paid legal plans and legal clinics. The pre-paid plans—which are offered with increasing frequency as a benefit to employees—function as a kind of legal health maintenance organization, where you pay an annual fee and are entitled to a specified amount of service from lawyers who take part in the network. Legal clinics tend to offer low-cost representation, often with less-experienced attorneys than those in private practices; simple procedures such as those that generally are billed at a flat rate generally can be handled cheaply by this kind of law office.)

If your legal needs are not routine and the amount of work involved is not predictable, then chances are you will pay *hourly rates* for your services. This is the most common form of billing and where most individuals worry that their legal bill will escalate, as rates go from $25 to $500 or more per hour, depending on the expertise of the lawyer, the complexity of the case, the size of the firm, and the amount of work that has to be turned down to accept your case.

Most lawyers keep a detailed record of how many hours they work for you, often breaking the time down into as much as tenths of hours. They keep a log of the time they spend on your case—and may charge a higher rate for courtroom time than office or telephone minutes.

This is where it is important for you to understand exactly when and why your lawyer is charging you. If the meter is running every time the lawyer picks up the phone—even if it is just to tell you that there is no progress on your case—that might wear your pocketbook thin.

Remember, too, that the lawyer's out-of-pocket expenses—ranging from court fees to messenger services, faxes, copying, and more—will show up on your bill too, added to the attorney's hourly bill.

If you fear an out-of-control hourly bill, find out if the lawyer will limit the amount you can be charged. Essentially this combines the flat-rate/hourly plans, giving you a maximum flat rate for the service you need, while charging you on an hourly basis if the necessary work can be done for less.

(To cut costs further, ask what you can do to help. Some lawyers will let you pick up and deliver documents or make a few phone calls to help gather information. This could not only save time and routine expenses, but it might make you better informed on the status of your case.)

Some lawyers charge *asset-based* or *percentage fees*, which are simply a sliver of the assets being managed or distributed. For example, a lawyer may earn a percentage of the assets in a will going through probate.

The problem with percentage fees is that they aren't always commensurate with the work involved to earn them. If there are major assets involved but only routine legal work—you are selling a $1 million home in a straightforward transaction, for example—you will be overpaying for the amount of service you get. In those situations press the lawyer to use an hourly or flat rate for the service, or ask for a cut in the percentage fee so that your bill is fair given the amount of work involved.

Lawyers accept *contingent fees* when they believe they have a case they can win, usually for a client who cannot afford to pay the other types of fee. Contingency fees only apply in situations where money is being claimed, notably personal injury and workers' compensation cases; some states forbid criminal and domestic-relations attorneys from accepting cases on a contingency basis.

If you win the case, the lawyer takes home a big cut—between 25 and 50 percent—of the spoils. Generally the lawyer gets one-third of your winnings (many states limit the maximum allowable fee), although a "sliding scale arrangement" in your contract may give the attorney a bigger cut if the case drags on or is appealed, and a lower percentage as the dollar value of the settlement rises.

If you lose the case, there are no winnings to split up and the lawyer gets nothing.

Win or lose, however, you will owe court costs. I recently saw a television ad for a lawyer who promised that clients would "never pay a single cent out-of-pocket" to try their case. Unless the lawyer agrees to pick up filing fees and the alike in the event of a loss, that statement most likely was false.

Those court costs are an important consideration in hiring a lawyer on contingency. To get the most for your money, you will want expenses to be deducted from the monetary award before the lawyer gets his or her cut. Say you win a $15,000 judgment; court costs are $3,000.

If the lawyer gets the first cut, they take one-third of $15,000—which is $5,000. Then you pay the court costs ($3,000) and you are left with $7,000 in take-home money.

If you pay the court costs first, then you reduce your $15,000 award by the $3,000 in expenses. That leaves you with $12,000, of which the lawyer gets one-third, or $4,000. You take home $8,000. Many contingency lawyers prefer to be paid before expenses are taken from the award, but the point often is negotiable. Be sure to negotiate it.

Retainers are monies paid to lawyers on a regular basis to make sure that an attorney will be available when needed. They are paid mostly by individuals and companies who have a regular need for service. (Many lawyers agree to take on work from individuals in exchange for an up-front payment for part or all of their services; they may call this a retainer but it typically amounts to a nonrefundable advance.)

But retainers are merely a method of payment, and not a charge for service; as a result you still must find out every time you need the lawyer's service whether the work is being done on an hourly or flat-rate basis.

If your lawyer asks for a retainer, consider this a down payment; if you have a big need for legal services, you could outspend the retainer and wind up with a bill. Make sure you have an idea how much service—hours of the lawyer's time—you should expect a retainer to cover.

Referral fees are paid if you go to a lawyer who refers your case to someone more expert in dealing with your problem. In exchange for the referral, the first lawyer may ask for a cut of the fee, an arrangement that may be prohibited by law depending on the circumstances of the case.

Both attorneys are entitled to a fee, so long as they both work the case. If the first lawyer steps out of the case completely, they should get no further payment.

If one lawyer refers you to another, ask if there will be a referral fee and, if so, how the arrangement is going to work. In most states the ethical rules governing lawyers say that a referral fee cannot be charged unless the client is aware of the situation and each attorney works on the case and splits the fee proportionately to the work they performed. Equally important, the referral fee cannot make the total bill unreasonably high.

One last thing to remember about fees: in some cases you can recoup attorney's fees and ancillary costs from the other side, but there is no guarantee. If you lose the case, you will be stuck with paying whatever fees and costs you have agreed to, and may even have to pick up the costs for your adversary.

What credentials will I have to deal with, and how important are they?

Law is not an area where you must see specific credentials to feel comfortable with a practitioner. The law degree and license speak volumes about someone having achieved the minimum standards for competency.

That said, there are some legal specialties—and about twenty states—where a lawyer can become a certified specialist, such as a "certified civil trial lawyer" or "certified tax lawyer." Nationally, for example, the American Trial Lawyers Organization has a credential for "certified trial lawyers," but most of the national law specialty groups

are set up more as membership organizations than educational/
credentialing institutions.

These credentials are valuable when you are looking for an attorney
with a particular expertise, since maintaining these designations
requires continuing education and some level of experience in the
field. Still they are hardly a necessity because they are not uniformly
administered. (Traditionally most lawyers were prohibited from calling themselves "specialists," even if they limited their practices;
some states continue to adhere to this outdated custom, which could
put the burden on you to find someone whose practice meets your
needs.)

You are looking for someone who is experienced in the kind of
matters you have; if you are presented with a credential, find out the
educational and experience requirements, and ask to see a code of
ethics, if there is one.

The one time you will want to be picky about credentials is if your
lawyer is going to wear two hats on your financial team. Some attorneys, for example, are also certified public accountants or financial
planners. If you intend to hire an attorney-CPA, for example, you
will want to make sure they have the appropriate accounting designations; if a lawyer doubles as a financial planner, you will want
some sort of advisory designation (because, unlike law, there is no
minimum standard of acumen to becoming a financial planner, and
lawyers who want to expand into that arena can hang out a shingle
regardless of whether they are qualified).

Where do I start my search?

When you need to hire a lawyer, you should start by talking to relatives and trusted friends who have been in a similar situation. Their
reference will go a long way, although it is important to remember
that every case is different.

There are legal referral services in many communities, many of
which will recommend a lawyer to evaluate your situation—often at a
reduced cost. Bar associations also make referrals according to specific
areas of law. Many of the referral organizations have minimum competency or experience requirements.

Even that is no guarantee that you will find the right lawyer,
however. Some of the referral services are essentially advertising for
lawyers, who pay for the right to have their name distributed. In
those situations there is no attention paid to a lawyer's skill.

Lawyers also can advertise now on television, in newspapers, on the radio, and in the phone book. This may help you remember their name, but it does not make them the best lawyer for your case. Moreover be careful of pricing issues; the advertising may talk about specific types of services and fees, but your case may not fall into the simple-and-straightforward category and you may not be able to get the advertised special.

The next chapter lists every state bar association. It will be a good place for you to get a few names. From there, call and arrange a few interviews. Most lawyers will agree to a free initial consultation, although many charge a nominal fee for their time; find this out before you set up the interview.

How do I check them out?

If you got a referral to a lawyer from the bar association or referral service, you should have asked if there was any record of the lawyer's disciplinary history. But since many of those listings are actually supplied and paid for by the lawyer, there may not be any negatives to speak of.

The Martindale-Hubbell Law Directory is a complete listing of domestic and international lawyers by state and specialty. It is available in most public libraries, and provides background information on how long a lawyer has been in practice, where and when they got degrees, and more. Unfortunately, that makes it a surface measure, since you will not find out whether an adviser has had complaints and malpractice suits field against them.

In fact that kind of crucial information is lacking almost everywhere you turn. As this book went to press, only one state—Oregon—made all complaints available to the public from the time allegations were filed. An American Bar Association study showed that another thirty-seven states will reveal grievance filings around the time when the bar's grievance committee has decided to issue charges against the attorney.

That can take awhile, and those charges can end in "admonitions" or "private reprimands," where only the lawyer—and possibly the aggrieved client—know what happened.

Regardless of those shortcomings, call your state or local bar association's grievance committee for any records it can provide pertaining to your prospective attorney.

In addition check with your local Better Business Bureau to see if there are any complaints filed there.

What should I ask during an interview?

Financier J. Pierpont Morgan once described what he wanted from his attorney. "I don't want a lawyer to tell me what I cannot do," Morgan said. "I hire him to tell me how to do what I want to do."

While none of us have Morgan's enormous fortune, we do want to hire his kind of lawyers, ones who will be able to help us achieve our goals.

Unfortunately, that may mean telling us what we cannot do. A good lawyer knows better than to waste time. You do not want a lawyer who is a "yes man," but rather someone who will argue on your behalf and also be ready to fight with you in order to keep you out of trouble. You need someone who knows and pays attention to details, and who does not let the little things slide.

As with every other type of financial adviser, you are shopping for trust, integrity, and ability, all of which will be hard for you to gauge during an initial interview. Obviously the way you make that determination depends on your needs. Someone seeking a divorce attorney is going to need different information than someone looking for defense counsel in a reckless driving case. Nevertheless, here are the questions to ask when sizing up a lawyer?

How long have you been practicing and in what areas of the law do you specialize?

In all financial relationships, you don't want to be a guinea pig. That's particularly true of law, where one misstep could put you on the wrong side of a judgment, whether it messes up your estate planning or, in extreme cases, sends you to jail.

What you want to find out is the scope of the practice, whether your current needs are a good fit either for the individual lawyer or the firm. It's not that a patent attorney can't write up a good will, but that you'd hate to find out what years of practicing intellectual property law have done to his or her skills as an estate-planning attorney.

If a lawyer has several specialities, ask how their workload is divided between those areas of the law. A lawyer might do real estate contracts and estate planning, for example, but their business may be heavily weighted toward the former; if you come in with a complex estate situation, they may not have the depth of experience you want—even though estate planning is supposed to be one of their specialties.

Be sure to find out how long a lawyer has had each specialty. They may have ten years of practice experience as a business lawyer, for example, but might only have branched into intellectual property a year ago. Make sure they pass muster in your area of need.

What continuing education classes have you taken? What certifications, if any, do you have?

Again you are looking to establish a lawyer's competency. The law is constantly changing and evolving; the lawyer who fails to keep up with it eventually will fall behind the times enough to where their clients suffer.

Who is your typical client?

You don't want actual names, so this question does not violate attorney-client privilege. What you want to find out is whether the average client is an individual or a business, and whether the average job resembles what you need done, both in terms of the legal matters being covered and, when applicable, the dollars involved. If tomorrow a book publisher wants to buy your memoirs, for example, and is offering a big six-figure advance, you would not want to hire an attorney whose experience negotiating book contracts was limited to deals worth only a few thousand dollars.

This is particularly important for any type of lawyer with whom you expect to have an ongoing relationship, where important papers—such as wills and estate-planning documents—are re-examined and updated every few years. If you are not a good fit for a lawyer's practice today, you may be even further out-of-sync in the future.

If you do not have the expertise to handle my case on your own, do you work with other lawyers? Under what circumstances would you allow them to take over the case?

You want to determine what makes a lawyer nervous enough to seek help or back away from a case.

Ideally you hire a lawyer who is as aggressive or conservative in their approach to work as you are in your approach to life. If you are the conservative type who likes everything buttoned down before proceeding, you might be concerned about a lawyer who never consults with others before making new maneuvers for clients.

Under what circumstances would you simply refer me to another lawyer?

There are good and bad answers to this question. The good answers involve a lawyer passing you on to a partner—or even an outsider—who is better suited for the job. It could also be that the lawyer is too busy to give your case the attention it deserves and believes you will be better served working with someone else.

The bad answer is that your case is not interesting enough or isn't likely to generate enough money.

If you went to a firm to interview a senior partner and find a fresh-out-of-school rookie handling your case, that could be a problem. Let the lawyer know that you intend to interview any lawyer to whom you are referred before signing up for that person's services.

Under all circumstances find out if the lawyer charges a referral fee.

Will anyone else be working on the case?

You're the one paying the bill, and you want to get what you pay for.

If the lawyer uses paralegals or junior partners to do the work, you will want to find out just how involved your attorney intends to be. It's dumb to pay for a figurehead. You also want to find out what, if anything, the involvement of others does to your projected costs; some firms have additional charges when paralegals and researchers get involved in a case.

How many active cases/clients do you work with at one time?

This is another good indicator of how likely the adviser is to work on your case. If they have a very heavy workload, your run-of-the-mill situation may not get the attention it deserves. Remember, however, that your will may be an everyday document to an attorney, but it is protection for your family, and not something you want the lawyer to squeeze between twenty clients with needs that may be perceived as more pressing.

There is one more major concern when it comes to a lawyer's caseload, namely "double-billing." This occurs when a lawyer goes to court for you and several other clients at the same time. While traveling, the lawyer catches up on other cases or reading—and sends bills for that time to every client whose file is in the briefcase.

You're paying for the lawyer's attention to your case, but it's not full attention.

The American Bar Association has condemned this practice, but it can't punish members for doing this.

If your lawyer's caseload seems heavy, ask whether he or she ever practices double-billing. It's not that the practice makes them a bad lawyer, necessarily, it's that you should get some sort of reduction in hourly rate if you don't have their full attention.

What are the potential outcomes of my case?

Any time there's an adversarial situation, one side loses. If every lawyer in those situations guaranteed a victory, half would be wrong.

Before you engage an attorney—particularly if you are paying on an hourly rate instead of contingency—you want an honest assessment of the strength of your case. This includes knowing whether the lawyer expects to settle the case or go to court—and the plusses and minuses to each of those resolutions—as well as whether a loss can be appealed and under what circumstances the lawyer would recommend it.

If the lawyer expects the case to go to trial, ask about trial experience, for there are plenty of attorneys who almost never set foot in a courtroom.

How can I improve my case?

You're paying someone for their guidance and judgment. If they believe you can make your case stronger, do it.

How do you work with clients?

Make sure a lawyer contacts you in all situations that effect your case, explaining the proceedings in plain English. Try to establish how often and under what circumstances you will hear from the lawyer, so you can decide whether that contact is sufficient for you to be satisfied.

In addition find out what paperwork, if any, the lawyer will give you copies of. A file of these papers can be a good thing if you have to change lawyers midstream.

Just how tough are you?

Many legal issues come down to a test of will and nerves, which side is going to break first or move the furthest from its demands.

You may say that you want an aggressive lawyer, but you may not be able to live with the outcome.

For example, some lawyers are particularly tough in negotiating insurance settlements. If they can't get the desired amount from the insurer, they may walk away from a settlement and risk getting the money in court. That could tie the case up for years—delaying how long it takes for you to get the money and, potentially, increasing your costs.

While you want someone who fights tooth-and-nail on your side, you may not want to pay the price such an aggressive lawyer exacts. Some particularly tough real estate lawyers, for example, will walk away from a house rather than giving up on the concessions they demand from buyers or sellers. Their desire to do the best deal is wonderful, but not if it costs you the dream house you had been looking for over several years.

Hire a lawyer who is as tough as you are, and who will demand nothing less than you would expect from yourself.

How are fees charged? How much are your fees and for what are they paid?

With all of the ways lawyers bill clients, you want to know specifically what is involved. You are always entitled to an itemized bill for the lawyer's services, but you would prefer to know in advance how those fees are calculated.

Some lawyers are always on the clock, meaning that your call to check with a lawyer on your case sets the clock in motion, as does your few minutes of small talk with the attorney. You do not want to be racking up charges while talking to your attorney about his family.

Find out the ground rules for being charged; will a five-minute phone call show up on your bill, or is that a free part of the lawyer's service? If you are charged, what's the rate going to be? Will you pay to have copies of important papers mailed to you?

If you are involved in a case that could have court costs, be sure to get a ballpark figure from the lawyer as to your out-of-pocket costs.

What other costs might I incur?

Just because your lawyer gives you a great hourly rate doesn't mean you are going to get off cheaply.

You might pay $1 per photocopy, $5 to receive a fax, or pay inflated tabs for secretarial work.

Lawyers really aren't supposed to profit on costs, but many do. They build depreciation, secretarial time, and anything they can think of into their charge for using the copier, for instance, so that you don't get off with the two-cents-per-page charge you can get from the corner office supply store.

Again there is nothing illegal about doing this, although the American Bar Association says that lawyers should only charge for "actual costs." That makes it hard to complain about after the fact because you agreed to pay the lawyer's costs.

Most lawyers do not want to sound like they are going to rip you off. They may decide to "waive" some of the higher charges if you press them for details in advance. If you don't ask about these charges up front, don't be shocked if your bill doesn't come back more padded than an adolescent's bra.

How can I reduce my costs?

Most lawyers will tell you that the easiest way to keep costs down is to tell the truth at all times, since anything else can come back to haunt you and make a case even harder.

It's not a bad answer, but it doesn't really apply to the cost-conscious consumer.

If you want to keep costs down, let your lawyer know and find out if you can pick up and deliver papers, photocopy documents, and do some of the more menial chores that can greatly inflate a legal bill.

You may also be able to cut costs by reducing the lawyer's work-load. You may want, for example, to have a lawyer review your real estate contract. If you have bought several homes over the years, however, you may not want to pay to have the attorney handle your closing (particularly if you live in a state where the lender's attorney generally does the work).

Be sure that you pay for necessary services and not for window dressing.

Who are the best lawyers in town—besides yourself—and why?

The legal community is tightly knit, particularly within specialties. You want someone who knows the competition, and gets along with those adversaries, because your case may boil down to cutting a settlement rather than going to court.

Use the list of lawyers who your prospective counsel admires as part of the hiring process too. They become references and should be asked the very same question; you want other lawyers to want to do business with your loved ones.

Could I get the names of a few recent clients who you have worked with?

Attorney-client privilege sometimes makes this a sticky issue, but if there is someone you can talk to who can act as a reference and tell you how this lawyer deals with clients, that would help cement your decision.

If they won't give you the names of clients, ask for professional references, perhaps the names of lawyers to whom they make referrals. When you call those colleagues, do not identify the person who gave you their name at first, saying "I was told you could be a reference for my attorney. I was wondering who you consider to be the best attorneys in town."

If your lawyer's name comes up, then ask why the reference feels that way. If it's not on the list, then ask why not.

How often will I hear from you?

You want to make sure that the lawyer's idea of the appropriate amount of time to spend with you is similar to your own. If you need hand-holding and a call from your attorney every day, then a lawyer who calls only when there is action on the case may not be active enough.

This helps forge your expectations for the relationship. If the adviser subsequently fails to call frequently enough, you will have set a standard that they are measurably under, which helps you decide if the lawyer is living up to their end of the agreement.

How can I terminate this relationship if I am not satisfied?

Never enter any financial arrangement without knowing how to get out of it.

How will we resolve complaints if I am dissatisfied?

Just because you know how to get out of the arrangement doesn't mean there won't be complaints to settle. Just as you want to know how to end the relationship before it starts, so do you want to know how any future disputes will be settled.

Most state bar associations offer arbitration committees that, for a fee, settle disputes that arise between clients and lawyers (usually over expenses). At the same time you could resolve those matters in small claims court.

Fees represent the biggest area of dispute between lawyers and their clients; find out whether the lawyer has had this kind of problem in the past and how it has been resolved. Then determine how it will be resolved if it happens in your case, preferably settling upon fee arbitration as the most fair solution to potential problems.

Have you ever had complaints filed with the bar association against you? Have you ever been sued for malpractice?

These questions may make a lawyer wince because it's an uncomfortable subject. But suits happen.

I know many outstanding lawyers who have had to defend themselves from clients whose expectations were not met and who decided to pursue the lawyer because they did not get the outcome they wanted.

If your lawyer has been sued, ask in general terms what happened and how the case was resolved.

More important, this will solidify your discussions of what to expect from both the current legal situation you are handling and the relationship, as well as how you will resolve any problems that arise before they reach this extreme.

Remember, the lawyer is not obligated to provide details of problem cases. You will have to use your intuition to help you determine whether past problems should send you off to visit someone else.

What happens next?

Once you have engaged a lawyer and taken care of your current needs, how often will you have contact with them? Will they call periodically to see if your will needs updating, for example, or if you need a new health-care proxy? When something else comes up in your life, will you be able to call them with a question—just to get a sense of the direction you want to go—and not be billed for it? Under what circumstances would a future telephone consultation—perhaps a second opinion on an estate-planning issue—become billable advice?

By defining what you want and describing the kind of ongoing relationship you desire with a lawyer, you lay the framework on which a successful relationship with a lawyer is built.

What are the danger signs to a relationship gone sour?

Even Perry Mason once lost a case; in real life, lawyers are likely to lose even more often than that.

You have the right to competent representation. Your lawyer is not always to blame if a case goes against you. If you are dissatisfied with your lawyer—whether they are doing a simple will or defending you in court—it is important to look at the reasons why. If a realistic view leaves you with a general complaint about the quality of your representation, then you may have an honest beef.

You should worry about the relationship with your lawyer if:

They appear to have lost interest or stopped working on a case. Unhappy clients often complain that a lawyer is not devoting sufficient time to the case. In fact the client might not be completely aware of the progress being made or of delays that are beyond the lawyer's control. Generally this boils down to a communications issue.

If the problem is more than miscommunication, write your lawyer a letter. This generally serves as a wake-up call because lawyers know it is a prelude to building a case against them for not doing their work.

In addition every case has a time limit, called a statute of limitations, within which it must be filed. And some paperwork must be filed immediately given the health and welfare concerns of the people involved. If your lawyer is in jeopardy of missing these kinds of deadlines, you need to either apply pressure to get the ball rolling or simply find someone who will take your case on now.

Your instructions are not being followed. With the exception of doing something illegal, such as lying in court, the lawyer's job is to advise a client of possible actions and outcomes and then take the path chosen by the client, regardless if that is the direction the lawyer wants the case to go.

If your lawyer is doing things in accordance with their own feelings, or pushing you very hard to do things their way without explaining the situation so that you come to the same conclusions on your own, question whether they respect you.

The bill is much more than you expected or was not properly explained. You have a right to an itemized bill. You should have discussed what those items would be ahead of time, so there should not be unhappy surprises in the end. If there are, contact the lawyer and ask about the unexpected charges; if the situation cannot be resolved that way, contact the local or state bar association to ask about the fee arbitration process.

There are any apparent conflicts of interest

A lawyer can't sit on both sides of the fence, representing clients on opposite sides of the same or related lawsuits. If the lawyer wants to do this, both clients must give permission; if you find out that your lawyer has breached this ethical standard, you will probably want to seek new counsel immediately.

One other thing to know about conflicts: a lawyer should not represent you if your interests conflict with their own. In other words, a lawyer should not write your will if you plan to leave the lawyer property or money in that will.

Your have not received your complete share of a settlement

If you believe that a lawyer has improperly taken or kept money owed you, it's a big problem. Contact the state and local bar association and get in touch with its disciplinary board if your money is not returned on short order; when you contact the bar association, ask about its funds for "client assistance" or "client security." These are funds put together by lawyers that may reimburse you if a court decides that your lawyer is guilty of fraud.

If I have a complaint, where do I go?

If something appears to be going wrong, talk to your lawyer first. If you are not satisfied after that, you have several options.

▪ If the lawyer is in a firm, go to the managing partner. If you are in a pre-paid legal plan, you would contact the plan administrator.

In either case they should try to resolve the complaint and get you the kind of representation you seek. That does not mean you will come away satisfied.

▪ Your state or local bar association can help you in several ways. The attorney's disciplinary committee can answer any questions you have about whether you complaint is legitimate. The fee arbitration committee can help you determine whether you have a beef over fees, and may be able to help settle any disputes.

If you believe the lawyer has stolen money from you, you will want to pursue restitution from the bar's client security fund. (You will also want to contact the police or your local district attorney.)

- You can sue your lawyer for malpractice. If the lawyer has been negligent and you have been damaged as a result, you can pursue reimbursement.

Of course, suing for malpractice involves another attorney, this one involved in handling professional liability cases.

How can I develop and build the relationship?

If you want to have a lawyer as part of your financial team, you need to plan regular visits as often as you have major life changes—children, buying a house, moving, etc.—and as infrequently as once every other year.

Ask the lawyer how often they want to be consulted with regard to your financial planning and other issues, and try to include them in estate-planning discussions with your financial adviser. (The latter is particularly important because the best estate plans can go awry if assets are not properly titled.)

And, if you like the lawyer you have dealt with, consult with them on other legal matters, if only to get a referral to another specialist who is likely to help you. All of these conversations help to ensure that you will feel comfortable with your attorney, regardless of when you actually need their services.

Here is a state-by-state listing of bar associations, including numbers for the general office and the referral service. If no referral number is listed, use the general number. There may also be a regional or local bar association that can provide you with more detailed information about lawyers in the community in which you live.

Alabama

415 Dexter Street
Montgomery, 36104
334-269-1515
Referrals: 800-392-5660

Alaska

510 L Street, Suite 602
Anchorage, 99501
907-272-7469
Referrals: 907-272-0352

Arizona

363 North First Avenue
Phoenix, 85003
602-252-4804
Referrals: 602-257-4434
        (Phoenix)
        520-623-6159 (Tucson)

Arkansas

400 West Markham
Little Rock, 72201
501-375-4605

California

555 Franklin Street
San Francisco, 94102
415-561-8200
Referrals: 213-622-6700
        (Los Angeles)
        510-893-8683
        (Oakland)
        714-835-8811
        (Orange County)
        916-444-7125
        (Sacramento)
        619-758-4755
        (San Diego)
        415-746-1616
        (San Francisco)

Colorado

1900 Grant Street, Suite 950
Denver, 80203
303-860-1112
Referrals: 719-636-1532
            (Colorado Springs)
            303-831-8000 (Denver)
            303-226-1122
            (Fort Collins)

Connecticut

101 Corporate Place
Rocky Hill, 06067-1894
860-721-0025
Referrals: 203-335-4116
            (Fairfield)
            203-525-6052
            (Hartford)
            203-562-5750
            (New Haven)
            860-889-9384
            (New London)
            203-753-1938
            (Waterbury)

Delaware

1225 North King Street
10th Floor
Wilmington, 19801-3233
302-658-5278

District of Columbia

1250 H Street NW
6th Floor
Washington, 20005
202-737-4700
Referrals: 202-626-3499

Florida

650 Apalachee Parkway
Tallahassee, 32399
904-561-5600
Referrals: 800-342-8011

Georgia

800 The Hurt Building
50 Hurt Plaza
Atlanta, 30303
404-527-8700
Referrals: 404-521-0777

Hawaii

PO Box 26
Honolulu, 96810
808-537-1868
Referrals: 808-537-9140

Idaho

PO Box 895
Boise, 83701
208-342-8958

Illinois

Illinois Bar Center
Springfield, 62701
217-525-1760

Indiana

230 East Ohio Street
4th Floor
Indianapolis, 46204
317-639-5465
Referrals: 317-269-2222

Iowa

521 East Locust Street
Des Moines, 50309
515-243-3179
Referrals: 515-280-7429

Kansas

PO Box 1037
Topeka, 66601-1037
913-234-5696
Referrals: 913-233-4322

Kentucky

514 West Main Street
Frankfort, 40601-1883
502-564-3795
Referrals: 502-583-1576

Louisiana

601 St. Charles Street
New Orleans, 70130
504-566-1600
Referrals: 504-561-8828

Maine

124 State Street
Augusta, 04332
207-622-7523
Referrals: 207-622-1460

Maryland

520 West Fayette Street
Baltimore, 21201
410-685-7878

Massachusetts

20 West Street
Boston, 02111
617-542-3602
Referrals: 617-542-9103

Michigan

306 Townsend Street
Lansing, 48933
517-372-9030
Referrals: 800-968-0738

Minnesota

514 Nicollet Mall, Suite 300
Minneapolis, 55401
612-333-1183

Mississippi

PO Box 2168
Jackson, 39225
601-948-4471
Referrals: 800-682-6423

Missouri

326 Monroe Street
Jefferson City, 65101
314-635-4128
Referrals: 800-392-8777

Montana

PO Box 577
Helena, 59624
406-442-7660
Referrals: 406-449-6577

Nebraska

635 South 14th Street
Lincoln, 68508
402-475-7091
Referrals: 402-435-2995 (Lincoln)
                402-341-4104 (Omaha)

Nevada

1325 Airmotive Way, Suite 140
Reno, 89502
702-329-4100
Referrals: 702-382-0504
                (Las Vegas)
                702-329-4101(Reno)

New Hampshire

112 Pleasant Street
Concord, 03301
603-224-6942
Referrals: 800-639-5290

New Jersey

CN973 Richard Hughes Justice
Complex
Trenton, 08625
609-984-7783
Referrals: 201-906-8444

New Mexico

PO Box 25883
Albuquerque 87125
505-842-6132
Referrals: 800-876-6227

New York

One Elk Street
Albany, 12207
518-463-3200
Referrals: 800-342-3661
                212-676-7373
                (New York City)

North Carolina

PO Box 25908
Raleigh, 27611
919-828-4620
Referrals: 919-828-1054

North Dakota

PO Box 2136
Bismarck, 58502
701-255-1404
Referrals: 710-255-1406

Ohio

PO Box 16562
Columbus, 43216
614-487-2050
Referrals: 216-253-5038 (Akron)
                513-381-8359
                (Cincinnati)
                216-696-3525
                (Cleveland)
                614-221-0754
                (Columbus)
                513-222-6022
                (Dayton)
                419-242-2000 (Toledo)

Oklahoma

PO Box 53036
Oklahoma City, 73152
405-524-2365
Referrals: 405-235-6022
      (Oklahoma City)
      918-589-6014 (Tulsa)

Oregon

5200 SW Meadows Road
Lake Oswego, 97035
503-620-0222
Referrals: 503-684-3763

Pennsylvania

100 South Street
Harrisburg, 17108-0186
717-238-6715
Referrals: 717-238-6715
      (Harrisburg)
      215-238-1701
      (Philadelphia)
      412-261-0518
      (Pittsburgh)

Puerto Rico

PO Box 1900
San Juan, 00903
809-721-3358

Rhode Island

115 Cedar Street
Providence, 02903
401-421-5740
Referrals: 401-421-7799

South Carolina

950 Taylor Street
Columbia, 29202
803-799-6653
Referrals: 800-868-2284

South Dakota

222 East Capitol
Pierre, 57501
605-224-7554
Referrals: 800-952-2333

Tennessee

3622 West End Avenue
Nashville, 37205
615-383-7421
Referrals: 423-266-5950
      (Chattanooga)
      423-522-7501
      (Knoxville)
      901-529-8800
      (Memphis)
      615-242-6546
      (Nashville)

Texas

1414 Colorado
Austin, 78711
512-463-1463
Referrals: 800-252-9690
      214-969-7066
      (Dallas)
      713-237-9429
      (Houston)
      210-227-1853
      (San Antonio)

Utah

645 South 200 E.
Salt Lake City, 84111
801-531-9077
Referrals: 801-531-9075

Vermont

35–37 Court Street
Montpelier, 05602
802-223-2020

Virginia

707 East Main Street, Suite 1500
Richmond, 23219-2803
804-775-0500
Referrals: 800-552-7977

Washington

500 Westin Building
2001 6th Avenue
Seattle, 98121-2599
206-727-8200
Referrals: 206-623-2551 (Seattle)
509-456-3655
(Spokane)
206-383-3432 (Tacoma)

West Virginia

2006 Kanawha Boulevard East
Charleston, 25311
304-558-2456

Wisconsin

PO Box 7158
Madison, 53707-7158
608-257-3838
Referrals: 608-257-4666
(Madison)
414-274-6768
(Milwaukee)

Wyoming

PO Box 109
Cheyenne, 82003
307-632-9061

21 *Hiring a real estate agent*

My parents have owned the same home for nearly thirty years. It will take a lot for them to sell it.

But a few years back, my father told me he had pretty well picked out the person he would use as a real estate agent when the time came to sell.

During the same conversation, he said that he planned to have a different person come in and do a market evaluation on the house.

When I asked why he wouldn't use the agent who would someday represent the property, he explained that he didn't want to trouble the guy when no sale was imminent. Instead, he would take up some stranger's offer for a free evaluation; that agent had no expectations, so would not be disappointed when my parents opted not to sign a contract.

That reaction is not uncommon. Most people work with a real estate agent only when they are buying or selling a home.

That makes sense. Real estate agents get paid on commission for doing a deal, so the idea of continuing the relationship past the point of a sale—when there is no commission to be made—is foreign to many people.

But a home is the single biggest investment most people ever make, and having a specialist who can help you determine the appropriate steps to take to get the most from that holding. You might think that the $10,000 in renovations you put into a home are going to come back to you in sales price, but an agent familiar with the local market may know better; you could have bought a particular type of house—say a townhouse—where there seems to be an upper limit as to what buyers will pay to be in the community. If you bought near that upper limit, you may not get the $10,000 in improvements back out of the home because prospective buyers may not be willing to pay that much for a townhouse.

Real estate agents are a valuable member of your financial team because they can help you think about the monetary impact of the altering the biggest piece of your investment portfolio. Just as most people wouldn't make a $10,000 change in their stock portfolio without consulting a broker, it is prudent not to make that big a change in your real estate portfolio without consulting an expert.

Obviously most people work with a real estate broker only when they are buying or selling. In hiring an agent, however, you should look both at how they get a deal done and what they are like afterward.

If you only work with a real estate agent during sale periods, you treat your home entirely as a "use asset," akin to a car, using and repairing it and getting whatever value possible from it when it's time to sell. Unlike a car, however, you probably expect your home to appreciate in value. The pre–baby boom generation and the front edge of the boomers lived through tremendous home-price appreciation; since the late 1980s, however, real estate price growth has slowed dramatically and even been negative in some parts of the country.

That trend puts a premium on managing your property. It's not that every quart of paint trickles down to the bottom line—or that you might not want to spend money for your own comfort, even if you will not be rewarded with a better sales price—but it does make it smart to consult with an expert every now and again.

"Realistically, real estate is a part of your investment portfolio and more and more people are treating their house as if it were a financial asset," says John A. Tuccillo, chief economist for the National Association of Realtors. "They want an expert on their house the same way they want an expert on mutual funds or estate planning, to help them decide if it's a good time to refinance or borrow against their equity, to expand or buy something new. You may only hire a realtor when you are buying or selling, but it's a good idea to have one who you can talk to every now and again."

Presumably that agent will be the one who served you when you bought or sold a home in the community where you live, or the one you are likely to work with years from now when it comes time to move. In a case like my parents', advice over several years could be a precursor to doing business down the road—which is why the real estate agent is willing to take the time now to have informal meetings—and to creating a very comfortable working relationship when the time comes to sign an actual listing contract.

Whether you are a buyer, seller, or just looking for someone to help you make smart decisions as a homeowner, here are the questions you will want answered before hiring a real estate agent:

Can I do this myself? If not, who should I deal with?

The short answer to this question is yes; the longer answer may be "Why would you want to?"

While the law does not require you to hire a real estate adviser when buying or selling a home, this is one area where the biased professionals actually present a pretty clear picture of what will happen to you if you go it alone.

Real estate agents typically say that they can get you a better price and sell your home more quickly and with less hassle. To some extent all of those points are probably true.

The main reason to represent yourself is to save money, generally a commission of between 5 and 7 percent of the sale price that gets paid to the agents involved in the deal. On a $150,000 house, that's a savings of between $7,500 and $10,500, which is hardly insignificant; depending on individual circumstances, that money can be the difference between making a profit on the home or having to bring a checkbook to the closing to settle up your losses.

But that assumes you can actually get to a closing on your own. Selling without representation is not a go-to-closing-free card. You have to do your own market analysis in order to price your house reasonably (but not too cheaply), pay all marketing costs, organize any and all open houses, and you have to find buyers without using the Multiple Listing Service, a computerized system where member real estate brokers and agents advertise and swap information on available homes.

And unless you have the cash to do a seller-financed deal, you probably lack the kind of financing muscle that a good agent can produce for a prospective homebuyer.

In other words, there's a reason why experts say that about 90 percent of all homes—give or take 5 percent and excluding new construction—are sold through an agent. Unless you have a strong desire, a lot of time, and a hot seller's market where buyers are flocking to new offerings, you probably will want to hire an adviser to help with the sale of your home.

For homebuyers, the issue is a bit different. There is no drawback to scouring the local newspapers, finding the right home and making appointments on your own. You miss out on access to the Multiple Listing Service, but you do get to see most of the for-sale-by-owner homes (which an agent might not show you, since they can't get even a small commission from many do-it-yourselfers.)

Dealing with the agent who handles the listing means you are dealing with the seller's broker, otherwise known as a conventional agent. Conventional agents always represent the seller.

But even if you go into a real estate office, sit down with an agent, and they help you find a home to bid on, they remain a conventional agent unless you have specifically contracted with them to represent you as a "buyer broker." In real estate terms, the conventional agent who brings the buyer to the bargaining table is a "subagent;" don't be fooled by the jargon.

Say, for example, you found an agent who showed you available listings in town. You find a home on which you bid, say, $135,000—but tell the agent you would go to $150,000. By law, the agent's responsibility is to look out for the seller's best interest—even if the agent has never met the seller—which means that your willingness to go to a higher price must also be communicated.

Obviously that's not a great bidding strategy.

But the fact that an agent works for the seller should not discourage you. For years conventional agents have been the only game in town, and it didn't stop people from buying homes at a fair market price.

Indeed there are plenty of conventional agents who will do everything in their power to represent you well. It is in their best interest, after all, for you to be happy, to find a home you love, to refer other people to them, and, perhaps, to someday sell your home through them.

What you should remember if you choose to work with a conventional agent is that they cannot tell you which home to buy (if you are looking at more than one home in the area, they represent both sellers and are not allowed to favor one), how much to offer (their job is to get the seller the listing price), and—with the exception of hidden defects which, because they are invisible, must be pointed out—cannot tell you what is wrong with the property (they are not allowed to influence you not to buy).

In addition a conventional agent is not required to provide you with a comparative market analysis—although many do—unless you ask for it.

The apparent conflict of interest of having a buyer's agent actually working for the seller is as old as the profession itself, but if the potential biases worry you, consider a buyer broker.

With a buyer broker, you sign a contract that says you will not look for a house with any agent for a specific period of time. The buyer broker comes to you with appropriate listings and handles every part of the negotiation, including pricing strategy. Many also help clients search for the best available financing and insurance and set up all inspections.

Shrewd buyer brokers also keep an eye on the for-sale-by-owner market, which means they may find homes that a conventional agent would ignore. (They do this because you are paying for their service, rather than the seller, so they get paid regardless of whether the house you buy is sold by the owner or an agent.)

The drawbacks to buyer brokers are that they are sometimes are discriminated against by conventional agents—which can affect how much (and how) you pay for their services—the exclusivity of the contract and another potential conflict of interest.

The discrimination issue is very big in some parts of the country, where resistance to the buyer-broker movement has been so strong that virtually no one attempts to work on behalf of buyers.

For anyone who has worked with conventional agents and jumped from one to the next, the exclusivity of a buyer-broker arrangement will seem a bit limiting. In addition one frequent complaint from people who have gone to buyer brokers and not been satisfied is that the broker got pushy as the exclusivity period neared its end.

As for the conflict of interest, that stems from the fact that most buyer brokers also work as seller's agents. It is possible to have an agent who is doing both sides of the deal, selling you one of their own listings; in that case—where they have to disclose the potential conflict—they are supposed to represent both you and the seller, which is close to impossible since they probably have too much information from each side to cut an honest deal.

Is my only choice to go with a full-service agent or go it alone?

There are discount real estate brokerages; the question is whether there are any where you live.

For sellers, a discount brokerage works like this: The agent puts you into the Multi-List, you do virtually everything else.

Okay, that may be a bit harsh, but you get very limited services, most revolving around the marketing of the house, and then you do the open houses, the showings, the price negotiations, and the rest. The agent then gives back up to half of their share of the commission when the sale is completed.

Let's go back to that $150,000 example. The listing agent normally would get half of the $9,000 or so commission on the property (assuming there is a subagent or buyer broker for the bidder). That would make your take about $2,250.

For buyers, the system works roughly the same way. The agent gives you a listing of the available homes in the area, but you set up appointments, negotiate the contracts, and all of the rest. If you do all of the work, you get to split the commission.

In both cases, however, you really are working on is a pay-as-you-go system. You get the full split of the commission if you do all the work; if you want the agent to step in and arrange for inspections, for example, that's going to cost you. If you want the agent to call your banker, *cha-ching!* goes the cash register.

That's not necessarily bad. You might be able to save money doing a lot of legwork and leaving the tasks you dislike to someone else. The important thing to find out up front how much those "extras" are going to cost you and what, exactly, you are being charged for.

Is there a difference between "brokers" and "agents?"

In terms of handling the purchase or sale of a piece of property, there is no real difference between a broker and an agent. A real estate broker, however, had to first qualify as an agent, taking the requisite classes and passing a licensing exam; moving up to broker requires additional class work, a certain amount of experience in the business, and another test.

By earning a broker's license, an individual earns the right to work independently and to open or operate a real estate office. An agent, meanwhile, must work for a broker.

Just because the broker is the Big Kahuna around the office does not make them a better adviser than one of their agents; plenty of agents have no desire to run an office, and plenty of brokers become office bound and lose some of their feel for the community. You should worry more about an adviser's knowledge of the community than about the hierarchical structure at a real estate office.

Am I better off working with someone from a brand-name office?

Since all member agents have access to the Multiple Listing Service, bigger does not necessarily mean better when it comes to your agent's firm. Supply and demand in your market, the property itself, and the initiative and energy of the agent will determine how quickly your home sells more than whether an agent runs a one-person shop or is affiliated with the local office of a giant national chain.

At the same time one of the key things you want from an agent is that person's contacts. If you are a buyer and you hire someone from the firm that does the most listings in the area, you are likely to get a chance to see those houses before they appear in the Multi-List. In a tight market that could be an advantage.

There is no guarantee that the bigger firm does more business in your area than the Mom-and-Pop shop, so the agents there don't necessarily have more pull with local bankers. They may have more pull with the local media, however, if they have a big advertising budget; that can lead to better display in the paper, access to television shows spotlighting area homes and more. And though no one at a big firm would ever admit this, it's no secret that some big firms encourage agents to show prospective buyers the firm's listings first, meaning that a pool of prospects may see your property only after all of the alternatives have been reviewed.

The crucial elements, however, will be the people involved and the access to the Multiple Listing Service. Finding an agent you have confidence in—assuming all of your choices are members of the Multiple Listing Service—is more important than who the agent works for.

What credentials will I deal with, and how important are they?

While there are designations that mean something in the world of commercial real estate—such as the Counselors of Real Estate designation that a select few members of the National Association of Realtors have earned—the truth is that there is no specific credential that makes one residential real estate agent superior to another. Your hiring decision will be based more on what you perceive they can do for you than on what plaques hang on the wall.

That said, make sure that your agent or broker is properly licensed by the state. Most states require brokers and agents to post their license in plain sight, but don't be afraid to ask for it.

The one designation that most consumers look for is that their adviser is a Realtor, which means an agent or broker who is a member of the National Association of Realtors. Of the 2 million real estate agents in the country, about 750,000 are Realtors.

The big plus for consumers is that Realtors adhere to the national group's code of ethics and conduct.

The Realtist designation essentially is parallel to that of the Realtor. It is awarded by the National Association of Real Estate Brokers, a group that tries to meet the needs of real estate advisers who are African American or from other minority groups.

How does an agent get paid, and is it negotiable?

By this point you know that a real estate agent gets paid in commission, but that does not mean there is no room to negotiate.

A small-but-growing segment of real estate agents will make flat-fee arrangements—essentially a different form of discount brokerage—where they agree to provide certain services for a prearranged fee. There still may be commission to pay for the broker who brings in the buyer, and there may be some work to do on your own behalf, but some experts believe that this type of agreement represents the future of discount pricing for real estate advisers.

And, in some of these cases, half of the flat fee must be paid up front, and is kept by the agent regardless of whether the home sells during the time of the listing agreement.

When it comes to buyer brokers, the commission issue also can get sticky. Technically you sign a contract that specifies what the broker is to be paid either as a percentage of the purchase price or on an hourly or flat rate for service. In practice, however, the seller's agent agrees to split the commission with the buyer broker, the same way they would give a share to a conventional subagent.

But you can't bet on the fact that you won't have to come up with money to pay a buyer broker. In areas where "Establishment" agents try to discourage buyer brokers, many seller's agents structure listings so that there is no splitting the commission with a buyer's agent. It's not fair—and it can often be negotiated around—but you still have to be prepared to pay up just in case. (There would also be no commission for a buyer broker if you buy a home sold by its owner, although this, too, can be negotiated.) Many sellers—and seller's agents—come around and pay for the buyer broker's services if they see a deal walking out the door.

As for negotiating commissions, that's a sticky issue with many real estate advisers. The problem with reducing the commission is that you may not get the same level of service or traffic; I have had a scary number of real estate agents say that they don't work as hard when the commission is reduced, and that they are reluctant to show their buying clientele homes where a less-than-normal commission is being paid.

Still, if you have a seller's market for homes—where it is easy to make properties move and where there are not many homes to be listed—there may be the leverage necessary to get agents competing for the business.

There are a lot of ways to play with commissions without necessarily insulting an agent. Find out if the commission can be shaved if the brokerage firm handles both sides of the deal; if the firm lines up your buyer, it doesn't have to share the commission, so it might be willing to take a bit off to entice you to sign up.

If you have an expensive home, ask for a commission that is staggered. For example, the commission could be structured to equal 6 percent of the first $100,000 in sale price, 5 percent on the second $100,000 and 4 percent thereafter. If the house is worth enough to generate a big commission—particularly in a seller's market where there are few available houses—this kind of structure may be appealing. In addition many brokers and agents won't negotiate commission because they don't like the principle of taking less money for their services; this may be a fair compromise, since it is not necessarily harder to sell a $400,000 home than a $250,000 home.

Last, if you have a home that is hard to sell—you live next to a toxic waste dump or, hopefully, some lesser evil—you might actually consider raising the commission. It is not out of line to pay a 10 percent commission for a home that is particularly tough to unload. Raising commissions, to a lesser degree, also helps generate traffic if you have a short time to move the house; just as brokers and agents don't like to work in situations where their rates are cut, they love situations that bring home extra money.

What should I ask during an interview?

If you are picking an agent to sell your home, the interview should occur at home—or at least with the property being a central part of the process. Invite several real estate agents from your area to do a comparative market analysis.

Even if there is no imminent sale and you just want some advice and the chance to start building a relationship with an agent, a market evaluation is the place to start. It's a service most agents gladly provide because they know it can lead to future business and referrals (which is precisely why the agent my father had never met before offered him the service in the first place).

Essentially you want the agent to walk through your home and get an idea of its pluses and minuses, to look for what you can do to make it more salable.

It will generally take the agent a few days to put together a market evaluation, which includes checking the prices of similar properties currently on the market, as well as prices of like homes that have sold in recent months.

You can interview a real estate counselor either when they do the walk-through or when they deliver the analysis; I prefer the latter because the evaluation always brings up more questions.

Here are some things you will want to go over with any agent. Some apply only to seller or buyer agents, others to both; some must be altered slightly to fit both types of agents.

How long have you been in the business? Is this your full-time job?

Full-time, experienced people are generally the way to go, although there may be nothing wrong with folks who have less experience but know the area very well.

Part-time agents are the best option only if you are looking to buy a home and don't want your search to be too active—the kind of thing where you could be satisfied seeing only one or two homes a month—but the problem is that they are not always going to be available when you need them. Remember, too, that a real estate agent's life heats up when a sale is pending; if they squeeze business in between a lot of other activities, they may not have sufficient time to handle the demands of the deal at its most delicate time.

Are you a broker or a sales agent?

As stated earlier, this is a minor concern. The reason you ask is to be sure that a broker has sufficient time to represent you effectively. If they are too busy managing the office or keeping tabs on their associates, they might be too much of an administrator to meet your day-to-day demands.

What continuing education classes have you taken?

Real estate sales practices keep changing. So do the laws governing many specific aspects of land ownership. You are always best off working with someone who keeps their education current and is trying to make themselves a better representative for you.

As long as you are asking about continuing education and background in the business, don't be shy about asking for a resume. There is no reason why a real estate agent should want to withhold that information from you.

How far afield do you go to get clients?

If you are a buyer and want to look in a region—such as Boston's South Shore area where I live—you want someone who knows more than one community. If, however, you want to live in a specific town or neighborhood, you may want someone who really specializes in local real estate and has superior knowledge of the community you want to call home.

As a seller, your concern when someone gets spread out is time. Since an agent can't be two places at once, having listings that are spread over a 25-mile radius can be a problem, particularly if you want your adviser to attend all showings of your home.

How many listings (buyers) do you work with at one time?

I know agents who say they can handle eight listings at once; I know others who claim to comfortably handle twice that many. There is no right number, but the amount of business an agent has right now does affect your service, ranging from how much time an agent might have to communicate with you to how often they will be able to show your home.

As with all advisory relationships, a lot of your decision will be based on instinct and who you feel you can trust. If you hear about a workload that sounds unreasonable, ask about it.

How many homes have you listed and sold in the last year? (How many buyers have you represented in the last year?)

Ask for a list of the homes the agent has sold in the last year, including both the list and sale prices. Real estate is not unlike financial planning or insurance, in that you want to be a lot like an adviser's average client.

If you have a $150,000 home (or that amount to spend on a new home) and the agent's sales sheet includes mostly homes valued at twice that much, chances are that you're not a good match.

Similarly you want to make sure that the agent sells your kinds of properties. If their sales in the last year have been mostly single-family homes and you have a condo (or want to buy a condo), they may not be expert at dealing in your kind of property.

Have any of your showings or sales included homes in my neighborhood?

Just because someone is the top agent at their firm does not make them the best for you. If they are not familiar with your neighborhood, if they can't describe it knowledgeably to a seller, you may be better off with someone else.

What is your standard commission?

You *must* ask. Enough said.

Do you accompany all buyers through my home?

This is a personal preference issue, but one that you want settled in advance. Many real estate agents use a "lock box," essentially a special key holder with a combination that is given to a buyer's agent. The buyer's agent brings clients to your home, opens the box and uses the key to show people around your empty home.

It's very convenient, particularly if you live a busy life and can't always be around the house to open the door for a showing.

At the same time many selling agents prefer to be present—or send their associates—for walk-throughs, hanging around to answer questions about the home.

You can consider it either a service or a privacy issue, but consider it in advance so that you can let the agent know your preferences. Remember, you want them to hire you as a client; if trekking to your house for each showing is more work than they care to do—but you think their presence is important—neither you nor the agent is going to be happy with the relationship.

What are you going to do to help the house sell?

The Multiple Listing Service is a no-brainer. You want to find out if the rest of the advertising will consist of newspaper ads, exposure on a local television show, glossy advertising giveaways, or, maybe, a radio transmitter that lets passersby get a description of the house 24 hours a day.

They get paid to market your house; if they can't come up with a good plan, you'd be better off doing this yourself.

Are you going to hold a broker's open house?

A broker's open house is designed to show your home to every other agent in town. Your agent will send a notice to every firm in the area, inviting interested agents to come for lunch and a look-see.

Don't kid yourself; there are plenty of agents who just come to eat, especially if your broker is known for putting out a good spread.

At the same time, for a few hours on a weekday afternoon, you will get some agents in your home who could decide it is perfect for someone they are working with.

Many agents choose not to do a "broker's open," particularly if the customer doesn't request it.

How often will you have weekend open houses?

This is both a marketing and lifestyle decision. For most busy people there are only so many weekends in a month that they can disappear from home for five hours without falling behind on housework, yardwork, or homework.

Too many open houses smacks of desperation, too few means that you aren't bringing potential buyers through your doors. Find a happy medium.

What are the positives and negatives of this house?

Few of us have a perfect house, no matter how much we love it. Ask an agent to tell you the home's best selling points and biggest drawbacks; you want to make sure the two of you perceive the house in the same way; otherwise, you could be in for a big disagreement on pricing.

What can I do to improve the house and make it easier to sell?

No one likes dumping money into a home they are about to move out of, but a coat of paint can do a lot to refresh an older home. And while prospective buyers generally don't purchase your furniture, they do notice the way you live; cluttered closets, for example, look small and make people wonder if they will run out of shelf space.

Ask what can be done to get your house in the best condition to be shown. Plan to do the work early, so that you don't have to rush around at the last minute before a prospective buyer shows up.

What price range would you suggest for my home and why? If the house stays on the market, when and by how much will we lower the asking price?

This is where they detail the comparative market analysis and tell you what they think you can get for your house. Obviously some level of agreement between you and the adviser is necessary.

What you are listening for is a fair market price based on current market conditions and the urgency of your need to sell, as well as a strategy that makes sense to you if there is a need to drop your price.

Don't be impressed by big numbers; some agents price everything high in order to impress potential clients. After the contract is signed, the house goes on the market at an inflated price before dropping to the more reasonable price suggested by less-aggressive (or, perhaps, more scrupulous) agents.

If the projected price is below your expectations, find out whether the agent's calculations or your impressions of the home are what is askew.

Make sure you know their feelings about how long a home should sit on the market before dropping a price because you do not want the relationship with the agent to deteriorate later if there are pricing surprises. Many homeowner-broker relationships sour when the parties disagree on the next pricing move; since you both make money on the sale of the home, you are teammates and you will function the best if you are in agreement on strategies before the game begins.

Who are the best agents in town—besides yourself—and why?

Unlike virtually every other form of financial adviser, real estate agents are in a cooperative situation. A lawyer can sit in a corner office and write and file paperwork for you, an accountant can crunch numbers, and a financial planner can develop a strategy all without consulting another soul.

But real estate agents can't close the deal without working with their peers. Real estate is a small community where most of the local players know of each other (at least by reputation). If your agent can't say a nice thing about anyone else in the field, then chances are that they don't work well with those people. That is not good.

Asking this question lets you see what an agent admires in his peers. It's also a pretty good list of professional references because the names you get represent the competition. If you call, say, a lawyer who the agent works with, there is a potential bias because the agent may routinely refer clients and the lawyer doesn't want to lose that business. The competition has no reason to say something nice, especially if they might be interested in your business themselves.

Could I get the names of a few recent sellers (or buyers) who you have worked with?

Unlike many other financial advisory relationships, where confidentiality and privacy are major concerns, you should have little trouble getting the names of references from a real estate agent. Property transactions are public record, so the confidentiality issue is moot.

Make sure they don't just give you the names of the friends or relatives who referred you in the first place, as in "Why don't you just talk to Uncle Morty about that. You know how he feels about me."

This is your biggest investment, and a bad adviser can cost you a lot of money, so make sure you talk to more than one reference. In fact try to find references who had to deal with this agent in different circumstances, possibly one whose home sold quickly and another whose house sat on the market for months. (Review the chapter on dealing with references to know what to look for in reference checks.)

What can I do to make myself a better buyer?

If you are buying a home, there are ways to make bids more attractive, such as being preapproved for a mortgage so that the deal can be written without a mortgage contingency.

This question will give you insight into the kinds of strategies a buyer broker thinks will work, both with lenders and sellers.

Can you assist with financing?

Real estate agents often track interest rates and have contacts with favorite lenders who can speed the application process. That not only comes in handy when you buy a home but years later, when your agent may be able to say who can help you pursue refinancing, home equity lines of credit, reverse mortgages, and other options. (A good real estate agent knows which bankers bend the rules—going against standard industry formulas that might make you a poor candidate for, say, a home-equity loan.)

Do I need a "reality check?"

A reality check is where an agent puts you in the car and drives you around to look at other properties. As a seller, they are showing you that your expectations are unreasonable compared to similar homes in similar neighborhoods. For buyers, a reality check may be to prove that you have too little money to afford the neighborhood and that perhaps you need to adjust your hopes and dreams down to the size of your wallet.

How often will I hear from you?

Obviously the agent should contact you the moment they have an offer (or a home they think might be right for you). The question is what happens when nothing is happening.

You will want to hear from your agent enough to quell your fears and to strategize about the price and marketing of a home (or whether to widen your search area because nothing is coming up in the neighborhoods you desire). Generally those conversations take place once a week, but you want to know what to expect because a lack of communication between you and your agent is a sign of trouble.

Are you planning a vacation soon?

Yes, it's personal question and one that only a seller will ask. Brokers and agents are entitled to vacations just like everyone else, but the hot time for activity on a home is when the listing is new, generally in the first three to four weeks after it is listed.

That's when every buyer who is in your price range and interested in your community—and every broker working with a prospective client in your area—will want to see the house. If you are putting your house on the market and need for it to sell quickly, you may not be comfortable having your agent on the road during the first few weeks.

Does a vacation automatically disqualify an agent? Absolutely not. There is an adage in the real estate business that when brokers go on vacation, all of their listings sell.

If I sign a contract, how long is the listing agreement good for? Can I change agents without paying a double commission (or would you get a piece of the deal no matter what)? How can I terminate the listing, and for how long after that are you entitled to payment?

The listing agreement is fraught with terms that are to the agent's advantage. Ask about them and read the agreement carefully. Picking the wrong agent is bad enough, but signing a restrictive contract can actually make the situation worse.

Some contracts force you to list with the agent for six months—you should never agree to more than three—and have no termination clause. Essentially this is like trying to force you to sell your house. Before entering a contract, you want to know exactly how you get out of it if you change your mind or dislike the service.

Paying a double commission can occur when you switch brokers; brokers know that losing a listing means losing a commission, and they want to cash in on their work—even if you didn't think their work was so great. So, if someone saw the house while they had it listed comes back to see it again later—when you have a new agent— and buys the home, they will try to get a commission for having brought you the buyer. This is the kind of language you do not want in your listing agreement.

Similarly, say you decide to test the waters—hoping, perhaps, to move to a better place in town—and put your home on the market. A few people come through, but no one makes a worthy offer, and you decide to terminate the listing. Five months later, one of the prospective buyers knocks on your door, wondering if you are still interested in selling and makes a great offer. If your listing agreement specifies that the agent gets a commission for six months after termination, you are going to pay a commission on the deal. Try to limit the time to, say, three months.

There are even listing agreements that could force you to pay a commission without selling the home, rewarding the agent for bringing you a "ready, willing, and able buyer." In most cases the agent who produces that buyer is going to make a sale. The deal, however, can still fall through; the buyer could get a job offer or transfer and could back out. You do not want to be on the hook for the commission, so make sure the agreement language does not force you to pay until the deal is done.

If you go over a standard agreement line by line, you can find at least the potential for unfavorable terms.

In general, listing agreements are designed to discourage you from taking advantage of an agent's time, then bolting to stiff the agent and do the deal on your own. That's fair and reasonable, up to a point; there's a fine line between planning to stiff a broker—which presumably you will not do—and protecting yourself and your options.

How will the process go when there is an offer?/What's the drill when we find a house to bid on?
For sellers, you want to be walked through the process of what is going to happen once a bid comes in, how the agent feels about

counteroffers and pricing strategy, and what they do to get the deal from start—the first contract with an acceptable offer—to closing.

Buyers, too, want to go over the way a bid works and what the broker's responsibility is when it comes to helping push the deal through.

What happens after the sale?

This gets back to the concept of developing a relationship so that your real estate adviser is with you after you have moved in.

When my wife Susan and I bought our first home, it had an attic that was ready to be turned into a master bedroom suite. The previous owners had started the work, all we needed was to finish the job.

Before hiring a contractor, however, we went back to the agent who helped us buy the house (the same agent we planned on using to sell it when the time came), and she advised against fixing up the room, warning that we would never get the money out. She provided a very compelling comparative analysis that saved us thousands of dollars because we took a loss on the house and are convinced that the extra room would not have generated enough difference in the sale price to pay for itself.

Find out if an agent is willing to consult with you periodically, to "come see what you've done to the house," and to advise you as to the value of adding a fill-in-the-blank (fireplace, new kitchen, addition, swimming pool, etc.). Their knowledge of the market can be a major asset to you, provided they are interested in you for more than your current transaction.

You are not talking about getting their tips for decorating or asking them to pick the color of your new shutters, so you are not going to see them very often. It may be a once-a-year cup of coffee or lunch.

Most agents like doing this because they are always curious to see what happens to a house after the sale. It's good for you as a homeowner because it helps you set your priorities, particularly as you near a selling period. If you expect to stay in a house for only a few years but have the choice of which repairs to make next—say replacement windows versus a replacement kitchen—the agent would probably advise you to make the repairs that will make the most difference in selling price (the kitchen). If you plan to live in the house for twenty more years, the windows might be the better investment now because they will save money on the heating bill.

Last, one reason to keep in touch with an agent is that it never hurts to have representation. You may not be in the market to sell your home, but few people would turn away an offer without at least reviewing it. If an agent knows your house and meets someone tomorrow who wants to move to your town and describes your house as their dream home, the agent may just pick up the phone and call with an unsolicited offer. If it's good enough, you might decide that it's a good time to move to something bigger. At the very least, it never hurts to listen—and you will never have a shot at an unsolicited offer if a broker or agent is not familiar with your home.

How do I check out a broker or agent?

You can check with your state to make sure that an agent still has license, but that is generally unnecessary (since agents work for brokers, the brokers have a vested interest in keeping you away from scoundrels).

That said, you should contact the local Board of Realtors to see if they have any record of disciplinary action against either the agent or the firm. (Not all Boards of Realtors will give out information on a member firm.)

Last, check with the local Better Business Bureau; if there has been any pattern of problems, it will show up in their files.

If you find any red flags, be sure to ask about them during your interview. You want to know what happened, how it was resolved, and what can be done to make sure that these problems never happen to you.

What do I ask references?

Ask client references all of the character questions that you went over with the agent during your interview. Find out how often they heard from the agent, how quickly the price was dropped, how they felt about pricing and marketing strategy, whether there were any unpleasant surprises—or pleasant ones, for that matter—in the whole process, whether the agent smoothed over any rough edges and trouble spots while the sale was pending, during the closing, and so on.

Then ask what is always the most important question: "If you were selling (or buying) again today, would you hire this agent again? If so, would you do anything differently that would make things even better the second time around?"

What you want to learn from references is whether there is anything you need to incorporate into your pre-hiring discussions with an agent, in order to be certain they understand—and are willing to meet—your expectations.

With professional references, including those competing agents whose names you got during the interview, you are looking for their opinion. What are the strengths that they see this agent having; are there any weaknesses. The most important question here is, "If you were selling (or buying) a home, would this agent be one of the three top candidates to get the job?"

You can't expect them to say that this person is "the one" because they have a lot of professional ties that they want to maintain. If they tell you that this person would be one of "five or six" they would consider, ask why they would have so many people; listen for whether the answer is trying not to break wide-ranging ties, or if they are hemming and hawing, trying not to say that your prospective agent does not have their full faith and confidence.

Remember, too, that in all reference situations, you would expect the agent to have given you the names of people who are going to say the right thing. If that does not happen, if the agent has misjudged how they are viewed by clients, colleagues, and/or competitors, then you need to consider where else their judgment might off when it comes to business relationships.

What are the danger signs to a relationship gone sour?

The biggest problems in real estate relationships tend to involve personality, communication, and interest.

Obviously you should not sign on with an agent—no matter how great their credentials or sparkling their resume—if you don't click. Chemistry is important because it is hard to build a trusting relationship when the person across the table from you gives you the willies.

Obviously going through a detailed interview and following the tenets put forth in this book should help you uncover a personality conflict before you sign an agreement. If a personality problem does surface, ask for a meeting between you, your agent, and the managing broker of the firm. The managing broker may be willing to reassign you to another agent rather than risk that you will terminate the contract.

While personality clashes account for the major problems, they are not the only warning signs to consider. Others include:

- Loss of interest. Almost every broker is excited about your business after first getting you as a client. But they may not be so excited when there is no movement. If your house isn't selling (or you, as a buyer, are extremely picky and are not willing to bid on any number of houses that meet your own definition of what you're looking for), keep an eye on whether your broker or agent is doing everything possible to make things work.

For sellers, that means the agent continues to place ads, hold open houses, and search for ways to make your home show better.

For buyers, it means trying to do a better job pinpointing exactly what it is you are looking for, reviewing your financial situation to see if there are other ways to help do a deal, and continuing to scour the area for new listings to show you.

One other point: Loss of interest may not have anything to do with you. While there are many long-time real estate agents, there also are many transients, who come into the field for awhile and then move on or pursue other careers. Just as you probably want to work with an agent who is full-time, you might be wary of an agent whose other interests make them so busy that they don't have the time or energy to work on your behalf.

- Lack of communication. During your interview, you set a standard for how often you should hear from the agent. Even if nothing is happening, there should be a phone call every week, assuming that is what you have agreed to.

Even if nothing is happening on the house and you have agreed to talk less frequently, there could be a communication problem—and a loss of interest, for that matter—if your agent does not return phone calls within six hours.

And, obviously, you do not want any surprises. If you call and find out that your broker has gone on vacation without telling you, that's a problem.

If you are a buyer, lack of communication can result in missed opportunities. By asking you a lot of questions, the broker gets an idea of how flexible you are in your needs—you need that fifth bedroom for an office, for example, but could get by with four bedrooms and some other space to work in—your willingness to do work and make renovations, and more. If they don't ask a lot of questions, particularly after you start looking at houses and your reactions tip them to what elements you consider crucial, then they are stuck with a rudimentary picture of what you want. They never find out how your thinking is changing as you go through the buying process, and that makes it more difficult to find a home that meets your needs.

- Failure to follow instructions. If you are buying a home and the first few houses the agent is trying to sell you are out of your price range or not even close to the description of what you want, chances are that the agent is trying to make you more like their average client and to fit you into their own comfort zone.

Don't go there. You control the relationship.

My wife Susan and I once worked with an agent—very briefly—when we were just starting to search for a home. We had very little free time and figured we were at least six to twelve months away from being financially ready to buy. We also had a very specific price range.

When the agent wanted to show us four homes a week, all of them just slightly above our price range, and kept trying to convince us that we could find a way to finance these homes, we felt pressured. The agent had stopped listening to what we wanted and was trying to bring us around to what she wanted, which was to sell a house in her favored price range.

- Maximum commission at your expense. It's understandable that agents hate the idea of reducing commissions, but it's shameful the way some unscrupulous agents nickel-and-dime buyers and sellers.

Say you have agreed on a deal, but the home inspection brings up a few issues. The buyer wants the price reduced, the seller agrees to make up the difference, but the real estate agent pushes to keep the original selling price and to have the seller "credit back" money at the closing.

That keeps the agent's commission the same, but benefits neither the buyer nor seller. The buyer is not only taking a bigger mortgage to meet the higher price but could face higher property taxes, since many communities use sales price as part of their valuation of the home. The seller is facing a larger capital gain on the home—assuming it was sold at a profit—as well as a higher commission.

Some agents will argue that they should keep the higher commission, even if the price is adjusted from the original deal. That's a compromise, but it still smacks of an adviser who is not putting your interests first. It is the agent's job to represent the house properly, and if anything comes up that alters the deal, that's a circumstance that an experienced agent should be prepared to deal with in a manner that is in the best interest of the customer. If you have problems like this one, contact the managing broker and complain.

- Incomplete disclosure or conflicts of interest. We have already covered the potential conflicts of interest in most real estate relationships. These days, however, there are plenty of agents who function as both a buyer broker and seller's agent, depending on the needs of their client. When an agent is listing your house and brings you a bidder who is not working with another real estate agent—or if they are your buyer broker and show you a house which they are listing for the seller—they are functioning as a "dual agent."

If that sounds like something you read in a spy novel, then you understand why you need to be careful around double agents.

As a seller, your concern will be if the agent is acting as a buyer broker. If not, then they are a conventional agent which means, as discussed earlier in this chapter, that they represent the seller. As a result, at least technically, there is no conflict of interest because all of their fiduciary responsibility is to you. (Be aware, however, that being a dual agent means not splitting the commission, which is why an agent may be particularly sweet on an offer that comes from someone they represent; if there are two offers on the table, or you believe a second offer is about to be made, you will have to gauge whether your agent's desire to seal the deal is in your best interest.)

If your agent has a contract to act as a buyer broker and as your selling agent, there is a big conflict of interest. Effectively the agent has a fiduciary duty to each of you, and it's tough to wear two hats. The agent may want you to sign a disclosure statement acknowledging that you understand the conflict of interest; that's fine and good, provided that you believe you are getting the advice you are paying for. If, for example, the agent cannot talk pricing strategy with you—they can't say how much the buyer is prepared to bid because that would break the trust of their buyer-broker client—then you may want to go to the managing broker of the office and ask for someone else to step in on your side during these negotiations.

If you are the buyer and your agent also has the listing of the seller, that's also a big conflict. Remember, the agent wants you to buy the house because they get to keep the entire commission.

Any time there is a dual agency situation, be very critical of your adviser's actions and make sure that they have your best interest at heart. If they do not—if they keep trying to steer you into a deal that benefits their other client or themselves—then you will have lost the trust that is a cornerstone to the relationship, and it's probably time to find a new adviser.

Where do I start my search to find the right agent?

Unlike most other financial advisers, there is not necessarily anywhere to go for a professional referral. Instead, most people find their agents by word-of-mouth, asking friends and neighbors who they worked with.

One suggestion on finding an agent is to start with your local Board of Realtors and find out which firms do the most business, then schedule appointments with the top-selling agents in those firms. That is no guarantee that you and the agent will be a match, but it does ensure that your candidates will all be very active members of the local real estate community. The big plus to this method for a buyer is that the most active agencies are likely to have the most listings and give you the chance to see the most houses before they go into the Multi-List and out to the rest of the world.

My favorite way to find an agent is to attend a few open houses in your neighborhood. As a seller, this helps you see how the agent represents a home and helps the owners get ready for a showing. In addition going to open houses and looking at homes through the eyes of a buyer is the kind of reality check that you asked after during the interview.

Attending an open house is also the best way to develop a relationship with an agent if you are looking for advice on managing your property but are not interested in selling right now.

After you have done a walk-through of a house—preferably something similar in price range to your own—talk to the agent. Chat with them about the local market and some of the broad home ownership issues in the area. They will invariably ask what you are looking for—they think you are a buyer and want your business, even if it is not to buy the house you are visiting—and then you can tell them that you are shopping for an agent or that you want advice on prioritizing your improvements so that you get the most for your home-ownership dollar.

This informal time will tell you a lot about chemistry. Coupled with the interview and market evaluation, it should be the beginning of a good, long relationship.

When it comes to performing background checks, getting referrals and filing complaints about real estate agents, state and local Boards of Realtors are a focal point of reference. Here are the addresses and phone numbers for the state boards:

Alabama Association of Realtors
PO Box 4070
Montgomery, 36103
334-262-3808

Alaska Association of Realtors
741 Sesame Street, Suite 100
Anchorage, 99503
907-563-7133

Arizona Association of Realtors
4414 North 19th Avenue, Suite R
Phoenix, 85015
602-248-7787

Arkansas Realtors Association
204 Executive Court, Suite 300
Little Rock, 72205
501-225-2020

California Association of Realtors
525 South Virgil Avenue
Los Angeles, 90020
213-739-8200

Colorado Association of Realtors
308 Inverness Way South
Englewood, 80112-5818
303-790-7099

Connecticut Association of Realtors
111 Founders Plaza
11th Floor
East Hartford, 06108-3212
860-290-6601

Delaware Association of Realtors
9 East Loockerman Street
Suite 315

Dover, 19901
302-734-4444

Washington DC Association of Realtors
1400 I Street, Suite 400
Washington, 20005
202-789-8889

Florida Association of Realtors
PO Box 725025
Orlando, 32872-5025
407-438-1400

Georgia Association of Realtors
3200 Presidential Drive
Atlanta, 30340
770-451-1831

Guam Board of Realtors
PO Box 5786
Agana, 96910
011-671-477-2081

Hawaii Association of Realtors
1136 12th Avenue, Suite 220
Honolulu, 96816-3793
808-737-4000

Idaho Association of Realtors
1450 West Bannock Street
Boise, 83702
208-342-3585

Illinois Association of Realtors
Box 19451
Springfield, 62703
217-529-2600

Indiana Association of Realtors
PO Box 50736
Indianapolis, 46250-2023
317-842-0890

Iowa Association of Realtors
999 Oakridge Drive
Des Moines, 50314-2197
515-244-2294

Kansas Association of Realtors
3644 Southwest Burlingame Road
Topeka, 66611
913-267-3610

Kentucky Association of Realtors
161 Prosperous Place
Suite 9
Lexington, 40509-1804
606-263-7377

Louisiana Realtors Association
PO Box 14780
Baton Rouge, 70898
504-923-2210

Maine Association of Realtors
RFD 4, Box 51
Community Drive
Augusta, 04330
207-662-7501

Maryland Association of Realtors
2594 Riva Road
Annapolis, 21401-7406
410-841-6080

Massachusetts Association of
Realtors
PO Box 9036
Waltham, 02154-1139
617-890-3700

Michigan Association of
Realtors
PO Box 40725
Lansing, 48901-7925
517-372-8890

Minnesota Association of
Realtors
5750 Lincoln Drive
Edina, 55436
612-935-8313

Mississippi Association of
Realtors
555 Park Drive, Suite 301
Jackson, 39208-8805
601-932-5241

Missouri Association of
Realtors
PO Box 1327
Columbia, 65205
314-445-8400

Montana Association of
Realtors
208 North Montana, Suite 105
Helena, 59601
406-443-4032

Nebraska Realtors Association
145 South 56th Street, Suite 100
Lincoln, 68510-2150
402-488-4303

Nevada Association of
Realtors
PO Box 7338
Reno, 89510
702-829-5911

New Hampshire Association
of Realtors
115 A Airport Road, Box 550
Concord, 03302-0550
603-225-5549

New Jersey Association of
Realtors
PO Box 2098
Edison, 08818-2098
908-494-5616

Realtors Association of New
Mexico
PO Box 4190
Santa Fe, 87502
505-982-2442

New York State Association of
Realtors
PO Box 122
Albany, 12260
518-463-0300

North Carolina Association of
Realtors
PO Box 7918
Greensboro, 27417-7918
910-294-1415

North Dakota Association of
Realtors
1120 College Drive, Suite 112
Bismarck, 58501
701-258-2361

Ohio Association of Realtors
200 East Town Street
Columbus, 43215
614-228-6675

Oklahoma Association of Realtors
9807 North Broadway
Oklahoma City, 73114
405-848-9944

Oregon Association of Realtors
PO Box 351
Salem, 7308-0351
503-362-3645

Pennsylvania Association of Realtors
4501 Chambers Hill Road
Harrisburg, 17111-2406
717-561-1303

Puerto Rico Association of Realtors
PO Box 8998
Santurce, 00910-0998
809-725-1325

Rhode Island Association of Realtors
100 Bignall Street
Warwick, 02888
401-785-3650

South Carolina Association of Realtors
PO Box 21827
Columbia, 29221
803-772-5206

South Dakota Association of Realtors
120 North Euclid
Pierre, 57501-2521
605-224-0554

Tennessee Association of Realtors
PO Box 121149
Nashville, 37212-1149
615-321-0515

Texas Association of Realtors
PO Box 2246
Austin, 78768-2246
512-480-8200

Utah Association of Realtors
5710 South Green Street
Murray, 84123
801-268-4747

Vermont Association of Realtors
PO Box 1074
Montpelier, 05602
802-229-0513

Virgin Islands Association of Realtors
3009 Orange Grove Shopping Center 13
Christiansted, 00820-4313
809-773-1855

Virginia Association of Realtors
10231 Telegraph Road
Glen Allen, 23060-4578
804-264-5033

Washington Association of Realtors
PO Box 719
Olympia, 98507
360-943-3100

West Virginia Association of Realtors
2110 Kanawha Boulevard East
Charleston, 25311
304-342-7600

Wisconsin Realtors Association
4801 Forest Run Road, Suite 201
Madison, 53704-7337
608-241-2047

Wyoming Association of Realtors
PO Box 2312
Casper, 82602-2312
307-237-4085

There are banks in this country that charge customers a fee for talking to a real person.

As callous as that sounds—and it only applies to certain routine transactions—that is actually an almost perfect marriage between typical bank and typical customer.

Banks, like any business, generally want to keep transaction costs low and stick to the formulas that generate profits.

At the same time consumers choose their banker on the basis of convenient branches, locations for automated teller machines, or the cost of a checking account. The customers then do their banking without ever leaving their car or talking to a person.

In other words, most people would never run up against that real-person fee.

Frequently I ask consumers if they "know" their banker. To my way of thinking, that means being on a "name basis" with someone who can recognize me and greet me by name without having to look at my deposit ticket.

Most people do not know anyone in their bank by name.

If all you ever intend to do is run a checking account, that is perfectly appropriate. But it also means that you are probably missing out on a higher level of service, and the lack of a relationship with your banker can cost you.

The typical consumer does not spend much time choosing or working with a banker. They consider the bank their depository institution and hope it will become their lender when they need a mortgage or car loan. While they might be aware of a bank's trust department or available insurance coverage or mutual funds, those extras are not why they chose their bank.

Most people I talk to have never interviewed a banker, and say that the first time they met with anyone from the institution it was to open an account. On that day the banker they met with took all of the data necessary to open an account and give them some starter checks. There may have been a cursory mention of other services—"Would you like a safe-deposit box?" or "Would you be interested in our trust department?"—but the entire experience couldn't have even qualified as a mental handshake between consumer and adviser.

Of course the big question is whether the average person needs to "have" a banker. After all, unlike a business that needs to find new and different ways to leverage assets to cut deals, or which needs to finesse financing so that it meshes with cash flow, an individual generally does not have those kinds of needs. Beyond a checking and savings account, perhaps some certificates of deposit or a money market and a safe-deposit box, typical consumer needs start to dwindle.

And while having a personal banker can be a big plus, it is hardly a necessity.

That said, you ought to know how to shop for a banking adviser so that you can decide if you want a personal banking relationship.

More than virtually any other type of financial adviser, bankers clearly break into the two groups, concerned either about doing transactions or developing relationships.

Transaction-oriented bankers want to get the job done, from the easiest services to more complex offerings, by keeping the vast majority of customer business "within the box." The box is the safe zone where the financial ratios work out to the bank's liking. If your numbers fit into the box, you get the loan; if not, hit the road.

Relationship banks, as the name implies, want relationships.

They don't just want your checking account business, but they want to handle as much of your money as possible, from mortgages and car loans down to establishing trusts and selling insurance or mutual funds.

Obviously you may not be comfortable with all of that—especially if you have an insurance agent and financial planner on your advisory team.

But if you ever want any treatment that is beyond the box—you want to buy an older used car, want to find out about lesser-known mortgages, or simply try to get the most for your banking dollar, you will want to find a banker with whom you can have a relationship.

Very often—but not always—that means turning to a community banker. Unlike the giants, who thrive on cookie-cutter offices churning out the standard deals, smaller banks tend to thrive on relationships. But whether it is a large or small institution, relationship banking is unique enough that you will have to ask for a meeting and the chance to sit down with the branch manager or vice president running the office.

My own case proves the benefit of this kind of approach to banking. My wife and I lived in Pennsylvania before moving to Boston; at the time of our move, interest rates had fallen to where a refinancing was attractive. In addition we had been unable to sell our house and wanted to lower payments so that it could be rented more easily.

I had been working with a local bank, to which I had moved our accounts, established our children's accounts, and taken a car loan. Moreover, since it was a small local bank, I knew the executives and was comfortable calling.

When I started mortgage shopping, I had been looking simply for the best rate, and had called the institutions that had the best rates in the area. My bank was not among them.

In each case the banks were going to charge me three points—a point is an up-front payment of a percentage of the loan—because the house was going to be a rental instead of a primary residence. While I was in the box as a customer—each bank wanted my business because I represented a good credit risk—I was out of the box on the good no points/no closing costs deals.

This was a distinct problem, since we hoped the house would sell within a year, meaning we would never pay off the points. Our choices appeared to be losing money on the rental or losing money on the points, neither of which was particularly attractive.

So I called "my banker" and told him of the situation and asked if there was anything he could do. Essentially I needed a short-term mortgage, with no points or closing costs.

A day later, my banker returned my call. His institution had been considering offering "interest-only mortgages," where the borrower simply pays the interest due and does not reduce principal. This would dramatically cut my payments—to the point where the home easily could be rented without being a drag on the family finances—and stop me from pouring more equity into a house which I expected to lose money on. The loan, in essence, was a one-year loan, that could be rolled over if the home didn't sell.

The benefit to the bank was that it was getting a good credit risk and lending money—if only on a short-term basis—at a rate higher than it could get by keeping the cash in its vault.

That banker's diligence in looking at the different options for me—searching outside the box for a solution that benefited a customer—was a lifesaver. And the banker admitted afterward that had I not been the type of customer who came in and asked questions and sought out solutions, that I never would have gotten the loan.

Therein lies one of the primary benefits of working with a banker. But bankers function in many different arenas. Because they sell so many products, they can offer a good counterbalance to other advisers; in some instances banks offer low-priced products too, particularly when it comes to basic term life insurance policies.

Here again there will be a difference between a relationship and a transaction banker. A relationship banker might notice an unusually large balance in your checking or savings account and call to suggest that perhaps you might be better served by putting the money elsewhere; if you approve, they may even call your accountant or financial planner with questions to integrate that cash into your money management agenda.

The result of this might be losing some of that money, as you could take tens of thousands of dollars and move it to the management of another adviser or into other products.

The transaction-oriented banker would not give you the call because they would rather have the money sit in your account—where it makes the most money for the bank.

If you are considering whether you need a relationship with a banker, here are the questions you will want to answer:

Can I do this myself?

The answer to this question is "Probably not, in terms of having the money necessary to meet all of your own financing needs, but almost certainly so in terms of feeling a need to have a working relationship with a banker."

No consumer—as opposed to business accounts—absolutely must have a banker on their financial team. Indeed, of all of the advisory positions you need to fill, banker is in many ways the least essential.

You can find someone to make loans or extend you credit and offer some counseling in a time of need, so you don't necessarily need to be working with a banker at all times.

Indeed, if you are a transaction-oriented customer, you can simply seek out the services of a lender if and when you need one. You might decide to work with a mortgage broker—someone who originates loans for other institutions—or to get car loan through the dealership, and to keep your accounts on drive-thru/by-machine/no-real-people basis.

Even if you have a relationship with a banker, you may still want to shop around with others when you are making transactions, if only because it is easy to shop rates by phone and you want to make sure you have a good deal.

But if you know that your goals and objectives are the least bit out of the ordinary, or if you simply want a financial adviser whose help is generally a no-cost add-on to a service you need anyway, then you will not want to do your banking in a vacuum.

Where do I start my search for a relationship banker?

Word-of-mouth is the best advertising for good bankers. Ask around, then try to mesh your needs with your desires.

You may need to find the lowest available mortgage rate, but want a banker who will do a lot of hand-holding throughout the buying process. That service may not come cheaply; you could be facing an interest rate that is a fraction higher.

Look at the advertisements and newspaper lists of the best available loan rates and the best account yields, then compare that to the suggestions you get from friends, relatives, and other financial intermediaries to see what banks score well on both counts.

Am I better off working with someone from a big or small bank?

Generally community bankers have the most interest in developing special relationships with ordinary customers. Their charters proscribe that they do the majority of work in the community in which they are located—as opposed to a large regional bank that has a greater area in which to meet requirements on offering services to the local community.

The other benefit to working with a small bank is that you generally will have a chance to meet the decision-makers, as opposed to working with a regional operation, where decisions on loans and more may be decided in some centralized location miles away from your branch.

That said, however, the truth is that it will be the people you work with rather than the size of the bank that counts.

Many large banks have private banking services and will assign you an individual banker if you have sufficient money tied up in your dealings with the institution. Others simply have individuals who are willing to work with people because it presents an unusual opportunity in a transaction-oriented institution.

The bottom line is that all banks provide roughly the same types of services, so remember that you are selecting a banker, not just a bank.

What credentials will I deal with, and how important are they?

For the most part the credentials of your banker will not be particularly important unless they are offering specific services that cross over into the realm of your other experts. If they offer to do financial planning or accounting—which might be included in some private banking services—you will want to qualify them the same way you would a financial planner.

How does a banker get paid?

Generally bankers offer basic services for free, as a value-added part of having an account. Of course the idea is to have you keep your money at the bank and take your loans there because that is how the bank makes its money.

That said, there may be charges for ancillary services, such as selling insurance or investments. If you cross the line from plain-vanilla banking services with clearly defined account charges into advice and salesmanship, make sure to find out whether the banker will receive any special compensation.

What should I ask during an interview?

You will be able to distinguish between transaction and relationship bankers almost immediately. If you walk in to open a new account and say that you want to take a few minutes interviewing the manager and talking about your banking needs and the bankers are not particularly eager or responsive, chances are you are not in the office of a relationship-oriented banker.

After all, if they can't be responsive to you as a customer opening a new account—or just considering opening an account or taking a loan—then when *are* they going to be responsive to you?

Because the interview is unusual for the banker, help your cause by bringing along some form of financial statement, so that you can talk to the banker about your assets, investments, cash flow, and more.

On the assumption that a banker will be interested in your business, however, you will want to ask these questions:

How long have you been at the bank?

In every advisory circumstance you want to know the breadth of experience of the person helping you. The longer your banker has been with the institution, the more they know the ins and outs of the bank's philosophy and the better chance they can finesse your unique circumstances into "the box," where the institution becomes comfortable doing business with you.

What are the basic accounts and services that are available?

You may already have this information by the time you sit down with a banker to find out what *else* he or she can do for you. But if you do not have open accounts at the institution, take a look at the menu.

From that you must cover ground germane to the opening of any account: minimum balance requirements and penalties, types of accounts offered, the ways those account works, and ancillary fees (such as the charge for talking to a live person).

Next, ask what else the bank can do for you, in terms of insurance, investments, credit cards and more—and ask after what kinds of discounts you can get if you do business with the bank in more than one area (do they give account holders a discount on insurance?).

You may not be interested in services like private banking and estate planning now, but you will be if you remain a customer of the bank for long enough.

Will I be dealing with you or someone else?

When you first walk into a bank and ask for a sit-down meeting, you likely will meet the manager on duty. When you explain that you'd like to have a personal relationship with a banker, someone you can bounce ideas off and who may get involved in helping to manage your money, make sure you find out who would become your personal banking adviser.

You may want to schedule a brief meeting with that person or have them sit in on your initial interview.

In addition many banks refer customers to other financial advisers. If a bank offers other advisory services but subcontracts the work out to others, you will want to know who those people are and complete a background check before accepting them as a member of your financial team.

Having reviewed briefly my financial statement, what kinds of suggestions would you have for me?

A big part of the reason to sit down and talk with a banker is to see what kind of creativity they bring to the table. You want someone who can offer a variety of solutions, preferably including some that you and your other financial helpers haven't thought of.

If you keep a high balance in your checking account, you would hope they might notice that and ask whether you need that money to live month-to-month or if you could put it into something that would provide a bit more yield.

If your planning is airtight, the planner won't have much to offer you. If it isn't, they should be able to come up with suggestions; after all, they want your business.

Are there any special costs or charges that I need to be aware of?

Always get a confirmation of costs, regardless of the financial adviser you are dealing with.

This is particularly true when you are doing some sort of transaction with your banker, such as a mortgage, refinancing, and more. You may not pay a specific hourly charge as you do with many other forms of advisers, but high account fees, closing costs, or points could make a financing deal less attractive than it sounds.

Does the bank stick to set formulas for determining who is eligible for a mortgage, home-equity loan, car loans, etc.?

Bankers have plenty of reasons to turn a loan down, and very few to approve them. The same can be said for most financing.

If a banker is bound and determined to stick to formulas, you are out of luck if your situation falls outside of those parameters. If you are interested in a particular type of financing, ask about the formulas that apply and whether there is anything you can do to make yourself (or the property involved in the deal) fall within the bank's guidelines.

In general, you will always want to ask the banker for suggestions on how to make yourself a better candidate for a loan and a better credit risk.

Can I get a copy of the bank's financial statements? How about bank-ratings reports?

This is public information that you could get on your own if you called the state banking commissioner and asked for a "call report." The bank shouldn't put you through the trouble; if you are going to share your finances with a banker, let him or her give you a peek at their numbers.

As for bank ratings, there are several services that rate the financial strength of banking institutions, notably Sheshunoff Ratings Services, Veri-banc, and Bauer Financial Reports. Ask about the highest possible rating for the service they show you. If the bank does not get the best rating, ask why not; it's probably nothing to worry about—unless they get very low ratings—but you'd like to be aware of potential problems in advance.

(When you ask this question, you should hear, pro forma, an explanation of bank insurance and how the protection applies to your accounts. If not, you will want to make sure you are protected—and you should remember that mutual funds sold through a bank do not have the deposit insurance of a savings account.)

You are looking for the signs of a healthy institution, particularly because troubled institutions often tighten up lending practices down the road and can make life miserable for borrowers who got in under the old rules.

How are decisions made here?

Find out who pushes the buttons, whether the person you are talking to is actually involved in, say, the loan-review process or if decisions are made in some remote office.

Obviously you tend to get the most options when you can work with the decision-makers and can be involved in the process of deciding what choices appeal to you most, instead of just being thrown into the box for one-size-fits-all options that may not fit you.

This is one advantage that smaller banks and thrifts tend to have over their regional competitors; decisions are made in the local office, by people who know the value of your business to both to their bank and to the community.

How will you work with my other advisers?

One of the key roles a banker can play on a financial team is to offer some options that might otherwise be overlooked.

A banker friend of mine recounted the story of a professional client whose accountant called. The executive had a house, some investment properties, and some good assets, but also some unsecured debt such as credit card expenses. The accountant knew that the $15,000 in unsecured debt was accruing interest at a rate of about 18 percent, or $2,700 per year.

The credit card debt is not tax deductible.

The accountant wanted to know what the banker could do, and the answer was refinance the mortgage on the home, with the unsecured debt added to the small amount that the executive owed. The result was that the unsecured debt became tax deductible and the client saved money.

That kind of work is not unusual.

If you talk to a banker about your situation and your options, they may have some ideas on ways you can save money or trim costs. If that happens, you may want the banker to talk directly to your other advisers, particularly if you need to establish any special accounts that might have specific tax or titling considerations.

What bankers in town—besides yourself—do the best job for their customers and why?

I like to ask this question to all advisers. Banking is a small community, and you will find out which qualities you banker admires in other bankers. If they do not place importance on the same things you do, it may be a sign of what you can (or can't) expect in the future.

What am I going to get from you that I can't get from every other bank in town that is clamoring for my business?

You may be a small fry today, but a smart banker will see you as a lifetime customer, someone he or she can make money off in many ways. Most banks are interchangeable, and a few are exceptional; make sure the banker convinces you that his or her institution will fall into the latter camp.

How do I check out a banker?

You've already done this, in the interview where you asked about financial ratings and discussed bank insurance. Learn how federal deposit insurance works—all of your accounts with one institution qualify for $100,000 in coverage—and exercise caution in crossing those limits, particularly if the bank-rating agencies do not give the institution its top grade.

What do I ask references?

When it comes to a banking, where so much of the business is cookie-cutter transactions, you would only want a reference in a situation where you are either doing an important transaction or you have some unusual circumstance that requires special attention.

In this case chances are good that the person who gave you a referral to a banker may suffice.

Specifically, you might want to know how accommodating and easy-to-work-with the bank is as you get ready to close on a home. Likewise, if you know that you have a debt problem and are looking for a consolidation loan, a friend with similar circumstances can probably give you all of the information you need to be able to work with the banker comfortably.

How can I build a relationship with a banker? Where does it go from the point where I open an account?

Even relationship-oriented bankers may not rush to call you all the time, but they will be happy to see your face when you stick it in their office door.

The more you stay in touch with the banker, the more you will get from the relationship.

This might mean bringing in an updated financial statement once every year or two, or stopping by with a copy of your tax return and asking for your banker's opinion of any moves you might make.

Banking is a mix of objective and subjective decisions. The more someone knows you and knows of you, the easier it its to take those subjective factors and make them work in your favor.

What are the danger signs to a relationship gone sour?

Bankers are no different than most other advisers. Signs of trouble boil down to two basic areas:

- Loss of interest. If you complete your immediate transactions and the banker is no longer interested in you, assume they were most interested in filling your pressing need. If you are trying to develop a relationship, you will want more than that.

▪ Lack of communication or incomplete disclosure. There should never be any surprises in a banking relationship. By law, most fees and costs must be explained in advance. If any banking service winds up with more out-of-pocket costs than anticipated, something is wrong.

The same applies to the returns you can expect on bank products such as certificates of deposit. In most cases rates and yields can be clearly explained; you should be able to say "Here is my money, what will it be worth at the end of X period of time?" and get a direct and concrete answer.

Another key element of communication involves explanation of how various products sold by the bank actually work. A money market account, for example, is covered by federal deposit insurance. A money market mutual fund is not. You should know the status of each investment, particularly if you have multiple products from the bank.

Last, if your banker won't give you a heads-up, they are not serving you appropriately.

Say, for example, you have a CD coming due with a finite window to withdraw the money or have it roll over. If you could do better by changing the term of the CD—because rates have jumped since the note was originally written—or if you will not get interest during the make-up-your-mind period between when the certificate comes due and when you decide to reinvest, you should be aware of that.

Likewise, if your loan has any restrictions that penalize you for early repayment, those should not be a surprise.

A banker is only a valuable member of your advisory team if they want to take part; when a banker proves to you that they only care about the next money-making transaction, you'll probably be better off limiting your contact to machines and drive-thru windows until you can find a new banker who will give you what you need.

In virtually every business and financial relationship, it never hurts to contact your local Better Business Bureau, just to make sure it has no complaints on file about the service providers you intend to work with. This is particularly true with real estate agents, insurance brokers, and others where there may not be any other easy way to check out a provider's service record.

Here are the addresses and phone numbers for most regional Better Business Bureaus across the country. They are listed alphabetically by the community they are in, and not by the name of the individual bureau, but most offer services for a county or wider area than just the city in which they are located.

If you are not sure which agency serves you—or if you are in one of the six states that is not served by a Better Business Bureau—contact the Council of Better Business Bureaus. The Council is a business-supported nonprofit organization that serves as the head-quarters for the local Better Business Bureaus. You can reach the national organization at the Council for Better Business Bureaus, 4200 Wilson Boulevard, Arlington, VA 22203. Phone 703-525-8277.

Alabama

The BBB Inc.
PO Box 55268
Birmingham, 35205
205-933-2893

BBB of North Alabama Inc.
501 Church Street NW
Huntsville, 35801
205-533-1640

BBB of South Alabama Inc.
707 Van Antwerp Building
Mobile, 36602
334-433-5494, 5495

The Better Business Bureau Inc.
Union Bank Building
Commerce Street, Suite 810
Montgomery, 36104
334-262-5606

Alaska

BBB of Alaska Inc.
3380 C Street, Suite 100
Anchorage, 99503
907-562-0704

Arizona

BBB of Maricopa County Inc.
4428 North 12th Street
Phoenix, 85014
602-264-1721

BBB of Tucson Inc.
50 West Drachman Street
Suite 103
Tucson, 85705
520-622-7651

Arkansas

BBB of Arkansas Inc.
1415 South University Ave.
Little Rock, 72204
501-664-7274

California

BBB of South Central California
Inc.
707 18th Street
Bakersfield, 93301-4882
805-332-2074

BBB of Inland Cities
PO Box 970
Colton, 92324-0522
714-825-7280

BBB of Central California Inc.
5070 North 6th, Suite 176
Fresno, 93710
209-222-8111

BBB of Monterey Inc.
494 Alvarado Street
Monterey, 93940
408-372-3149

BBB Inc.
510 16th Street
Oakland, 94612
415-839-5900

Sacramento Valley BBB
400 S Street
Sacramento, 95814
916-443-6843

BBB of San Diego Ltd.
Union Bank Building
525 B Street, Suite 301
San Diego, 92101-4408
619-234-0966

BBB of San Francisco
33 New Montgomery St. Tower
San Francisco, 94105
415-243-9999

BBB of Santa Clara Valley Ltd.
1505 Meridian Avenue
San Jose, 95125
408-978-8700

BBB of San Mateo County Inc.
PO Box 294
San Mateo, 94401
415-347-1251

BBB of Tri-Counties
Suite C
402 East Carillo Street
Santa Barbara, 93101
805-963-8657

BBB of Mid-Counties
111 North Center Street
Stockton, 95202
209-948-4880, 4881

Colorado

BBB of the Pikes Peak Region Inc.
3022 North El Paso
Colorado Springs, 80933
719-636-1155

Rocky Mountain BBB Inc.
1780 South Bellaire, Suite 700
Denver, 80222
303-758-8200

BBB of Northern Colorado Inc.
1730 South College Avenue,
Suite 303
Fort Collins, 80525
303-484-1348

BBB of Southern Colorado Inc.
432 Broadway & Grant
Pueblo, 81004
719-542-6464

Connecticut

BBB of Western Connecticut Inc.
PO Box 1410
Fairfield, 06430
203-374-6161

BBB of Northern Connecticut
Inc.
2080 Silas Deane Highway
Rocky Hill, 06067
203-529-3575

BBB of Southeast Connecticut
Inc.
100 South Turnpike Road
Wallingford, 06492
203-269-2700, 4457

Delawre

Kent Sussex BBB Inc.
PO Box 300
Milford, 19963
302-422-6300 (Kent)
302-856-6969 (Sussex)

BBB of Delaware Inc.
2055 Limestone Road, Suite 200
Wilmington, 19808
302-996-9200

District of Columbia

BBB of Metropolitan Washington
1012 14th Street, NW
14th Floor
Washington 20005
202-393-8000

Florida

BBB of West Florida Inc.
13770 58th Street, North
Suite 309
Clearwater, 33520
813-535-5522
813-957-0093 (Sarasota &
Manatee Counties)

BBB of South Florida Inc.
Lee Collier Division
3089 Cleveland Ave.
PO Box 2155
Fort Myers, 33902
813-334-7331, 7152

BBB of Northeast Florida Inc.
3100 University Boulevard South
Suite 239
Jacksonville, 32216
904-721-2288

BBB of South Florida Inc.
16291 Northwest 57th Avenue
Miami, 33014-6709
305-625-0307

BBB of Central Florida Inc.
132 East Colonial Drive
Suite 213
Orlando, 32801
305-843-8873

BBB of Northwest Florida Inc.
210 Intendencia Street
Pensacola, 32597-1511
904-433-6111

BBB of Port St. Lucie Inc.
1950 Port St. Lucie Boulevard
Suite 211

Port St. Lucie, 34952
407-878-2010

BBB of Palm Beach, Martin &
St. Lucie Counties
2247 Palm Beach Lakes
Boulevard, Suite 211
West Palm Beach, 33409-3498
407-686-2200

Georgia

BBB of Metropolitan Atlanta Inc.
100 Edgewood Avenue
Suite 1012
Atlanta, 30303
404-688-4910

BBB of Augusta Inc.
624 Ellis Street, Suite 106
Augusta, 30901

BBB of West Georgia–East
Alabama Inc.
8 13th Street
PO Box 2587
Columbus, 31902
404-324-0712, 13

BBB of the Coastal Empire Inc.
6822 Abercorn Street
PO Box 13956
Savannah, 31416-0956
912-354-7521

Hawaii

BBB of Hawaii Inc.
1600 Kapiolani Boulevard
Suite 714
Honolulu, 96814
808-531-8131

Idaho

BBB of Treasure Valley Inc.
409 West Jefferson
Boise, 83702
208-342-4649

BBB of Eastern Idaho Inc.
545 Shoup, Suite 210
Idaho Falls, 83402
208-523-9754

Illinois

BBB of Chicago & Northern
Illinois Inc.
211 West Wacker Drive
Chicago, 60601
312-444-1188

BBB of Central Illinois Inc.
109 Southwest Jefferson Street
Suite 305
Peoria, 61602
309-673-5194

Indiana

BBB of Elkhart County Inc.
722 West Bristol Street, Suite H-2
PO Box 405
Elkhart, 46515
219-203-5731

Evansville Regional BBB
119 Southeast Fourth Street
Evansville, 47708
812-422-6879

BBB of Northeastern Indiana Inc.
1203 Webster Street
Fort Wayne, 46802
219-423-4433

BBB of Northwest Indiana Inc.
4231 Cleveland Street
Gary, 46408
219-980-1511

Central Indiana BBB Inc.
Victoria Centre
22 East Washington Street
Suite 310
Indianapolis, 46204
317-637-0197

BBB of Northeastern Indiana Inc.
320 South Washington Street
Suite 101
Marion, 46952
317-668-8954, 55

Ball State University BBB
Whitinger Building
Room 150
Muncie, 47306
317-285-5668

BBB of Michiana Inc.
50985 US 33 North
South Bend, 46637
219-277-9121

Iowa

BBB/Quad Cities
Alpine Centre
2435 Kimberly Road, Suite 110-N
Bettendorf, 52722
319-355-6344

Cedar Rapids Area BBB
1500 Second Avenue, SE
Suite 212
Cedar Rapids, 52403
319-366-5401

BBB of Central & Eastern Iowa
615 Insurance Exchange Building
Des Moines, 50309
515-243-8137

BBB of Siouxland Inc.
318 Badgerow Building
Sioux City, 51101
712-252-4501

Kansas

BBB of Northeast Kansas
501 Jefferson, Suite 24
Topeka, 66607
913-232-0455

BBB Inc.
300 Kaufman Building
Wichita, 67202
316-263-3146

Kentucky

BBB of Central Kentucky
154 Patchen Drive, Suite 90
Lexington, 40502
606-268-4128

The BBB Inc.
844 South 4th Street
Louisville, 40203
502-583-6546

Louisiana

BBB of Alexandria-Pineville
1407 Murray Street, Suite 101
Alexandria, 71301

BBB of South Central LA Inc.
2055 Wooddale Boulevard
Baton Rouge, 70806
504-926-3010

BBB-Tri Parish Area
300 Bond Street
Houma, 70361
504-868-3456

BBB of Acadiana Inc.
100 Higgins Road
PO Box 30297
Lafayette, 70593
318-981-3497

BBB of Southwest Louisiana Inc.
1413-C Ryan Street
PO Box 1681
Lake Charles, 70602
318-433-1633

BBB of Northeast Louisiana Inc.
141 De Siard Street, Suite 300
Monroe, 71201
318-387-4600

BBB of Greater New Orleans Area
Inc.
1539 Jackson Avenue, Suite 400
New Orleans, 70130
504-581-6222

The BBB
1401 North Market Street
Shreveport, 71107
318-221-8352

Maine

BBB of Maine Inc.
812 Stevens Avenue
Portland, 04103
207-878-2715

Maryland

BBB of Greater Maryland Inc.
2100 Huntington Avenue
Baltimore, 21211
301-347-3990

Massachusetts

The BBB Inc.
8 Winter Street
6th Floor
Boston, 02108
617-482-9151

BBB of Metro West
One Kendall Street, Suite 307
Framingham, 01701
508-872-5585

BBB of Cape Cod & the Islands
78 North Street, Suite 1
Hyannis, 02501
508-771-3022

BBB of Merrimack Valley
316 Essex Street
Lawrence, 01840
508-687-7666

BBB of SE Massachusetts Inc.
106 State Road, Suite 4
North Dartmouth, 02747
508-999-6060

BBB of Western Massachusetts
Inc.
293 Bridge Street, Suite 324
Springfield, 01103
413-734-3114

BBB of Central New England Inc.
32 Franklin Street
PO Box 379
Worcester, 01601
508-755-2548

Michigan

BBB of Detroit & Eastern
Michigan Inc.
150 Michigan Avenue
Detroit, 48226-2646
313-962-7566

BBB of Western Michigan Inc.
620 Trust Building
Grand Rapids, 49503
616-774-8236

Minnesota

BBB of Minnesota
1745 University Avenue
St. Paul, 55104
612-646-4631

Mississippi

BBB of Mississippi/Biloxi Branch
2917 West Beach Boulevard

Suite 103
Biloxi, 39531
601-374-2222

BBB of Mississippi/Columbus
Branch
105 Fifth Street
Columbus, 39701
601-327-8594

BBB of Mississippi Inc.
510 George Street, Suite 107
PO Box 390
Jackson, 39205-0390
601-948-8222

BBB of Mississippi/Meridian
Branch
PO Box 5512
Meridian, 39302
601-482-8752

Missouri

BBB of Greater Kansas City Inc.
306 East 12th Street, Suite 1024
Kansas City, 64106
816-421-7800

BBB of Missouri & S. Illinois
5100 Oakland, Suite 200
St. Louis, 63110
314-531-3300

BBB of Southwest Missouri Inc.
205 Park Central East, Suite 509
PO Box 4331 GS
Springfield, 65806
417-862-9231

Nebraska

Cornhusker BBB Inc.
719 North 48th Street
Lincoln, 68504
402-467-5261

BBB of Omaha Inc.
1613 Farnam St., Room 417
Omaha, 68102
402-346-3033

Nevada

BBB of Southern Nevada
1022 East Sahara Avenue
Las Vegas, 89104
702-731-9877

BBB of Northern Nevada
991 Bible Way
PO Box 21269
Reno, 89515

New Hampshire

BBB of Granite State
410 Main Street
Concord, 03301
603-224-1991

New Jersey

BBB of Greater Newark Inc.
34 Park Place
Newark, 07102
201-642-INFO

BBB of Bergen, Passaic &
Rockland Counties
2 Forest Avenue

Paramus, 07652
201-845-4044

Ocean County BBB
1721 Route 37 East
Toms River, 08753
201-270-5577

BBB of Central New Jersey Inc.
1700 Whitehorse
Hamilton Square, Suite D-5
Trenton, 08690
Mercer County
609-588-0808
Monmouth County
201-536-6306
(Middlesex County
Somerset County
Hunterdon County)
201-329-6855

BBB of South Jersey Inc.
16 Maple Avenue
PO Box 303
Westmont, 08108-0303
609-884-8467

New Mexico

BBB of New Mexico Inc.
4600-A Montgomery, NE
Suite 200
Albuquerque 87109

BBB/Four Corners Inc.
308 North Locke
Farmington, 87401
505-326-6501

BBB of Santa Fe
1210 Luisa Street, Suite 5

Santa Fe, 87502
505-988-3648

New York

BBB of Western New York Inc.
775 Main Street, Suite 401
Buffalo, 14203
716-856-7180

Long Island BBB
266 Main Street
Farmingdale, 11735
516-420-0500

BBB of Metropolitan New York
Inc.
257 Park Avenue South
New York, 10010
212-533-6200

BBB of Rochester, Inc.
1122 Sibley Tower
Rochester, 14604
716-546-6776

BBB Inc. Serving Central NY, the
North country, & the Southern
Tier
100 University Building
Syracuse, 13202
315-479-6635

BBB of Westchester, Putnam and
Duchess Counties
30 Glenn Street
White Plains, 10603
914-428-1230, 31

120 East Main Street
Wappingers Falls, 12590
914-297-6550

North Carolina

The BBB of Asheville/Western
North Carolina Inc.
801 BBB & T Building
Asheville 28801
704-253-2392

The BBB of the Southern
Piedmont Inc.
1130 East Third Street, Suite 400
Charlotte, 28204
704-332-7151

BBB of Central North Carolina
Inc.
3608 West Friendly Avenue
Greensboro, 27410
919-852-4240, 41, 42

BBB of Catawba County
PO Box 1882
Hickory, 28603
704-464-0372

BBB of Eastern North Carolina
Inc.
3120 Poplarwood Drive
Suite G-1
Raleigh, 27604
919-872-9240

The BBB Inc.
2110 Cloverdale Avenue
Suite 2-B
Winston-Salem, 27103
919-725-8348

Ohio

BBB of Akron Inc.
137 South Main Street, Suite 200

PO Box 596
Akron, 44308
216-253-4590

BBB of Stark County Inc.
1434 Cleveland Avenue, NW
Canton, 44703
216-454-9401

Cincinnati BBB Inc.
898 Walnut Street
Cincinnati, 45202
513-421-3015

The BBB Inc.
BBB of Central Ohio Inc.
527 South High Street
Columbus, 43215
614-221-6336

BBB of Dayton/Miami Valley Inc.
40 West Fourth Street, Suite 280
Dayton, 45402
513-222-5825

Mansfield Area BBB
130 West 2nd Street
PO Box 1706
Mansfield, 44901
419-522-1700

BBB Serving NW Ohio & SE
Michigan Inc.
425 Jefferson Avenue, Suite 909
Toledo, 43604-1055
419-241-6276

Wooster Area BBB
345 North Market
Wooster, 44691
216-263-6444

BBB of Mahoning Valley Inc.
311 Mahoning Bank Building
PO Box 1495
Youngstown, 44501
216-744-3111

Oklahoma

BBB of Central Oklahoma
17 South Dewey
Oklahoma City, 73102
405-239-6084

BBB of Tulsa
6711 South Yale, Suite 230
Tulsa, 74136
918-664-1266

Oregon

Portland BBB
610 Southwest Alder Street
Suite 615
Portland, 97205
503-226-3981

Pennsylvania

Lehigh Valley BBB of Eastern
Pennsylvania
528 North New Street
Bethlehem, 18018
610-866-8780

Capital Division of BBB of
Eastern Pennsylvania
53 North Duke Street
Lancaster, 17602
717-291-1151

BBB of Eastern Pennsylvannia
1930 Chestnut Street
PO Box 2297
Philadelphia, 19103
610-496-1000

BBB of Western Pennsylvania
Inc.
610 Smithfield Street
Pittsburgh, 15222
412-456-2700

BBB of Northeastern
Pennsylvania Inc.
601 Connell Building
6th Floor
PO Box 993
Scranton, 18501
717-342-9129

Puerto Rico

BBB of Puerto Rico
PO Box 70212
San Juan, 00936
809-756-5400

Rhode Island

BBB of Rhode Island
100 Bignall Street
Bureau Park, Box 1300
Warwick, 02887-1300

South Carolina

BBB of the Midlands
1830 Bull Street
Columbia, 29201
803-254-2525

BBB of the Foothills
311 Pettigru Street
Greenville, 29601
803-242-5052

BBB of Coastal Carolina Inc.
PO Box 8603
Myrtle Beach, 29578
803-448-6100

Tennessee

BBB Inc.
Park Plaza Building
1010 Market Street, Suite 200
Chattanooga, 37402
615-266-6144

BBB of Greater East Tennessee
Inc.
900 East Hill Avenue, Suite 165
PO Box 10327
Knoxville, 37939-0327
615-522-2552

Memphis Area BBB Inc.
1835 Union, Suite 312
PO Box 41406
Memphis, 38174-1406
901-272-9641

BBB of Nashville/Middle
Tennessee Inc.
506 Nashville City Bank Building
Nashville, 37201
615-254-5872

Texas

BBB of Abilene Inc.
3300 South 14th Street, Suite 307

PO Box 3275
Abilene, 79605
915-691-1533

BBB of the Golden Spread
6900 I-40 West, Suite 275
Amarillo, 79106
806-358-6222

The BBB Inc.
1005 MBank Plaza
Austin, 78701
512-476-6943

BBB of Southeast Texas Inc.
476 Oakland Ave.
PO Box 2988
Beaumont, 77704
409-835-5348

BBB of Brazos Valley Inc.
202 Varisco Building
Bryan, 77803
409-823-8148, 49

BBB of the Coastal Bend Inc.
4535 South Padre Island Drive
Corpus Christi, 78411
512-854-2896

BBB of Metro Dallas Inc.
2001 Bryan Street, Suite 850
Dallas, 75201
214-220-2000

BBB of Paso Del Norte Inc.
Better Business Building
1910 East Yandell
El Paso, 79903
915-545-1212

BBB at Fort Worth Serving
Tarrant, Johnson, Hood, Wise,
Parker & Palo Pinto Counties Inc.
709 Sinclair Building
106 West 5th Street
Fort Worth, 76102
817-332-7585

BBB of Metropolitan Houston
Inc.
2707 North Loop West, Suite 900
Houston, 77008
713-868-9500

BBB of the South Plains Inc.
1015 15th Street
PO Box 1178
Lubbock, 79408
806-763-0459

BBB of the Permian Basin Inc.
Airport Road 20
PO Box 6006
Midland, 79711
915-563-1880

BBB of San Angelo Inc.
1207 South Bryant
PO Box 3366
San Angelo, 76902-3366
915-653-2318

The Better Business Bureau
1800 Northeast Loop 410
Suite 400
San Antonio, 78217
512-828-9441

BBB of Central East Texas Inc.
3502-D South Broadway
PO Box 6652

Tyler, 75711-6652
214-581-5704

BBB of Waco Inc.
6801 Sanger Avenue, Suite 125
PO Box 7203
Waco, 76714-7203
817-772-7530

BBB of South Texas Inc.
PO Box 69
Weslaco, 78596-0069
512-968-3678

BBB of North Central Texas Inc.
1106 Brook Street
Wichita Falls, 76301-5009
817-487-4656

Utah

The BBB Inc.
385 24th Street, Suite 717
Ogden, 84401
801-399-4701

BBB of Utah
1588 South Main Street
Salt Lake City, 84115
801-487-4656

Virginia

BBB of Greater Hampton Roads
Inc.
3608 Tidewater Drive
Norfolk, 23509
804-627-5651

BBB of Central Virginia Inc.
701 East Franklin, Suite 712

Richmond, 23219
804-648-0016

BBB of Western Virginia Inc.
121 West Campbell Avenue
Roanoke, 24011-1290
703-342-3455

Washington

Tri-City BBB Inc.
127 West Canal Drive
Kennewick, 99336
509-582-0222

BBB of Greater Seattle Inc.
2200 Sixth Avenue
Seattle, 98121
206-448-8888

BBB of the Inland Northwest
South 176 Stevens
Spokane, 99204
509-747-1155

The BBB Inc.
1101 Fawcett Avenue, #222
PO Box 1274
Tacoma, 98401
206-383-5561

BBB of Central Washington Inc.
418 Washington Mutual Building
PO Box 1584
Yakima, 98907
509-248-1326

Wisconsin

BBB of Greater Milwaukee
740 North Plankinton Avenue
Milwaukee, 53203
414-273-1600

25 *How to get a group of individuals to function as one unit*

Donald Trump practices the art of the deal with a cadre of support people in tow.

Warren Buffett, considered by many to be the greatest investor of all time, has a financial team that includes Charles Munger, one of the nation's most astute business observers in his own right. His former stockbroker, Bill Ruane, runs the hugely successful Sequoia Fund, one of the most successful mutual funds in history.

In fact virtually every famous financier and member of the money elite has a financial team.

Their dealings of course are far from the average person trying hard to figure out which mortgage is best or whether to purchase an individual stock or mutual fund with the annual Christmas bonus.

Still they are cut from the same cloth—people seeking counsel in order to make the best decision.

Why not the rest of us? We need a financial team as much or more as the people who are on the *Forbes* magazine's list of the richest people in the world, if only because we can less afford to make money mistakes.

If you expect to hire a multitude of experts to meet needs at various times in your life, then it makes sense to build and manage a team of experts, coordinating your efforts and getting a cohesive strategy instead of piecing together a patchwork of different ideas and philosophies.

And let's face it, the vast majority of people—no matter how determined they are to manage their own affairs—will need to work with bankers, lawyers, investment consultants (brokers, financial planners, and assorted others), accountants or tax preparers, insurance providers, and real estate agents. The advisers will help to manage your money, secure or work out loan agreements, buy real estate, insure the whole kit and caboodle, and pay taxes on whatever can't be sheltered.

With the team approach, you cover all of the angles in each of those transactions, making sure that you not only think of the investment possibilities of what to do with, say, an inheritance, but also the tax liabilities. You look not only at the legal ramifications of setting up a trust but the financial options for managing the money within it.

As your lifestyle, finances, and goals change, you have a team that knows you and can make sure that your moves fit in with an overall strategy, rather than merely buying products that may solve your current needs but not maximize your long-term earnings or savings potential.

And by developing a network, you should get superior counsel and expertise from advisers who will come to know you as more than just another file number.

The team-building process does not change the way you hire each of your specialists but rather the way in which you work with them. Even there the modification is minor; you interact with these people individually but also schedule the occasional brainstorming session so that they can meet and work with your other helpers.

Essentially you hire each specialist normally—as laid out in the book—and then orchestrate a meeting of the minds on crucial matters. The only additional burden the team approach puts on your advisers is that each must be able to work well with the others. Anyone who, for the benefit of a client, is not willing to check their ego at the door, probably does not deserve a spot on your financial team.

After all, even if your players are top experts in their field, your lifetime needs are likely to encompass their knowledge and beyond.

Take a case that I once heard from a leading financial planner, who was brought in to consult with an insurance agent and estate-planning attorney.

The client had been lucky enough to amass a lot of money and wanted to donate a substantial amount of money to charity.

The attorney suggested a "charitable-remainder trust," an instrument designed to let the client (and his spouse, upon his death) make a donation yet retain a flow of income from the money. When both spouses died, the money set aside for the trust would then go to charity.

To fund the trust, the client was told to transfer some of his stock portfolio. While most of the stocks had capital gains—he had been lucky enough to pick long-term winners—a few issues had losses, amounting to about $20,000.

The client was just about to complete the move when he brought in the planner for a second opinion. The planner recognized that putting the stocks with losses directly into the trust would mean missing out on a tax deduction. Instead of simply moving the assets, the client sold them, realizing the losses—which he could then use to offset other winnings for tax purposes—and then putting the proceeds of the stock sale into the trust. (He correctly chose not to sell the stocks with the gains, however, because that would have triggered a tax bill.)

Complicated? Yes.

Ordinary? Absolutely.

Every day, there are financial situations that cross disciplines, that flow from insurance to investment management to law to taxation.

Let's look at a more common situation, one that doesn't require some huge estate for tax-planning purposes.

Say, for example, you have a bank certificate of deposit coming due. Your banker, doing his job as your adviser, contacts you before the rollover date. In reviewing your options for the money, the banker suggests you do something more aggressive with the money and shows you several attractive options, running from safe tax-free mutual funds to more aggressive stock funds.

By itself, the advice sounds good because you are juicing up the returns of a slow-moving asset.

There are countless people who take advice like this without consulting any other experts, including those they already have hired. Literally hundreds of financial advisers have related cases of how well-meaning friends, relatives, and advisers messed up the best-laid of financial foundations.

Armed with the banker's advice, however, the right thing to do might be to consult with your broker, accountant, or financial planner. A quick phone call might reveal that moving the certificate-of-deposit money into mutual funds lowers a cash cushion that was built into your planning for liquidity purposes, or that a move into a tax-free fund is not needed given your tax circumstances.

The banker in this case isn't overstepping his role by making the suggestion. It is his or her role to advise you on how you might improve returns. Ideally, however, the banker would know that you pursue a team approach, would see the certificate of deposit coming due, and would notify you—and possibly arrange to talk with your other team members.

If that sounds like a Pollyanna situation—that such consultations and basic advice simply never happens in the real world—it should. It almost never does happen, not because advisers are unwilling to work as a team but because investors don't ask them to.

"Some people get partial planning from a lot of people," explains Ross Levin of Accredited Investors in Minneapolis, a former president of the International Association of Financial Planners. "They do a little bit of everything that sounds good, and wind up with a hodgepodge, a collection of investment advice instead of a plan.

"They may just take sales advice from a few different people, without ever getting a second opinion. Or it might be that they have jumped around from adviser to adviser, keeping from each whatever sounded good or performed well, but never keeping their plans—financial, tax and estate—up-to-date. Or maybe they aren't happy with the way their investments are going, so when an insurance agent or banker offers investment advice, they take it and it goes against what they had set up with their financial planner. Then, to fix it, they wind up paying taxes or penalties or they give up interest (income)."

Over a lifetime of dealing with financial affairs, you will undoubtedly find advisers who claim to be able to do more than one job—you will find out in the next chapter how to decide whether to take that bait—or who say they (or their firm) can offer one-stop shopping.

They may indeed be able to deliver, but having multiple team members allows you to view each situation from different perspectives, get second opinions, bring in additional specialists when unique needs arise, and get the most from your advisory relationships.

Best of all, good advisers like working in a team approach because they know that the process stimulates discussions that will help not only you but their other clients.

"Every adviser you hire has their own level of expertise," explains Ginger Applegarth of Applegarth Advisory Services in Winchester, MA. "When they work together, they raise that collective level. Everyone becomes more aware of what you want, and the different advisers all want to make sure that you get the best help and pro-

tection, so they will raise questions and try to make sure that everything gets taken care of to your best advantage.

"Good advisers want to learn from each other; they don't just want
you to do better, they want to take the practice knowledge they gain
from your case and apply it, if it is applicable, to their other clients."

At a bare minimum, your financial team should consist of an
investment adviser, an accountant or tax preparer, an insurance
adviser, and an estate-planning lawyer.

A banker may also have a role on the team, depending on whether
they provide real personal services, as opposed to being merely a
conduit to the institution. A real estate agent probably will not work
with you financial team on a regular basis, unless you are managing
multiple properties or are making estate plans that involve your
home.

Stockbrokers are a question mark for your financial team. If they
are securities salespeople working strictly on commission, their interests may not be in sync with the rest of the team (they will obviously
want to see as much money as possible diverted toward your stock
portfolio and will have little concern for the rest). If they function as
an investment adviser or money manager, however, or if they need
to be aware of specific long-term strategies that could affect the suitability of their investment decisions, you might want to include
them in the process.

(It is worth noting that insurance agents also get paid on commission and could have the same conflicts as a broker. Still you will
want them to have a role in the team, particularly as you move
toward estate-planning and asset-protection strategies.)

And if you are among those people who still believe that a financial team is only for the Donald Trumps in this world, consider the
cost of maintaining those advisers each year. A financial planner, for
example, might charge 1 percent of the assets they manage, while an
accountant could charge up to $200 per hour (it could be signifi-
cantly less than that, depending largely on where you live and the
supply-and-demand factors at work there), an insurance adviser (either
straight commission or $100 to $200 an hour if you are dealing with
a fee-only adviser), and a lawyer (fees vary widely).

In general, you will spend more on an adviser when you first hire
them than in subsequent years. But, as you get your team rolling and
up to speed—and depending on your assets—an annual outlay of
$1,500 to $3,000 per year should allow you to run your finances with
a team of advisers.

That's probably more than you would like, but less than you would expect, especially when the team approach can provide more comprehensive money management and can make sure that you maximize the dollars spent on each adviser.

As you hire advisers, here are some things to consider that will allow you to manage them as a team and maximize their potential not only in an individual specialty but as a safety net to make sure that you are always moving in the most efficient path toward your goals.

Make sure each adviser is aware of the others

Throughout the hiring process and as you grow into a relationship, you will want each of your advisers to know about the others. For the most part, that is going to be easy because you may involve your advisers in the selection process.

Say that the first adviser you hire is a lawyer. That relationship is developing when you decide it is time to hire someone to do your taxes. One logical person to contact for a referral is the lawyer, who automatically knows that you are planning a change in your financial situation.

Once you have the referral, make sure that the lawyer knows that you may, at some point, want a group consultation.

If an adviser is uncomfortable with the idea of working with a particular person you have hired to advise you, find out why. Perhaps they simply prefer the person to whom they make referrals; this should not sway your decision because, as you learned in chapter 5, there are a lot of reasons (including kickbacks and other professional perks) why people make referrals. But if an adviser has had past problems dealing with a prospective new team member or if something they have heard makes them reticent to deal with a new adviser, that should raise a red flag over your selection.

If advisers know they will be working in a team, they will want that team to be the best one possible, the one where they get along the best and have the most expertise at the table.

Each adviser will know a few players in another specialty; you may be introducing them to someone new or simply providing them with a chance to catch up with old friends, but the one thing you can be sure of is that any adviser who knows they will be part of a team is going to want to make sure that all of your other financial helpers know what they are doing.

Define each adviser's role; make sure all advisers' are fully aware of your wishes

Some advisers are true specialists. You may get a lawyer, for example, who writes wills but who doesn't handle insurance and charitable trusts (often key areas for having a team).

Other advisers are generalists, crossing divergent lines because that is where their own interests—or those of their clients—have led them.

No matter which type of adviser you hire, you will want each one to know exactly what they were hired for. You do not want the insurance adviser second-guessing the financial planner, and visa versa. You want them working in concert.

That means that each should not cross the lines and recommend or sell you another financial product or service without consulting the others. Let's go back to that banker example I used earlier, the one who advised you on how to handle a CD that was maturing, and assume the banker knows you have a financial team in place.

If the banker starts pushing other products without consulting the rest of the team—or if they encourage you to make your decision before you can contact your other advisers—then they obviously have their own interests at heart. It's not just that they are not a good team player, it's that they probably aren't a good adviser.

If, however, the banker encourages you to contact the others and informs you of the products he would recommend at the bank, you can consider those products if and when the other advisers concur with the banker that moving the money to a faster horse is a good idea, in keeping with the rest of your plan.

Throughout the hiring process, you worked to determine what an adviser can and should do for you. Make sure that each one understands that role, particularly as you plan to have the whole team confer occasionally and would not want one of your helpers to discover at that time that they play a more limited role in your financial life than you had led them to believe.

Hire a quarterback

One adviser is going to have to become the captain of your team, the person who coordinates the overall efforts of everyone to make sure that you are going in the right direction.

While the next chapter warns about picking double agents, many people agree that the best kind of leader for an advisory team is either a financial planner who also is expert in taxes or an accountant who has a financial planning credential.

Of all the specialties, financial planning and accounting are the two that have their hands in virtually every aspect of your financial lives, the planner because their job is to coordinate your finances and help you reach a lifetime's worth of goals, the accountant because taxes are inevitable in every phase of your financial life.

The job of your quarterback or captain is to make sure that all planning is properly constructed and implemented. If you are saving to pay for a college education, for example, they would want to make sure that your plans maximize not only your savings but potentially keep you eligible for any grant or assistance programs out there; if you are engaged in estate planning, they would want to make sure that your assets are re-titled so that the plan can be carried out or, as mentioned earlier in this chapter, that the execution of your plan maximizes your potential tax savings.

This is the person who will make sure everything is in order, that the efforts of your advisers are coordinated, and that nothing has been overlooked. Of all members of your financial team, this is the one you will meet with most often, perhaps once every quarter or six months compared to an annual checkup with the rest of your counselors.

Ideally your quarterback will be well-connected in the local community, so that they know many people in the other advisory roles; not only will this make them more likely to know the helpers you have chosen, but it will allow them to get qualified second opinions if they feel the need to consult with someone outside your team. Despite all of your efforts to hire the best advisers, this kind of outside consultation may still be necessary; you can't expect anyone— even your team quarterback—to be an expert in every aspect of managing your affairs.

Have occasional group meetings

About once every year, you should get together with your team to review your progress toward your financial goals, discuss any changes in lifestyle or major events that occurred since the last meeting, and make sure everything is up to date.

The team approach may actually save you time in this manner; if not for this one meeting, you would be calling or meeting the other advisers every time there is a significant change in your life.

If a group meeting is not practical, consider meeting with each expert individually, with your team captain in tow.

A group meeting allows you to go over your finances specialty by specialty, and lets each adviser hear why moves were made, what goals you have for each specialist, and allows them to ask questions and review each others work. Effectively you will get second opinions and questions and double-checks by having the advisers interact because each one of your players will want to know what the other is doing. They also will want to make sure they are giving you the best advice going forward such that, for example, the banker will want to know what is going on so that they don't tell you the wrong thing to do the next time a CD comes due.

Never let advisers argue in front of you

Whether you bring the advisers together for a face-to-face meeting or have them take part in a conference call, don't let them battle in front of you.

For starters, this kind of argument smacks of unprofessionalism. It is usually a play for a bigger role on the team, but it is almost guaranteed to have bad outcomes, not the least of which is that it undermines your confidence in the team members. If they are second-guessing each other, you may start to get nervous about your decisions; in that case both advisers are diminished.

"There are major wars going on in the financial planning industry—CPAs and attorneys versus financial advisers, people with one credential versus people with another," says Dick Wagner, a past president of the Institute of Certified Financial Planners and a principal in the Denver advisory firm of Sharkey, Howes, Wagner and Javer. "That should never spill over into how someone deals with a client. Unless the client has picked a real idiot to do his taxes, everyone should defer to the [accountant] on tax issues, or the financial planner on investment issues.

"If there is conflict, it should happen away from the client—and the client should want it that way, so that the advisers work issues out privately and make combined recommendations, rather than everyone dancing around in the open trying to steal away a little bit of business."

Advisers should ask questions of each other in your presence, but it should never deteriorate from informational material into something where one counselor is questioning the competency of another.

If your advisers don't agree, ask them to sit down with you individually. You can then hear both sides and be the arbiter but never let one adviser badmouth another member of your team. Those nasty little arguments build the kind of tension that can quickly sabotage the process and make all of your financial helpers feel uncomfortable. In addition you will want to make your decision without the in-front-of-you bickering because such arguments could give an adviser an idea of what they must do—present forceful arguments and undercut the other experts—to become the most powerful player on the team.

Maintain control

Just because you have multiple advisers working together to meet your interests does not let you off the hook. You still have the ultimate decision-making responsibility.

When you have the team together as a group, ask contrarian questions—"What could go wrong? What IS the worst that could happen?"—so that everyone is sure to examine the downside and to protect you from it.

Most teams not only have a captain, they have a manager. That is your job.

Consider having an outsider review team performance every two or three years

As hard as this may be to believe, even a team approach is no guarantee that you will reach your goals. "Groupthink," where everyone gets on the same page and overlooks key concerns, is a real possibility, no matter how much you guard against it.

Unless you are comfortable doing this yourself in your role as manager of the team, you may want to get an independent audit of your performance. If that's the case, every few years you will want to engage an accountant or financial planner—another quarterback type—to review what your experts have done and to make sure it is comprehensive, performing to expectations and serving your needs.

You also may want outsiders to review the work of team members on an as-needed basis, such as when trusts are drawn up. (You should never sign a trust agreement without a second opinion from a lawyer working at a different firm than the one who drew up the papers.)

This kind of review won't come cheap, so make sure you see the potential benefits and don't do it so regularly that it becomes redundant, layering a new cost on top of what you already pay your hired guns.

If an independent audit turns up problem areas—bases left uncovered or holes in your financial security blanket—you may want to reconvene the team to address those issues, or you may want to make a few trades and kick the underperformers off your squad.

Remember, none of this team stuff is inherently different from what you would do if you managed each adviser individually. This whole book, after all, has been about managing your managers.

But, in the long run, paying that little bit extra for your advisers to function as a unit, probably will come back to you in the form of enhanced returns and security. That may not represent the "art of the deal" to Donald Trump, but it should sound pretty good to the rest of us.

26 *Utility infielders; can one adviser handle two jobs?*

Financial advisers of all stripes like to compare their work to that of doctors.

They are, after all, specialists helping to solve and cure a patient's financial ills.

In the medical field, however, failure to refer a patient to a necessary specialist actually can be considered malpractice.

In financial services, failure to refer to a specialist is common practice. It is fairly common for a generalist—in financial planning, banking, accounting, or law in particular—to stray into areas that are not their bread-and-butter because that is what the service calls for.

Your banker, for example, may be able to sell you investments, insurance, and offer trust services, areas that might otherwise be reserved for a financial planner, insurance agent, or lawyer. Some lawyers offer accounting and tax services, others do financial planning beyond establishing trusts and preserving assets. Some accountants, meanwhile, do financial planning and may offer an ability to establish trusts and handle legal documents. Brokers can offer a lot of bank-lookalike services and, along with insurance agents, financial planning.

And financial planners can offer practically anything.

There is a good chance over the course of your financial relationships that one or more of your advisers will want to cross the boundaries of their traditional role, hoping to sell you another product or to capture more of your assets under management.

There is nothing particularly nefarious about this. Presumably, they feel they have the necessary expertise, and understand your situation because of their primary role as one of your financial helpers.

Essentially, they are offering one-stop shopping, a convenience that most people desire.

That's where the problem arises.

Just because someone is a good accountant does not make them an outstanding financial planner, and visa versa. Even advanced credentials are no guarantee; the fact that a counselor studied for a certificate in another specialty does not make them good at that secondary job, especially if it is no more than a sideline business.

With that in mind, you will have a choice to make if your adviser volunteers to take one an expanded role as your needs grow.

"Unlike medicine, financial planning is too young to have rules about what makes for good practice," says Robert N. Veres, publisher of *Inside Information*, a trade newsletter about the financial planning industry. "You see people trying to wear a lot of different hats, and it is not always the best thing. It takes a lot to be good at any one specialty, let alone trying to practice in two distinct areas. I think it may be asking too much of someone to have them be your expert in two specialties."

In many financial fields, the best practitioners stick to their knitting and bring in others, or make referrals, when necessary. If one adviser has the most prominent role, that person may act as a team leader, quarterbacking your work with a number of advisers.

Indeed the team approach discussed in the last chapter is another reason to be careful before letting one adviser expand into two roles. Because of the natural overlap of each advisory position, there will always be an easy opportunity to get a second opinion, or a chance to run one adviser's work past another.

Before dismissing the idea of letting one adviser serve dual roles, however, let's examine the benefits.

The most notable one is convenience, the idea of one-stop shopping. The second big benefit is that you already know the adviser (and the adviser knows you); if you have picked that counselor carefully, you can avoid the legwork of choosing a new player for your team.

Convenience is a big issue. Remember that most people want a relationship with a financial adviser to have three qualities—cheap, easy, and successful—and it certainly is easy to let one adviser take on an expanded role. In our busy lives, having an adviser play dual roles allows you to keep tabs on two parts of your financial life with one phone call.

And, presumably, the first relationship has been successful or you wouldn't want to enter the second, so it's easy to project good things upon the adviser who does a good job for you and wants to take on more.

The second issue, the pre-existing knowledge of you as a client reducing the legwork also is true, to a point.

If you do not perform your due diligence and make sure the adviser is capable of handling your needs in a second arena, you will be unhappy with the results.

You do not need to go through a full-blown interview again, but you do want to make sure that your adviser is as qualified in their second field as they are in the first. And you probably want to interview at least one person who specializes in the second field, so that you can weigh the potential difference in service from someone whose primary business is, say, insurance and someone who sells insurance as a sideline.

A good adviser should want you to ask those questions, rather than be offended by your questioning their expertise. Having worked with you—particularly if you put them through the rigorous questioning advocated in this book—they should understand that you are cautious in your approach to advisers and that you want the best possible representation.

If they, instead, question your loyalty or make you feel guilty, then you need to re-think the entire relationship. Each of your financial advisers, no matter their position, should give your best interests their highest priority.

It will always be in your best interest to make sure you have the highest-quality representation.

There is something of a parallel between financial advice and baseball in this instance. In baseball, a utility infielder is someone who can play more than one position; the reason that they get this opportunity is often, but not always, because they aren't good enough to start at any one position.

If you have an adviser who wants to play two positions, you need to be sure they can "start" at both spots on your team.

To do that, you will want to have an initial interview covering the new territory. You can dispense with the questions that define the relationship, in that you already know the adviser's manner. You should not avoid asking the what-are-your-qualifications questions— as laid out in the chapter 8—plus any other applicable questions that cover the new ground that you and the adviser are considering exploring together.

In addition to those queries, and regardless of the advisory position involved, you should add the following:

Do you do the (fill-in-the-blank) work yourself?

There are a lot of full-service financial firms that can take you from cradle to grave, offering planning, accounting, brokerage, insurance, and legal services all under one roof.

Advisers in these firms may have more than one specialty, or may farm the work out to someone else.

There is nothing wrong with your broker or money manager relying on the insurance expert to do the needs analysis and process your information before making recommendations. You simply want to know up front whether your adviser is handling the work or passing it to a partner, and who will be dealing with you.

If there is another partner involved, you will probably want to do a background check to make sure they are qualified for the tasks at hand.

(You may also want to ask your adviser if they get some sort of bonus for bringing the extra business to the firm; if they do—and you agree to sign on—tell them that you want some of that bonus back as a price discount. If they get this type of referral fee, however, you might also question whether their advice to do more business through them and with the firm is really in your best interest.)

What percentage of your clients work with you in both of your specialties?

One of the basic tenets of for any counseling situation is that you want the adviser to be particularly comfortable working with people in your situation. If an adviser has a dual role with the majority of his or her clients, that makes not only for ready references but tells you that they can function efficiently in both roles.

If, on the other hand, only one in ten clients actually uses this person as a dual adviser, the new specialty is nothing more than a sideline business. At that point you need to question whether the adviser has the expertise of someone who makes the new specialty their primary business.

For example, say your accountant sells financial planning services but only to one client in ten. It is reasonable to wonder whether they will have the kind of knowledge, expertise, and interest offered by their competition, namely a planner who spends all day, every day helping people manage money.

If your needs are minimal, you might feel very comfortable with your accountant and hire them for financial planning help. If, however, you have a major money management job, the more expert planner might be your choice.

What percentage of your time do you spend dedicated to the new specialty—and to continuing education in this field—compared to the role in which you are currently my adviser?

Again you are qualifying the adviser's expertise. You don't want to be a guinea pig.

If the adviser is trying to build a dual clientele and the time spent on this side of the business is growing, that should raise your comfort level; conversely, you might not feel particularly comfortable with a financial planner who is dabbling in estate planning.

Remember, too, that your adviser will probably not cut you a price discount for this work, which means you will be paying as much for a part-time worker in a particular specialty as you could be paying for a full-time expert.

That brings us to the next question:

How do you get paid in the new advisory role?

This is absolutely critical because not every financial specialty pays the same way.

There are, for example, financial planners who use the "fee-only" label as part of their allure. But their work on a flat-fee basis may only apply to planning; if you purchase insurance from them, you could be paying commissions.

Check to make sure there are no pricing surprises.

Why do you want to have me as a client on this side of your business?

In chapter 6 which advises against hiring friends to be your financial helpers, this question is one of the key things to ask if you are going to do business with someone you have a personal relationship with.

The adviser who wants to take on two roles on your financial team should understand that they are jeopardizing their primary relationship. If something goes wrong, they will lose you as a client altogether.

That being the case, try to find out their motive in seeking you out. Are you simply an easy mark, a way to expand and generate some extra business, or do they believe your financial relationship has evolved to the point where you need additional help, notably assistance that they are qualified to provide?

If they do not have a good reason for wanting to expand the current relationship—beyond the mere paycheck you can provide—then consider who benefits the most from turning one adviser into a double agent.

Why should I come to you instead of someone who is specifically dedicated to my new field of interest?

Normally you interview a few people for each spot on your financial team; those interviews give each counselor the chance to impress you and convince you that they are the best qualified, most compatible person to work with.

Make an adviser convince you of their expertise and sincerity before handing them two roles on your advisory team. If they don't have compelling reasons to make you want to do business—that is, they have the same expert credentials as full-time practitioners in a field and they are familiar with your finances already—then chances are you will be better off sticking to the one-field, one-expert line of thinking.

Remember, it may be common practice for an adviser to wear two hats, but it may also border on malpractice if they can't do each job equally well.

27 *Breaking up is hard to do*

In one episode of the television sitcom *Caroline in the City*, the lead character complains that she is just no good at ending relationships.

She couldn't bring herself to change dry cleaners—no matter the quality of his work—until after he died. And at that, she gave the eulogy at his funeral.

Rather than tell her hairdresser she was seeking a new look from someone else, she explained that she was moving to Norway. He bought it, until bumping into her at a party (when she hastily agreed to go rushing back to him).

Of course Caroline is a fictitious character.

The main difference between a character like her and real people like us is that we could never pull that Norway thing off in the first place.

Ending relationships is never easy. The mere thought smacks of confrontation, hardship, betrayal, and a whole range of emotions that most of us would rather avoid.

Still, when a member of your financial team is not doing their job and meeting your expectations, you must take stern tones with them, express what you want and be prepared to dismiss them if the business side of the relationship does not improve.

When it comes to managing your affairs, remember one basic rule: Business is business. No matter your personal feelings for someone, they don't belong on the team if they can't do the job to your satisfaction.

Even if you don't hire a friend or relative—and chapter 6 explained why you probably don't want to do that—this is never easy. Chances are you will become friendly with your advisers as the relationship

grows. Assuming they can deliver on the business side of the relationship, that's a good thing. If they can't deliver in business, however, the budding friendship becomes a problem; most people would
be doubly reluctant to give a friend the boot.

Worse yet, you might not be as lucky with, say, a poor financial
planner as Caroline was with that dry cleaner. Your adviser could
have a long, healthy life ahead.

Typically people want to end financial relationships because their
expectations are not being met. If the real estate agent doesn't sell
the house, for example, you might decide not to renew the listing—
an easy dismissal to make because the contract to sell the house
is finite, as opposed to the unwritten, I-use-the-same-person-forever
mentality that comes attached to many banking, accounting, legal,
and investment relationships.

In chapter 10 on keeping control of your players, the mantra you
were supposed to repeat was "I'm the boss." Nowhere is that more
applicable than when you are thinking of getting rid of a player on
your team.

You might recall the story of Jim, the poor clod who lost the
investing contest and most of his clients. Until the investment contest ran in the newspaper, his clients had ceded control over their
investments to him; they were following blindly because he was
supposed to be the best broker in town. When his contest performance struck a familiar chord with his own clients, they re-took
control and re-shaped the relationship, either cutting Jim loose or
limiting his work and meeting with him to re-establish expectations
(which presumably did not include a 40 percent loss in an up year
for the stock market).

Obviously you will want to jettison your adviser in cases where you
suspect fraud, wrongdoing, or any sort of problem. In those cases you
should not only dismiss the adviser but file complaints and pursue
legal remedies to get your money back.

But short of those extreme cases, there are plenty of situations
where an advisory relationship just doesn't work out, where you feel
let down by the goods and services offered and believe you would be
better off working with someone else.

If a relationship sours for any reason and you think the best course
of action may be to dismiss your adviser, the firing process is simple
and straightforward:

Step 1: At the first sign of trouble—when service does not jibe with your expectations—tell the adviser your concerns

If the adviser pooh-poohs your concerns, explain that it's your money that is involved. For that money, you deserve, at the very least, an explanation as to why your expectations are not being met. If no explanation is forthcoming, you know that the adviser isn't taking you seriously.

If that's the case, skip step 2 and go directly to step 3.

Step 2: Redefine the relationship

You have explained what the trouble is, now set out to fix it.

This is not a place to lower your expectations, but you should make sure that your hopes for the relationship are reasonable. It would be unreasonable to expect a banker to make you a loan for which you are not qualified; it would be reasonable for the banker to suggest alternative means of financing that might suit your needs, and to explain how the new options work and will affect your overall financial health.

It is unreasonable to expect a tax preparer to cut your taxes by taking deductions they would rather not sign their name to, but it is very desirable to talk with them about all manner of deductions for which you qualify, even if a particular credit or benefit is worth just a few bucks. After all, it's your money.

It can even be the basic levels of service that need to be looked at. If—as has happened in my own home—an insurance company is raising premiums when they are supposed to go down (thanks to a clean driving record), consistently sends incorrect bills and is just plain sloppy, you have a right to ask the agent to clear up the problems. In signing up for the insurance, you could never have anticipated these varied woes, and they are not the agent's fault, but if the agent won't go to bat for you, it's a relationship that needs to be redefined.

One difficult area to redefine is on return on investment. Presumably you and your broker or financial planner set targets based on your investment profile. But many advisers are chastised by customers not for missing their return targets but for not "beating the market."

That is particularly ironic because a diversified investment portfolio, by design, will not beat the market. It encompasses more and different types of risk than the simple market baskets—such as the Dow Jones Industrial Average—that people use as benchmarks.

If you no longer believe the adviser has the acumen to reach the investment targets that you set together—and your unhappiness stems from the adviser's actions, rather than a downturn in the market that brings everyone down—then a change is in order. If, however, performance has lagged its targets but has been reasonable given current market conditions—virtually no investor, no matter how savvy, makes money every year—then setting a new performance standard is probably a bad idea. (If you tell a financial planner to achieve 25 percent returns in the next year or lose you as a client, you encourage the adviser to gamble. They can go hellbent-for-leather to achieve the gains and keep you as a client by taking extraordinary risks. If the move backfires, you lose a lot of money and they wind up losing you as a client—the exact same outcome they could have achieved by remaining conservative. If you don't believe a team member can hit your targets, find someone who can.)

So the idea in redefining the relationship is to revisit the things you were seeking when you first signed up and to review how your needs have changed and how you see things differently now that you have had time to get used to having an adviser.

Make a list of what you want from the adviser, including the services you are getting currently and the areas where he or she falls short. Prioritize your wants, giving the adviser a chance to see where the service they have been providing is not meeting your key needs.

Realize, too, that the adviser may decide to drop you as a client, which is not necessarily a bad outcome, particularly if they refund some of your payment to salve your dissatisfaction. The adviser may work with all clients on one level, and your desire for something else may simply not fit their profile.

Throughout the hiring process the idea was to find advisers who wanted to "hire" you as a client. If they no longer value you as a customer, you would be better off knowing now.

If the adviser is willing to refocus his or her efforts to keep you as a client, you should decide on a trial period. If you are still not satisfied after, say, six months or a year, you will move to:

Step 3: Drop the ax

The moment you are not satisfied with an adviser's performance, you should be preparing for this action. The key element is the bond of trust and confidence you are supposed to have with your counselors; once that is gone, so too is the adviser.

If you have obligations to fulfill—the listing contract with a real estate agent, a management fee with a planner, or the unexpired term of a certificate of deposit—you will have to live up to them. If you believe the situation is desperate, examine the cost of an early escape—paying remaining fees now but foregoing services due, paying early withdrawal penalties, and the like. In some rare cases it is worth making your changes immediately, rather than letting time compound mistakes.

Before kicking someone off your team, however, do some advance preparation. You may need to have records transferred or to take possession of some securities; you will want a place for those records and securities.

You may also need to be prepared to move some money around. If you leave a brokerage firm, for example, you may need to pull money out of mutual funds run by the house—although you can probably leave the funds in place and the account open until you have hired a new adviser. (The major brokerage firms are getting to the point where they will allow you to leave monies in place even if your account is managed by a broker from another firm, but it will be some time before that is universal.)

Transferring assets is a pain; make sure you know the rules and can avoid screwups that could cost you at tax time. Find out the rules involved before making a change; get the necessary information so that your new adviser—whenever they are hired—can help you move your money.

The actual dismissal should be clean and concise. If you need to notify the firm in writing, make the note short and say only that you no longer intend to use the adviser's services after a specific date, by which time you want to have possession of all pertinent records and paperwork.

If the adviser or a supervisor wants to discuss your decision, be brief and firm. This is where the situation can get ugly and emotional, and you don't need that. Worse yet would be to wind up like Caroline and the hairdresser and rush right back into a situation that you have already deemed untenable. You should not be badgered, pestered, or otherwise bothered about making a decision that is clearly in your own best interest.

Having dispatched with the adviser, you are ready for:

Step 4: Hire a replacement

If you did not go through the full-blown, it's-a-lot-of-work process described in this book while picking your last adviser, then you should be ready to change your interview and preparation style.

If you picked the departed helper by the book, you need to start over again and try to figure out how to avoid making the same mistake twice. Ask yourself what went wrong with the relationship and what impressed you during the interviews that never came through afterward.

Make sure the new adviser knows that you are coming out of a bad relationship and express your concerns, what went wrong and what you expect from whoever you hire as a replacement.

Ask how they would react in similar situations, and whether they consider your expectations with the previous adviser to have been unreasonable. Be honest about the circumstances, so that an adviser may pull themselves out of the running if you sound like a client they cannot work with. (You jettisoned the last adviser because they did not return your phone calls every time the market burped; an adviser who acts the same way would not want you as a customer.) Use the list of your expectations developed under step 2 of the dismissal process to let the new adviser see your priorities and to help them understand where the relationship soured.

Once you have found a new partner for your financial team, they should review the work of the departed player, keeping whatever is worthwhile. It's especially important that they justify investment changes, as such decisions have tax consequences and may be motivated by self-interest (the new broker gets commissions when you sell the old stocks and purchase new ones, creating an incentive to say that stocks purchased under your previous brokerage relationship were dogs).

The new relationship comes with no guarantees that it will be better than the old one, but if you learn from experience and hire by-the-book, you should not have to go through many advisers in order to find one that you can keep for a lifetime.

Firing and replacing team members will not be fun and should not be entered into lightly, but neither is it enjoyable to feel like you aren't getting your money's worth. Ultimately what will be fun is having an adviser with whom you can have a long and prosperous relationship.

The Last Word

If you have made it this far into the book, you are nothing if not persistent.

That, or you took shortcuts.

Either way, it is an appropriate metaphor for the use of this book in your efforts to hire financial helpers.

Your job in selecting and managing advisers is to screen out the rogues, scoundrels, incompetents, personality problems, and the greedy. What you should be left with are people whose expertise matches your current and future needs, and whose style and manner provide the guidance and counsel you desire.

There is no question that the selection process proscribed in this book can be overkill. If you are persistent and dogged in your pursuit of the most appropriate financial representation, this book will screen out those advisers who do not have the attention span or desire to meet your demands. It will also weed out the bad guys, since you will no longer be an easy mark; your confidence and trust will be too hard to gain, and there will be easier targets for them to pursue.

At the same time you do not need to follow every suggestion in order to determine an adviser's qualifications and your comfort level. Just as you may have skipped around in the book to seek out specific bits of information, so can you pick and choose the type of data you want to get from an adviser.

The question is whether you know enough about each adviser—or type of adviser—to leave stones unturned while searching for a helper.

For example, my colleagues at *The Boston Globe* routinely tell me when they have interviewed a financial planner I know. When I ask if they have interviewed—or plan to talk with—other planners before signing up, most say no.

At most, they intend to talk with one other planner.

That still leaves them one short of the minimum number of recommended interviews.

Obviously I would prefer they did the due diligence necessary to be absolutely certain they were pleased with any adviser, but my colleagues—and the readers of this book—are busy people. Following the recommendations—choosing advisers in advance, doing the requisite interviews, and then actively keeping those relationships going—takes time and effort that is pretty hard to justify if you consider yourself a good judge of character.

I can live with that, and so can you.

There is nothing to say that my busy colleagues won't be perfectly happy with the first planner they interview, or that everyone who needs to hire an adviser on the spur of the moment—say picking an estate attorney after a parent has died and their property needs to be divided or repositioned—will face a disaster.

But, as with anything else in finances, it is a risk-reward trade-off. You must balance the risk that your judgment and good fortune will not hold up against the reward of the time you save with the shortcut.

Most of the time, things turn out fine. But if things go wrong, the time you saved will probably not be worth it.

So decide which approach you plan to take, whether you need to go completely by the book or whether you can adapt this approach to your lifestyle and needs. You need not make all of your hiring decisions at once; start now on hiring those advisers whose services you expect to need in the next three to five years. Do your interviews and make a short list so that you can make your choices with the least amount of disruption in your life.

My job in writing this book was to develop a way to draw out information that will help you eliminate the bad guys. That meant developing a process that would be hard for laggards to pass.

If you give an adviser the full wax job, you virtually guarantee that you will find competent representation. It may not be the absolute best choice you could make, but it is unlikely to be someone who rips you off or makes you feel abused. Make the methods in this book work for you, based on how much you know about an adviser or a specialty; use as much or as little of the selection process as you believe is necessary, but remember that it is better to overqualify advisers than to take risky shortcuts.

I can't stress enough that the majority of advisers I meet in all of the specialties are, at a bare minimum, competent and well intentioned. They may balk at doing so much work to get your business because they are not the bad guys.

Still don't be afraid to make an adviser jump through some hoops. If they won't work hard to win your business, you can only imagine how they might respond once they have it.

No matter whether you put a few suggestions from this book into play or carry your copy into an interview and make an adviser answer every last question, remember one thing: as the prospective client of a financial adviser, you are entitled to overkill. You are allowed to worry, fret, and sweat over the small stuff.

It's your money. Use your knowledge to make the most of it; hire advisers who help you make more of it.

Index